T0376556

Fairness Issues in Educational Assessment

Fairness and ethicality have been at the center of the debates on the appropriate use of educational tests since the 1960s. Particularly in high-stakes contexts, it is clear that fairness should be a major concern to both the test developers, and to those being tested, given that the fairness of a test is so intertwined with its validity.

Fairness Issues in Educational Assessment aims to shed more light on the issue and bring to sight some of the ways in which test fairness can be addressed. The contributions, written by some of the most prominent figures in educational assessment, address both theoretical and practical aspects of test fairness. The wealth of ideas presented here will be valuable to novice researchers and help them appreciate both the joy and complexity of conducting fair educational measurement.

This book was originally published as a special issue of *Educational Research and Evaluation*.

Hossein Karami is a Lecturer in the English Department, Faculty of Foreign Languages and Literatures, at the University of Tehran, Iran. His areas of interest include validity and fairness, especially in the context of language testing. His work has appeared in various journals including *Educational Research and Evaluation*, *RELC Journal*, *Psychological Test and Assessment Modeling*, *TESOL Journal*, and *Asia Pacific Education Review*.

Fairness Issues in Educational Assessment

Edited by
Hossein Karami

Routledge
Taylor & Francis Group

LONDON AND NEW YORK

First published 2016
by Routledge
2 Park Square, Milton Park, Abingdon, Oxon, OX14 4RN, UK

and by Routledge
711 Third Avenue, New York, NY 10017, USA

Routledge is an imprint of the Taylor & Francis Group, an informa business

British Library Cataloguing in Publication Data
A catalogue record for this book is available from the British Library

ISBN 13: 978-1-138-64794-7

Typeset in Times New Roman
by RefineCatch Limited, Bungay, Suffolk

Publisher's Note
The publisher accepts responsibility for any inconsistencies that may have
arisen during the conversion of this book from journal articles to book chapters,
namely the possible inclusion of journal terminology.

Disclaimer
Every effort has been made to contact copyright holders for their permission to
reprint material in this book. The publishers would be grateful to hear from any
copyright holder who is not here acknowledged and will undertake to rectify
any errors or omissions in future editions of this book.

Contents

Citation Information

The chapters in this book were originally published in *Educational Research and Evaluation*, vol. 19, issues 2–3 (February/April 2013). When citing this material, please use the original page numbering for each article, as follows:

Editorial
Fairness issues in educational assessment
Hossein Karami and Magdalena M.C. Mok
Educational Research and Evaluation, vol. 19, issues 2–3 (February/April 2013)
pp. 101–103

Chapter 1
Ongoing issues in test fairness
Gregory Camilli
Educational Research and Evaluation, vol. 19, issues 2–3 (February/April 2013)
pp. 104–120

Chapter 2
A "conditional" sense of fairness in assessment
Robert J. Mislevy, Geneva Haertel, Britte H. Cheng, Liliana Ructtinger,
Angela DeBarger, Elizabeth Murray, David Rose, Jenna Gravel, Alexis M. Colker,
Daisy Rutstein and Terry Vendlinski
Educational Research and Evaluation, vol. 19, issues 2–3 (February/April 2013)
pp. 121–140

Chapter 3
The unfairness of equal treatment: objectivity in L2 testing and dynamic assessment
James P. Lantolf and Matthew E. Poehner
Educational Research and Evaluation, vol. 19, issues 2–3 (February/April 2013)
pp. 141–157

Chapter 4
The quest for fairness in language testing
Hossein Karami
Educational Research and Evaluation, vol. 19, issues 2–3 (February/April 2013)
pp. 158–169

Chapter 5

Decisions that make a difference in detecting differential item functioning
Stephen G. Sireci and Joseph A. Rios
Educational Research and Evaluation, vol. 19, issues 2–3 (February/April 2013)
pp. 170–187

Chapter 6

Identifying differential item functioning in multi-stage computer adaptive testing
Mark J. Gierl, Hollis Lai and Johnson Li
Educational Research and Evaluation, vol. 19, issues 2–3 (February/April 2013)
pp. 188–203

Chapter 7

Assessing statistical aspects of test fairness with structural equation modelling
Rex B. Kline
Educational Research and Evaluation, vol. 19, issues 2–3 (February/April 2013)
pp. 204–222

Chapter 8

The formalization of fairness: issues in testing for measurement invariance using subtest scores
Dylan Molenaar and Denny Borsboom
Educational Research and Evaluation, vol. 19, issues 2–3 (February/April 2013)
pp. 223–244

Chapter 9

Generalizability theory and the fair and valid assessment of linguistic minorities
Guillermo Solano-Flores and Min Li
Educational Research and Evaluation, vol. 19, issues 2–3 (February/April 2013)
pp. 245–263

For any permission-related enquiries please visit:
http://www.tandfonline.com/page/help/permissions

Notes on Contributors

Denny Borsboom is a Professor of Psychology at the University of Amsterdam, The Netherlands. His research interests include the methodological foundations of psychology, the conceptual problems in psychological measurement, and the construction of network models for psychopathology. His research has recently appeared in *Frontiers in Psychology*, *Journal of Research in Personality*, and *Journal of Intelligence*.

Gregory Camilli is professor in the Department of Educational Psychology at Rutgers University, New Brunswick, NJ, USA. He is currently re-examining the issue of identifying school-level effects in mathematics for NAEP and TIMSS data learning using a hybrid model combining multilevel analysis with item response theory. His research has appeared in journals including *Reading Research Quarterly*, *Journal of Educational Measurement*, and *Journal of Educational and Behavioral Statistics*.

Britte H. Cheng is a Senior Educational Researcher for SRI International, based in Menlo Park, CA, USA. Her research focuses on the design and impact of learning technologies, instruction and assessment in K-12 math and science. Her work considers systemic issues of educational practice and policy, including the investigation of processes and designs that cross learning contexts and settings.

Alexis M. Colker served as a consultant to the Principled Science Assessment Designs for Students with Disabilities project at SRI International, based in Menlo Park, CA, USA. She specializes in assessment and learning.

Angela DeBarger is a Senior Research Scientist at the Center for Technology in Learning at SRI International, based in Menlo Park, CA, USA. Her research focuses on using principles of Evidence-Centered Design and Universal Design for Learning to inform the design of innovative technology-supported classroom assessments for formative purposes and large-scale assessments.

Mark J. Gierl is Professor of Educational Psychology and Director of the Centre for Research in Applied Measurement at the University of Alberta, Edmonton, Canada. His research interests include educational and psychological measurement, focusing on cognitive diagnostic assessment; assessment engineering, including cognitive modelling, automatic item generation, and automated test assembly; differential item and bundle functioning; unidimensional and multidimensional item response theory; psychometric methods for evaluating test translation and adaptation.

Jenna Gravel is a doctoral student in the Graduate School of Education at Harvard University, Cambridge, MA, USA. Her research interests focus on Universal Design for Learning and the impact that this framework has on student learning. Prior to beginning her doctoral program, she worked as a Project Manager and Research Associate at CAST, based in Wakefield, MA, USA.

Geneva Haertel is Director of Assessment Research and Design at SRI International's Center for Technology in Learning, based in Menlo Park, CA, USA. Her research interests focus on the implementation of evidence-centered assessment design (ECD) in K-16 educational settings for general education students and students with special needs. She is interested in the application of ECD in assessment, curriculum, and video game contexts.

Hossein Karami is a Lecturer in the English Department, Faculty of Foreign Languages and Literatures, at the University of Tehran, Iran. His areas of interest include validity and fairness, especially in the context of language testing. His work has appeared in various journals including *Educational Research and Evaluation*, *RELC Journal*, *Psychological Test and Assessment Modeling*, *TESOL Journal*, and *Asia Pacific Education Review*.

Rex B. Kline is Professor of Psychology at Concordia University in Montréal, Canada. His areas of research and writing include the psychometric evaluation of cognitive abilities, cognitive and scholastic assessment of children, structural equation modelling, the training of behavioural science researchers, and usability engineering in computer science. He is the editor of the forthcoming book *Principles and Practice of Structured Equation Modeling* (4th ed., 2016).

Hollis Lai is a PhD candidate with the Centre for Research in Applied Measurement and Evaluation in the Department of Educational Psychology, Faculty of Education, at the University of Alberta, Edmonton, Canada. His research interests include technology in assessment, automatic item generation, and assessment engineering.

James P. Lantolf is the Greer Professor of Language Acquisition and Applied Linguistics at Pennsylvania State University, State College, PA, USA. His research focuses on sociocultural theory and second language development. He is co-author of *Sociocultural Theory and the Genesis of Second Language Development* (2006), editor of *Vygotskian Approaches to Second Language Research* (2000), and is currently completing work on a new book with Matthew Poehner, *Sociocultural Theory and the Pedagogical Imperative in L2 Classrooms*.

Johnson Li is Assistant Professor in the Department of Psychology at the University of Manitoba, Winnipeg, Canada. His research interests include educational and psychological measurement and quantitative research methods, with an emphasis on bootstrap procedures, meta-analysis, reliability and validity evaluations, cognitive diagnostic assessment, and computer-based testing.

Min Li is Associate Professor in the College of Education of the University of Washington, Seattle, WA, USA. Her research focuses on the validity and reliability issues of large-scale tests and classroom assessments in science. She is planning to explore how students respond to the test items and how assessment practice can improve student learning, which may involve interdisciplinary collaborations with teachers and scientists.

Robert J. Mislevy is the Frederic M. Lord Chair in Measurement and Statistics at the Educational Testing Service, and Professor Emeritus at the University of Maryland, College Park, MD, USA. His research interests apply developments in psychology, statistics, and technology to practical problems in educational assessment.

Magdalena M.C. Mok is Chair Professor of Assessment and Evaluation at the Department of Psychological Studies, and Co-Director of the Assessment Research Centre at The Hong Kong Institute of Education. Her research focuses attention on the integration of assessment and self-directed learning to enhance instruction and learning.

Dylan Molenaar is an Assistant Professor of Psychometrics at the University of Amsterdam, The Netherlands. His research interests include item response theory, factor analysis, response time modelling, intelligence, and statistical modelling of genotype by environment interactions.

Elizabeth Murray is a Senior Research Scientist/Instructional Designer at CAST, based in Wakefield, MA, USA. Her research interests focus on applying technology to math and science instruction.

Matthew E. Poehner is Associate Professor of World Languages Education and Applied Linguistics at Pennsylvania State University, State College, PA, USA. His research examines the use of Vygotskian theory as both a lens for understanding second language development and a basis for educational activities that promote it. He is the author of *Dynamic Assessment: A Vygotskian Approach to Understanding and Promoting L2 Development* (2008) and co-author (with James P. Lantolf) of *Sociocultural Theory and the Pedagogical Imperative in L2 Classrooms* (forthcoming).

Joseph A. Rios is currently a doctoral student in the psychometrics program and a Senior Research Assistant in the Center for Educational Assessment at the University of Massachusetts–Amherst, MA, USA. His methodological research has focused on differential item functioning effect size guidelines, subscore reporting, as well as variance component and standard error estimation procedures in generalizability theory.

David Rose is a Developmental Neuropsychologist and educator whose primary focus is on the development of new technologies for learning. In 1984, Dr. Rose co-founded CAST, a not-for-profit research and development organization whose mission is to improve education, for all learners, through innovative uses of modern multimedia technology and contemporary research in the cognitive neurosciences. His most recent book is *Universal Design for Learning: Theory and Practice* (with Meyer and Gordon, 2014).

Liliana Ructtinger works as a Research Analyst at the SRI International Center for Technology in Learning, based in Menlo Park, CA, USA. Her work spans preschool mathematics and technology, science curriculum and assessment development, and informal learning.

Daisy Rutstein is an Educational Researcher at SRI International, based in Menlo Park, CA, USA. Her research interests include applying an Evidence-Centered Design approach to the development of assessments in education.

Stephen G. Sireci is Professor of Educational Policy, Research, and Administration, and Director of the Center for Educational Assessment at the University of Massachusetts–Amherst, MA, USA. His specializations include test development, computer-based testing, validity theory and test validation, and issues in assessing students with disabilities and linguistic minorities.

Guillermo Solano-Flores is Professor of Educational Equity and Cultural Diversity at the University of Colorado at Boulder, CO, USA. His research examines the intersection of language and validity in large-scale assessment, especially the testing of linguistic minorities and the testing of linguistically diverse populations in international comparisons.

Terry Vendlinski is the Co-Director for Assessment Research in SRI International's Center for Technology in Learning, based in Menlo Park, CA, USA. His research focuses on applying Evidence-Centered Design to the development of the next generation of large-scale assessments, to gamebased assessments, and to classroom formative assessment.

INTRODUCTION

Fairness issues in educational assessment

It has long been argued that validity is "the only genuine imperative" in educational assessment (Messick, 1989). The outcome of such an emphasis on validity is clear: Every attempt should be made to ensure that the inferences and interpretations made on the basis of test scores are justified. Such an enquiry into test validity will encompass virtually every stage of test development and use, from the early conception of the test to the evaluation of the consequences. With the exception of some counterarguments such as Borsboom, Mellenbergh, and Van Heerden (2004), this has been the mainstream thinking about validity for the last couple of decades.

Messick (1989) identified two major threats to validity: construct underrepresentation and construct-irrelevant variance. The former happens when the totality of the construct is not captured by the test. That is, some parts of the construct are left out. Construct-irrelevant variance, on the other hand, occurs when some factors, irrelevant to the construct of focus, affect test score variance. Not only do these two factors threaten test validity, they can also affect the fairness of the test if different groups of test takers are differentially affected. This is indeed the traditional definition of fairness, where fairness is defined as comparable validity. Cole and Moss (1989), for example, define bias, or unfairness, as the "*differential validity of a given test score for any definable, relevant subgroup of test takers*" (p. 205, italics in original).

It appears that validity and fairness are tightly interwoven. In fact, Kane (2010) argues that validity and fairness are related approaches towards answering the same fundamental question: "Are the proposed interpretations and uses of the test scores appropriate for a population over some range of contexts?" (p. 177). It is evident that fairness should be a major concern for test developers and users alike, especially in high-stakes contexts. The higher the stakes involved, the more pronounced the need for evidence supporting test fairness.

Systematic fairness enquiry in educational assessment has begun since at least the 1960s (Angof, 1993). Much work has been undertaken since then (for overviews, see Camilli, 2006, this issue; Holland & Wainer, 1993). This special issue and the papers included here are also another attempt at bringing into focus some of the issues involved.

The special issue is roughly divided into two parts. The first four papers (Camilli; Mislevy et al.; Lantolf & Poehner; Karami) are more of a theoretical nature, while the remaining five papers (Sireci & Rios; Gierl, Lai, & Li; Kline; Molenaar & Borsboom; Solano-Flores & Li) discuss psychometric aspects of fairness. We would not hesitate to point out that this is at best a rough sketch as theoretical discussions may also include statistics and vice versa, and no dichotomies may exist after all.

The first paper, by Gregory Camilli, provides an overview of the "ongoing" issues in test fairness. Individual and group basis for fairness evaluation, statistical methods and their limitations, employment testing, classroom assessment, and procedural and substantive due process are dealt with in this paper. Camilli provides a detailed discussion of the kind of issues that appear under each of these categories.

Mislevy and colleagues argue for a "conditional" definition of fairness as opposed to the traditional "marginal" approach. The new approach is based on the idea that equivalent surface features may not provide equivalent evidence about learners and that surface features "that differ in principled ways for different learners can provide equivalent evidence". Their approach infuses the evidence centered design (ECD) with principals of universal design for learning (UDL) and the general diagnostic model (GDM) and offers a unified approach towards applying the conditional conception of fairness in practice.

Lantolf and Poehner discuss fairness issues from a totally different perspective, that of dynamic assessment (DA). Unlike the traditional approach which aims for standardization in its zeal for fairness, the authors argue that due to the nature of DA, the test users may have to modify some aspects of the testing process relative to the needs of the particular individuals. Specifically, they argue that "while standardizing every aspect of the testing process has been prioritized in most approaches to assessment, DA addresses fairness through what at first blush appears to be "unequal treatment".

Hossein Karami discusses fairness issues in the context of language assessment. He provides an overview of some of the fairness frameworks that have been proposed and discusses their relative merits. He argues that fairness enquiry in language testing has been most limited to an appraisal of the psychometric properties of the tests along with their consequences. Few empirical studies exist on the value implications of the constructs embodied in the tests. The paper also discusses critical language testing and its implications.

Sireci and Rios provide an overview of the critical decisions that researchers should make in applying Differential Item Functioning (DIF). DIF analyses are increasingly applied in the psychometric circles to investigate the proper functioning of the items across groups of examinees. Sireci and Rios show how the decisions made at each stage of DIF analysis may affect the results. The issues addressed include the choice of the DIF detection method, selection of the groups and the conditioning criteria, the need for replication, and the application of effect size tests.

Gierl, Lai, and Li examine the performance of the CATSIB, a modification of Shealy and Stout's (1993) SIBTEST for CAT contexts, in detecting DIF in the context of multistage computer adaptive testing. They are specifically concerned with the performance of the CATSIB with different samples sizes and differing item difficulties. The criteria for the evaluation of the CATSIB includes Type I error and power rates. Their results generally indicate that CATSIB has the best performance with large samples.

Rex Kline discusses aspects of fairness that can be analyzed in the context of Structural Equation Modelling (SEM). He is specifically concerned with the application of multiple-group confirmatory factor analysis (MGCFA) to investigate the measurement invariance. An empirical example is provided to illustrate the process and the issues that may arise in each step.

Molenaar and Borsboom review the problems that can arise in investigating measurement invariance through the linear factor model. They address four issues: nonlinearity of the latent variable to subtest relation, suboptimality of the total score as a proxy for the latent variable measured through the item scores, non-normality of the subtest score, and differences in the nature of the latent variable at the item level as compared to the latent variable at the subtest level. The problems are then discussed through an empirical example with data from an IQ test.

Solano-Flores and Li treat fairness issues in the context of Generalizability Theory. The authors draw on the empirical studies they have conducted where they utilize G theory in the assessment of linguistic minorities. They illustrate how the failure to include a facet such as the heterogeneity of the linguistic groups in measurement designs can affect test results. Their paper ends with two suggestions. First, linguistic minorities should be included in the piloting of the tests. Second, separate generalizability indices should be calculated for different proficiency levels, and the minimum number of items to be included in the test should be determined based on the dependability indices obtained for the group with the greatest measurement error.

We hope that these papers help extend the discussions of fairness in educational assessment as the impact of educational measurement on the stakeholders is getting more and more crucial. Finally, we gratefully acknowledge the reviewers who have provided valuable comments on the papers that appear in this special issue.

References

Angoff, W. H. (1993). Perspectives on differential item functioning methodology. In P. W. Holland & H. Wainer (Eds.), *Differential item functioning* (pp. 3–24). Hillsdale, NJ: Lawrence Erlbaum Associates.

Borsboom, D., Mellenbergh, G. J., & Van Heerden, J. (2004). The concept of validity. *Psychological Review, 111*, 1061–1071.

Camilli, G. (2006) Test fairness. In R. Brennan (Ed.), *Educational measurement* (pp. 221–256). New York, NY: American Council on Education & Praeger series on higher education.

Cole, N. S., & Moss, P. A. (1989). Bias in test use. In R. Linn (Ed.), *Educational measurement* (3rd ed., pp. 201–219). Washington, DC: American Council on Education & National Council on Measurement in Education.

Holland, P. W., & Wainer, H. (1993). *Differential item functioning*. Hillsdale, NJ: Lawrence Erlbaum Associates.

Kane, M. (2010). Validity and fairness. *Language Testing, 27*, 177–182.

Messick, S. (1989). Meaning and values in test validation: The science and ethics of assessment. *Educational Researcher, 18*(2), 5–11.

Shealy, R., & Stout, W. F. (1993). A model-based standardization approach that separates true bias/DIF from group differences and detects test bias/DIF as well as item bias/DIF. *Psychometrika, 58*, 159–194.

Hossein Karami
University of Tehran, Tehran, Iran

Magdalena M.C. Mok
Hong Kong Institute of Education, Tai Po, Hong Kong

Ongoing issues in test fairness

Gregory Camilli

School of Education, University of Colorado at Boulder, Boulder, CO, USA

In the attempt to identify or prevent unfair tests, both quantitative analyses and logical evaluation are often used. For the most part, fairness evaluation is a pragmatic attempt at determining whether procedural or substantive due process has been accorded to either a group of test takers or an individual. In both the individual and comparative approaches to test fairness, counterfactual reasoning is useful to clarify a potential charge of unfairness: Is it plausible to believe that with an alternative assessment (test or item) or under different test conditions an individual or groups of individuals may have fared better? Beyond comparative questions, fairness can also be framed by moral and ethical choices. A number of ongoing issues are evaluated with respect to these topics including accommodations, differential item functioning (DIF), differential prediction and selection, employment testing, test validation, and classroom assessment.

Introduction

In the attempt to identify or prevent unfair tests, quantitative analyses are often used to determine whether test items or test scores have equivalent meaning for different groups of examinees. Other instances of unfairness are not easily characterized in this manner. For example, a test may include items that are culturally insensitive, or test administration may occur in a distracting environment. This suggests a single theory or conceptual umbrella for capturing all potential threats to test fairness is not feasible. Furthermore, there are few contemporary illustrations to guide fairness evaluation in the literature showing how test bias has been prevented or rectified – other than situations in which a problematic item has been detected and removed from a test. Thus, fairness evaluation and implementation is often a pragmatic activity based on an eclectic set of analyses to determine whether due process has been accorded to either a group of test takers or an individual.

In both the individual and comparative approaches to test fairness, counterfactual reasoning is useful to clarify a potential charge of unfairness: Is it plausible to believe that with an alternative assessment (test or item) or under different test conditions an individual or groups of individuals may have fared better? An important related issue is how high the burden of proof should be for admissible counterfactual evidence. That is, should the counterfactual be probable, reasonable, or merely plausible? A third issue concerns what recourse should be offered given a successful challenge to the hypothesis that a test is fair, namely, what should the recourse be for demonstrated unfairness?

In this paper, a number of particular issues are examined including the individual and group basis for fairness evaluation, statistical methods and their limitations, employment testing, classroom assessment, and procedural and substantive due process. While the material on employment testing is unique to the US, these procedures may be useful for informing or examining procedures elsewhere in the world. Indeed, this is not just a controversial topic in the US, and the American experience succinctly demonstrates points of social and scientific contention.

Individual and group fairness

The 1999 *Standards for Educational and Psychological Testing* (American Educational Research Association [AERA], American Psychological Association [APA], & National Council on Measurement in Education [NCME], 1999) is intended to provide criteria for the evaluation of tests, testing practices, and the effects of test use, where the term *test* here is used to specify a broad range of assessments including particular tests, scales, inventories, and instruments. The *Standards*, for short, reflect a broad vision of test fairness:

> A full consideration of fairness would explore the many functions of testing in relation to its many goals, including the broad goal of achieving equality of opportunity in our society. It would consider the technical properties of tests, the ways test results are reported, and the factors that are validly or erroneously thought to account for patterns of test performance for groups and individuals. (p. 73)

Twelve criteria pertaining to fairness are given in the *Standards*. Nine refer to groups or subgroups, and three to individuals or aspects of individuals, suggesting the broad categories of *group* and *individual* fairness (Ferdman, 1989). Along a second dimension, six standards refer to interpretation, reporting, or use of test scores; three to differential measurement or prediction; and three to equity or sensitivity. Below, the ideas of individual and group fairness are explored in more detail. This material is key to understanding methods of fairness evaluation corresponding to the descriptions of features along the second dimension.

Individual fairness

Individual fairness requires standardized conditions of testing in which students are treated comparably. This type of fairness is denoted as equity. However, the term *comparable* is not equivalent to *equal*. For example, some students have recognized difficulties, such as dyslexia, that interfere with their test performance, while others may be English language learners. Both of these backgrounds may lead to lower performance under standard testing conditions. Thus, for their scores to be *comparable* to other test takers, accommodations may be required to offset conditions that prevent full demonstration of ability. This may consist of allowing extra time for slow readers, but may also include reading or translating a mathematics item to accommodate language issues. The goal is to prevent influences irrelevant to the test to create advantages or disadvantages that result in higher or lower test scores (Messick, 1989). In sum, if a test or test item is equitable, it is presented to individuals under impartial conditions, meaning that no individual student is favoured over another in *demonstrating what they know or understand*.

A charge of unfairness might be the argument that a different set of testing conditions would have allowed an examinee to demonstrate his or her true capacity. Of course, this counterfactual requires that the proposed altered condition (e.g., a testing accommodation such as extended time, extra breaks, or glossaries for non-native speakers of a language) would not provide an unfair *advantage*. To determine the appropriateness of an accommodation, an experiment could be conducted in which groups of students – those who qualify for an accommodation and those who do not – are randomly assigned to accommodated and standard testing conditions. Helwig and Tindall (2003) carried out such an experiment with read-aloud accommodations for a mathematics test for both general and special education students to determine whether accommodations provided a better assessment of the proficiency of the latter. Their results suggest that accommodations can be reasonable (most of the students were diagnosed with learning disabilities), but actionable information may be ambiguous. Moreover, they a found that teachers could identify with a probability no greater than chance students who would benefit from accommodations. In a meta-analysis of 11 studies on accommodations for English language learners (ELL), Kieffer, Lesaux, Rivera, and Francis (2009) found that only one of seven typical accommodations had a relative positive impact – providing English dictionaries or glossaries. Yet, even in this case the average effect size was small ($d = .15$) and suggests that in some studies, accommodations increased the achievement gap between ELL and non-ELL students.

Major testing programmes nonetheless have procedures for requesting and granting accommodations. For example, the College Board requires documentation that includes a statement of the specific disability, educational history, evaluative test results (and credentials of the evaluator), explanation of a student's functional limitations, and specific accommodations requested (College Board, 2012). It can be argued along these lines that accommodations constitute a salient and pragmatic feature of test fairness beyond psychometric considerations. This is true despite the unarguable psychometric value of an accommodation in particular cases. In legal reasoning, there is a distinction between *probable cause* and *reasonable suspicion* as standards for proof. In oversimplified terms, probable cause "exist[s] where the known facts and circumstances are sufficient to warrant a man of reasonable prudence in the belief" of a conclusion (Congressional Research Service, 2006). On the other hand, reasonable suspicion of a cause–effect linkage is more than a hunch or intuition. It is a standard "considerably below preponderance of the evidence", but must flow from generalizations drawn on the basis of experience (Congressional Research Service, 2006, p. 1). With accommodations, it seems prudent and feasible to use the lesser standard: In some documented cases, it could be shown that an accommodation did enhance a student's score given an alternative test administration with no accommodation. However, this type of information is more an existence proof than a pattern with broad generalization.

Another aspect of individual fairness involves treating test takers with dignity and sensitivity. This aspect of testing may have no counterfactual stated in terms of alternative tests or test conditions: It is no defence of a charge of unfairness in this regard to argue that examinees were treated badly but equitably. It is also no defence to demonstrate equity if the objectives upon which a test is based are themselves faulty. Bouville (2008) noted that

> Giving credit to students because their name starts with a B is not any less fair than giving them credit because they have the correct answer .... Fairness of treatment is no fairness at all when it means applying rules that are themselves unfair: it merely propagates the fairness or unfairness of pre-existing rules. (p. 2.)

This is why test validation is an essential element in the analysis of fairness. The test should measure what it is intended to measure, but what the test does measure should be defensible logically and ethically. Testing conditions and test content should also avoid stereotyping, culturally offensive material, and other negative implications – regardless of whether these factors have an effect on test performance or testing conditions are standardized. Sensitivity problems can potentially lead to statistical bias and thus faulty interpretation of test scores, but establishing a convincing causal link between insensitivity and test performance is difficult, at best (requiring an unethical experiment). Rather than attempt to adduce the effect of cultural insensitivity on test performance, it should be recognized that cultural norms may be more damaging or hurtful to individuals in other ways than underestimation of ability. The process of screening items for negative social content is called *sensitivity review*, and is a well-established feature of many testing programmes that occurs prior to operational testing.

Group fairness

It is often the case that issues of individual fairness are of concern, but statistical methodologies for test fairness often focus on group comparisons. In addition to race and ethnicity as groups of interest, other methods of classification include, but are not limited to, social class, language, urbanicity, and the like. The categorization of individuals into groups must be done with caution, and this point is illustrated below with respect to race.

In October 1997, the Office of Management and Budget (OMB) in the US released new categories for collecting data on race and ethnicity (OMB, 1997). The new racial categories established were White, Black or African American, Asian, Native Hawaiian or Other Pacific Islander, and American Indian or Alaska Native. In contrast to racial categories, several ethnic categories were designated. For designating ethnicity, the categories were Hispanic or Latino and Not Hispanic or Latino. While there was no "multiracial", individuals could select one or more races – recognizing that designations of race are becoming more complex and nuanced. Ethnicity is at least as nuanced as race, involving issues of language, race, place of origin, values, and heritage.

The charge of unfairness is often, if not inevitably linked to social bias. The argument in favour of establishing the classification in this regard is that it is the source of the social bias that creates the classification, not those who are using it to investigate potential bias. That is, a classification may indeed be socially constructed, but the central issue concerns the rationale or *causes* underlying the classification. Beyond these causes, there are also *effects* to consider, and this raises a central question in test fairness of how cause and effect are linked. Quantitative methods can improve an understanding of the link between cause and effect, but arguments solely based on the authority of statistical methods are both flawed and obfuscating (e.g., Camilli, 1993).

Statistical evidence of unfairness

To evaluate bias statistically, a counterfactual question is useful. In particular, the question is how an individual or a group would have fared on a test (or a particular test item) had the test materials or conditions not presented an obstacle to demonstrating full proficiency. The difference between the observed outcome and the counterfactual outcome constitutes the effect, but the link between cause and effect cannot be established in individual cases. Some have suggested causality cannot be determined without the possibility of random assignment to factual and counterfactual conditions (Holland, 1986). Without a controlled comparison, a scientific link below the threshold of reasonable cause, if one is to be made, must be established in a process which could be based on other criteria such as either expert judgement or legal precedent.

With classifications of individuals, an initial sign of unfairness is an average difference among different groups. However, it is important to understand the extent to which an average test score difference is artifacts of a test or testing conditions rather than differences in true ability or proficiency. An observed difference does not necessarily imply unfairness. To give a simple example, consider the difference in average running speeds over a fixed distance for two groups (A and B), using different stopwatches. In contrast, statistical bias arises when the stopwatches do not measure time identically. In this case, at least part of the group difference in average running speed is due to the different watches. If stopwatch B runs more slowly than stopwatch A, group A is advantaged. In short, test fairness does not imply equal outcomes across individuals or groups. The purpose of a fairness investigation is to sort out whether the reasons for group differences are due to factors beyond the scope of the test (such as opportunity to learn or level of achievement) or artificially dependent on testing procedures.

There are two broad categories of analyses for examining the comparability of scores across groups: item-level analysis and prediction of a criterion measure. Both are intended to identify instances in which a test procedure is the source of group differences rather than true differences in ability. The first category is often labelled *differential item functioning* (DIF), while the second is conveniently referred to by the phrase *differential prediction*. Though the phrase test bias is often used to describe this latter category, the phrase differential prediction more accurately conveys the meaning, while the term fairness is bound to a particular use of a test in selecting candidates. It is the *selection procedure* that is described as fair or unfair, not the test itself. Differential item functioning and prediction are discussed more fully in the next sections.

Differential item functioning

Absent an external criterion, procedures were developed using the other items on the test: An item of interest had a group performance difference relatively larger than the group differences for other items. Holland and Thayer (1988) formalized the concept of relative item performance and introduced the term *differential item functioning* to convey this concept more clearly. Differential item functioning (DIF) is said to occur when examinees from groups A and B have the *same degree of proficiency* in a certain domain but different rates of success on an item. The DIF may be related to group differences in knowledge of or experience with some other topic beside the one of interest. The term DIF is synonymous with nonequivalent measurement, whereas unfairness can only be established if measurement differences are factors irrelevant to the test construct: There is no direct route from differential measurement to an inference of unfairness.

Sensitivity and specificity

Most testing programmes examine test items for group difference in measurement properties. An item is flagged when a statistically significant difference between two groups is found. However, due to statistical uncertainty, some flags are false positives. New testing techniques have resulted in a vast improvement in the reduction of false positive errors (e.g., Penfield & Camilli, 2007). However, there is tension between Type I and II errors. Type II errors occur when an item functions differentially, yet a statistical test fails to flag the item. These concerns are often described in terms of specificity and sensitivity. A test with perfect sensitivity would correctly identify all items with DIF (or no false positive): A test with perfect specificity would correctly identify all non-DIF items; that is, all items identified as having no DIF in truth have no DIF (or no false negatives). Unfortunately, there are no perfectly sensitive and specific tests for DIF. More importantly, as a test is designed to become more sensitive, it often becomes less specific. It seems most reasonable to tip the trade-off toward sensitivity at the expense of specificity because many flagged items are not automatically rejected, but reviewed for substantive interpretations of unfairness. Only if a plausible link can be offered is an item modified or deleted. Thus, additional safeguards exist (causal linkage and minimum effect sizes) for false positives.

Explanations of DIF

Bronfenbrenner and Crouter (1983) and Bronfenbrenner (1986) argued that research that relates a macrosystem such as group identity to an outcome of interest employs a *social address model*. While such a model might correctly reveal a statistical connection between group (the "address") and individual outcomes, it would not clarify the processes that might explain the connection. In other words, the address tells you where you are, not how you got there. One significant limitation to DIF analysis results from classifying individuals by social address rather than educational histories. Implicit assumptions are made, for example, that individuals with a common race or ethnicity have the same experience when within-group variability may be greater than between-group differences (Reese, Balzano, Gallimore, & Goldenberg, 1995).

Examples of social address classifications are race, ethnicity, religion, political inclination, and so forth. The different routes to this address contain the desirable or even necessary information for explaining variance in an outcome of interest. Recall that with DIF techniques, the link between cause and effect is usually required in order to remove or modify an item from a test. A successful link entails uncovering the mediating processes which link different developmental outcomes with the address label (De Graaf, 1999). However, this information is typically not available or not used in DIF analysis. Moreover, to the degree that the classes used as the basis of a DIF analysis are heterogeneous, there is a very low chance that the mediating processes are strongly correlated with the address labels. Because many individual influences are submerged in a "social address," it is likely that the use of such classifications will not provide a very powerful means of detecting differential measurement. Consequently, the failure to reject hypotheses of differential measurement does not provide convincing support that a test item is fair. In sum, a cause–effect link can rarely be established, though modest success has been encountered with linguistically homogeneous groups (Schmitt, Holland, & Dorans, 1993). This tends to minimize the effect of Type I errors because test items are typically modified or removed only if a plausible link can be established.

Differential prediction

Differential prediction requires a criterion construct by which a person or student can be deemed successful in a given activity, and is often motivated by the need to select candidates that are more likely to be successful on the job. The idea is to select examinees using their scores on the predictor or qualifying variable. Unbiased prediction is obtained when the same prediction equation holds for two or more groups. In other words, procedure is illustrated (see Camilli & Shepard, 1994, Figure 1.1A). Despite the difference in group distributions on the predictor (disparate impact), the test has equal predictive validity for two groups because they share the same regression line. For any given qualifying score, individuals have the same expected criterion performance, regardless of group membership.

Suppose candidates are chosen for a position with a qualifying examination, and the qualifying score is used to make a prediction regarding the candidates' likelihood of success on a criterion. For example, the Law School Admission Test (LSAT) is used to predict 1st-year grade point average (GPA) in law school. Then, as Cleary (1968, p. 115) suggested, differential prediction occurs if the criterion score predicted for a particular group is different from that of other groups given the same qualifying score (see Camilli & Shepard, 1994, Figure 1.1B). While many different models of selection based on a qualifying score have been proposed (see Camilli, 2006, for a brief review), the model most often employed is that of (a) using a common regression line across groups and (b) setting a cut-off point along the qualifying score continuum.

In the case of differential prediction, a common regression line used to select candidates for college or a job would lead to overprediction of performance for one group and underprediction for another, leading to an *unfair selection process*. An initially obvious solution to this problem is to use different prediction equations. However, such a solution is not feasible: Using different qualifying scores for different groups would itself be perceived as unfair outside of a technical community. More important, as a number of authors have argued (Borsboom, Romeijn, & Wicherts, 2008; Cronbach, Rogosa, Floden, & Price, 1977; Lord, 1960; Millsap, 1998, 2007), test scores with measurement error – which means all tests – will have different prediction equations for two groups with mean separation, even when there is no DIF in test items. Camilli, Briggs, Sloane, and Chiu (2013) further showed that differential selection can be quite large in some cases with a test composed of items with equivalent measurement properties.

A related issue with criterion prediction is whether a test may underrepresent the qualities desired for success (construct deficiency). However, this is more of an assumption underlying an analysis of differential prediction (along with construct contamination) than an issue to be investigated with differential prediction. Content validity along with expert review and job analysis are often the methods for examining the latter two qualities of a test.

Other fairness perspectives

Above, a number of limitations were examined for both differential item functioning and differential prediction. A broad perspective of test fairness requires coverage of still more issues in which test use is consequential to individuals. One such issue that stirs controversy is selection in employment testing. A perspective on the current situation in the United States is given, but the essential elements of this debate are likely to be relevant internationally. Second, test fairness is examined in the framework of test development. Third, a perspective on classroom testing is given, recognizing that this is the most prevalent kind of testing in the US and elsewhere.

Legal issues in employment testing

For some, fairness requires treating people as individuals, and for others, fairness requires taking into account the collective representations that matter in society. Levin (2003) frames this fairness debate in terms of a distinction between the individual and group perspective:

> Proponents of the individualistic perspective argue that it is unfair to pay attention to ethnicity because ethnic group memberships should not influence the opportunities and outcomes of individuals in society. Proponents of the group perspective, on the other hand, argue that it is unfair not to take ethnicity into account because of the power differentials that exist between ethnic groups in society. According to this latter perspective, ignoring ethnic group

membership obscures the significant ways in which these power differentials influence the opportunities and outcomes of members of different ethnic groups. (p. 8)

Both aspects of fairness must be considered in an evaluation of employment selection. The message from social address theory should not be taken to imply that the "social labels" have no inherent meaning; indeed, stereotyping and historical discrimination are directed precisely toward the "label" rather than the individual. In turn, this provides the starting point for a legal due-process perspective.

Title VII of the Civil Rights Act of 1964 concerns discrimination in employment practices, and the Equal Employment Opportunity Commission (EEOC) was created to provide guidance and enforcement regarding Title VII. Section 703(a)(2) declares it unlawful to limit, segregate, or classify his employees or applicants for employment in any way which would deprive or tend to deprive any individual of employment opportunities or otherwise adversely affect his status as an employee, because of such individual's race, color, religion, sex, or national origin. The EEOC in 1966 interpreted Title VII discrimination to consist of employment practices intended to discriminate or to treat people of protected status differently from others, but also includes practices having a harmful affect on members of certain groups (Hartigan & Wigdor, 1989).

Title VII provides for challenges to employment practices that adversely affect such groups – whether the outcome was intentional or not (Griggs v. Duke Power Company, 1971). Adverse impact, which is a measurable outcome derived from the Title VII term "adversely affect", has come to denote the selected proportions of people from groups with protected status relative to unprotected or majority groups. Adverse or disparate impact in employment decisions has been defined as a substantially different rate of selection that creates an imbalanced workforce with respect to a group with protected status. Note that the adjective *disparate* rather than *adverse* impact is used in the Civil Rights Act of 1991, PL 102-166). In particular, the usual threshold for adverse impact is established if the selection rate for one group is less than 80% (known as the 4/5 rule) of that for the group with the highest selection rate according to the *Uniform Guidelines on Employee Selection Procedures* (EEOC, 1978). However, courts have not rigidly interpreted statistical criteria for demonstrating disparate impact, and disparate impact by itself is not a sufficient basis for establishing violation of equal protection. Thus, the 4/5 rule is a guiding principle, and courts have also admitted evidence based on both statistical and practical significance (e.g., Gregory v. Litton Industries, 1972).

The demonstration of disparate impact establishes the grounds for legal challenge, i.e., a prima facie argument, and the effect of Title VII was to place the burden of proof on employers in the context of adverse impact given successful demonstration of disparate impact (e.g., demonstrating the 4/5 rule). To defend practices that result in alleged disparate impact, defendants may challenge the plaintiff's statistics or present three types of information on test validation:

(1) Criterion-related validity: A statistical correlation between scores on a selection test and job performance on a sample of workers.
(2) Content validity: A demonstration that the content of a selection procedure is representative same of important job-performance tasks.
(3) Construct validity: A demonstration that (a) a selection procedure measures a construct, and (b) the construct represents an important capacity for successful job performance.

It is the test user's responsibility to determine how to satisfy these three criteria, and this may include the use of previous validity studies (though the procedure for selecting previous studies must be consistent with the validation strategy). The third strategy above of construct validity is not well-developed in the content of the *Uniform Guidelines*. Construct evidence might take the form of showing that in previous validity studies test scores (for the test in question) correlated with the same requisite work behaviours in the context of different jobs, whereas concurrent validity evidence should concern correlations in the context of jobs with substantially the same work behaviours.

A selection practice should be justified by demonstrating it is job related and consistent with business necessity (Civil Rights Act of 1964), though there is some uncertainty of whether the word *consistent* is interchangeable with *necessary* (Grover, 1996). Arguments based on the "rational" relationship between a selection procedure and job performance are an insufficient defence (Washington v. Davis, 1976). If another feasible selection procedure is available that results in less disparate impact, that alternative procedure should be included in the validity study. If other alternatives result in even less disparate impact, the burden of evidence is on the plaintiff to uncover and demonstrate these practices. In any event, the Civil Rights Act imposes liability if the defendant refuses to adopt a validated selection practice that results in less disparate impact, if it can be identified.

Underneath the surface of this terse description, controversy surrounding the application of current employment selection policies is rampant. This is revealed by an exchange of views on a paper by McDaniel, Kepes, and Banks (2011b), "The Uniform Guidelines Are a Detriment to the Field of Personnel Selection", which appeared in the journal *Industrial and Organizational Psychology* (Volume 4, 2011).

McDaniel et al. (2011b) argued that the *Uniform Guidelines* encourage the "use of selection practices unsupported by scientific evidence" (p. 495). They further maintained that disparate impact is an unavoidable fact and that differential prediction does not exist. Perhaps most important, they also argue that with the "scientific" advance established by validity generalization, there is little need, if any, for local validation studies (that is, situational specificity is largely a myth) in response to Title VII challenges: "From the perspective of scientific knowledge, meta-analytic evidence largely eliminates the need for local validation studies" (p. 500). The bottom line in this argument appears to be the claim that disparities in selection ratios (e.g., the 4/5 rule) "should not generally trigger federal intervention in personnel selection practices" (p. 495). Consistent with this position, Barrett, Miguel, and Doverspike (2011) advocated removing the disparate impact theory of discrimination entirely from Title VII policies.

McDaniel et al. (2011b) identified three "tactics" used against the modification of the *Uniform Guidelines*:

> First, employers can document the costs associated with complying with the Uniform Guidelines. These include labor and other monetary costs associated with defending employee selection systems. There are also economic costs associated with using lower validity selection measures in hopes of reducing adverse impact .... Second, employees of federal regulatory agencies, human resources consultants, and labor lawyers seeking to preserve their jobs can manufacture uncertainty about scientific findings. If the price is right, one can find a "scientist" to testify to almost anything. Third, regulatory agencies and other interested parties (e.g., consultants, lawyers, and expert witnesses) can engage in delay tactics (e.g., litigation, requiring parallel studies and fighting over access to raw data) to avoid revising the Uniform Guidelines. (p. 509)

McDaniel et al. (2011b, p. 507) expressed the hope that given President Obama's mixed-racial heritage, an Obama-endorsed congressional effort to force a revision of the

Uniform Guidelines is less likely to be labelled as racially motivated. Finally, they faulted the *Uniform Guidelines* for not addressing the diversity-validity dilemma (pp. 506–507).

One would be incorrect to conclude that this point of view represented an endpoint along a continuum of disagreement. In more vigorous response, Sharf (2011) labelled the *Uniform Guidelines* as a "tool of political advocacy" and "the civil rights bar's hostility to job-related selection procedures that adversely affect preferred groups is based on their stealthy redistributive advocacy of equal employment" (p. 537). Sackett (2011) viewed the current *Uniform Guidelines* as a policy/political document rather than a scientific/professional document and maintains "it is thus inappropriate to rely on them as the basis for one's professional opinion" (p. 545), and further, the

> appropriate bases for testimony in selection cases are the peer-reviewed literature and the consensus documents that reflect concepts and procedures that have gained acceptance in the scientific community, namely, the *Standards for Educational and Psychological Testing* (American Educational Research Association, American Psychological Association, & National Council on Measurement in Education, 1999) and the *Principles for the Validation and Use of Personnel Selection Procedures* (SIOP, 2003). (p. 545)

Sackett also clarified that the key rationale for testimony inconsistent with the Standards or Principles is to provide a recommendation that is "is not a scientific claim, but rather some other factor, such as avoiding scrutiny from a regulatory agency" (p. 546).

In contrast to the views above, Tonowski (2011) argued that "One purpose of the *Uniform Guidelines* is clearly to address public policy regarding the use of tests and other selection procedures" (p. 527). Indeed, McDaniel et al. (2011a) suggested this should be the case in identifying the limitations of the *Uniform Guidelines* in addressing the diversity-validity dilemma. Tonowski also pointed out that a set of revised *Standards* will shortly be published, and the *Principles* may have to be revised accordingly prior to an attempt to revise the *Uniform Guidelines*. In addition, it seems likely that an agency or committee charged with revision tasks would itself require a complex selection process for members, and it is not clear whether such a committee could arrive at a consensus on key issues. However, Reynolds and Knapp (2011) suggested a broad outline for projects that might usefully serve to guide revision.

Outzz (2011) argued "there is credible evidence refuting that situation specificity is a "myth" (p. 529). He noted that "Ironically, the use of meta-analytic methods has revealed that other assessment tools or combinations of tools can result in validity equal to, if not higher than that for cognitive ability tests and produce less adverse impact...." (p. 531). In the *Principles* (Society for Industrial and Organizational Psychology [SIOP], 2003) in contrast, it is stated that generalized evidence can be used to support test validation claims given a "compelling argument for its application to the situation of interest" (Outzz, 2011, p. 530). In fact, it is explicitly stated in the *Standards* (AERA, APA, & NCME, 1999) that "The test user is ultimately responsible for evaluating the evidence in the particular setting in which the test is to be used" (p. 11) (also see *Standards* 1.1 and 1.20).

Brink and Crenshaw (2011) provided a counter-pole to the views presented in the focal paper. They argued that many of the criticisms lodged by McDaniel et al. (2011b) are adequately addressed in the *Uniform Guidelines*, but also in questions and answers (Q&As) provided by the Equal Employment Opportunity Commission (EEOC, 1979, 1980), which McDaniel et al. omitted from their discussion. The thesis of Brink and Crenshaw is that

> the majority of their arguments [McDaniel et al., 2011a] are either incorrect assertions, beliefs presented without basis in established fact, or trivial in terms of implications for practitioners –

none are significant enough for the *Uniform Guidelines* to be considered a detriment or rise to the level of calling for the *Uniform Guidelines* to be rescinded. (p. 547)

A selection of the critiques offered by Brink and Crenshaw includes the role of validity generalization (VG), the gap in selection test means for White and minority job candidates, and the roles of science and law in employment regulations. First, they argued that both the constructs and methods of measurement must be similar for VG to apply to a local test, and "Though the Principles address VG, they do not support its cavalier use" (p. 548). Second, they noted that while McDaniel et al. (2011a) provided evidence of group differences on many important selection variables, one was notably absent from their list: job performance. This is important to consider because the Black versus White gap in performance is considerably smaller than many other predictors of job success. Exclusive use of cognitive measures may focus too narrowly on the knowledge and skills required for effective job performance. Finally, Brink and Crenshaw (2011) argued that "science/practice and law should mutually influence one another and that a perfect match between science and law is a noble goal but difficult to attain the idea", and "it is egocentric to suggest that science takes precedence over law" in federal employment regulations (p. 552).

Despite the stark disagreement over the role and use of the *Uniform Guidelines* among industrial and organizational psychologists, there is agreement on some issues. First, practical significance (effect size) and statistical significance have been conflated in some legal proceeding (Jacobs, Deckert, & Silva, 2010). Some clarification in employment regulations would be helpful despite the fact that a cutoff for establishing a disparate impact review is a social construction rather than a scientific standard. Second, the method of *synthetic validity* provides a promising tool because it has the potential to combine generalized evidence and local context into a principled validity argument (Mead & Morris, 2011). However, as Russell (2010) noted, citing Milkovich and Newman (2007), it is estimated that "only about 20% of a typical firm's jobs have external labor markets" (p. 340). This poses a strong challenge for selection research on external evidence. Third, it would be useful to clarify whether the enduring observed score gaps on cognitive variables is an appropriate legal basis for rejecting the disparate impact theory of discrimination (Hanges, Aiken, & Salmon, 2011). After all, this argument would itself hinge to some degree on a legally suspect classification.

It is unlikely that any resolution on these matters is forthcoming, mainly because it is not clear what alternatives to current employment regulations might be palatable. Barrett et al. (2011) proposed the vague recommendation that "researchers should collaborate and engage in a professional discussion of ethnic group differences in test scores" (p. 535). And as McDaniel et al. (2011a) observed, the courts are unlikely to change their practices without fundamental changes to the Civil Rights Act of 1991. Yet, these authors other than seeking to "foster constructive debate" (2011a, p. 570), admit "no substantive experience in how to resolve the unfortunate situation with the *Uniform Guidelines*" (2011b, p. 509). Ultimately, the manner in which McDaniel et al. (2011a) responded, in their rejoinder, to the challenge of Brink and Crenshaw (2011) suggests little common ground: "the commentary [Brink and Crenshaw] appears ideologically driven, in part, because it assumes that it is acceptable for governmental officials to manipulate and deny research findings to advance political goals" (p. 569), and "We encourage individuals and professional organizations to continue this debate until detriments to the professional practice of personnel selection have been neutralized" (p. 570).

It is important to recognize that the applicability of Title VII challenges was reduced in 2001 when the Supreme Court ruled in Alexander v. Sandoval (2001) that disparate impact arguments could not be brought to federal courts by individual citizens (right of private action), as had been the case for the previous 35 years. This has effectively rendered disparate impact viable only in the context of Office of Civil Rights administrative enforcement actions (Welner, 2001), and this opinion may reduce the number of venues in which evidence, psychometric or otherwise, of disparate impact is salient. However, as dire as this situation sounds, a discrimination charge in employment selection is most likely to be unsuccessful. For example, in 2010 about 73,000 private-sector Title VII discrimination charges were filed for which the EEOC found no reasonable cause in about 70%; moreover, about 18% were closed for administrative reasons. Reasonable cause for the belief that discrimination had occurred was found by the EEOC in only about 5% of the cases, though charging parties had meritorious resolutions in about 20% of the cases leading to 229.8 million USD in benefits. Thus, discrimination charges do not have resolutions in which the charging parties benefit (meritorious resolutions) about 9 times out of 10. On the other hand, meritorious resolutions resulted in an average of about 16 thousand USD per charge in benefits (EEOC, 2010).

Test development

Though test validation was briefly discussed above in the legal perspective, more details on the test development process are useful. Collecting validity evidence is a cornerstone of test development which can be broken down into several distinct components including construct, content, concurrent, and predictive. However, the most common, if not convincing, evidence of validity for large-scale assessment is built into procedures for developing a test. Many problems associated with test validity may be avoided in the pre-operational stages.

Test items are written according to an overall plan in large-scale assessment programmes. This plan is sometimes called a content-by-process matrix, or more simple a test blueprint. Often, this plan is guided by a set of standards based on a formal curriculum; this implies that a good test is tightly aligned to both a curriculum and a test blueprint. The latter are also aligned in a coherent system of educational practices. Though standards documents typically do not provide enough detail for writing specific test items, intermediate tools can be used to articulate test blueprints with standards documents. For each "standard", an organization may develop a set of topics and indicators within those topics describing particular skills or content. In other words, indicators and other tools, as policy interpretations of a curriculum, are used to provide explicit information to item writers. For example, several hundred indicators may be defined for an assessment, where each indicator is linked to a standard within a content area for a test composed of 40–50 items. In the alignment process, content expertise and expert judgement are essential tools, and test validation is partially accomplished by setting forth both the design decisions and expert review process in a formal document often referred to as a technical manual or report.

After development, test items go through several stages of screening. Initially, items are reviewed by substantive experts to identify intrinsic ambiguities. They are further reviewed by expert panels for sensitivity to social and cultural content. In a second stage, items are piloted of samples of students for a number of reasons. An example of a problem that might arise with respect to fairness is the use of the word "snow" with student population having very little experience with snow. This problem might be detected with either sensitivity review or possibly DIF analysis. Test items often undergo a third stage of pretesting to determine if groups of items work together as expected. In short, a number of steps take place that in part address fairness issues that include match to the test blueprint and content standards, suitable cognitive processes, unfamiliar or insensitive language, inappropriate difficulty, and so on. Thus, fairness rather than being a property of a test is more accurately viewed in terms of the coherence of the claims within an educational system. Other steps to enhance validity occur in test administration, scoring, and score reporting.

Not all problems can be resolved prior to formal administration. As summarized by Kane (2010),

> A basic case for the validity of the proposed interpretation and use (i.e., the generic interpretive argument) is typically made during test development. This development stage tends to have a confirmationist bias, because it is an integral part of developing an assessment that is designed to support certain interpretations and uses.... (p. 181)

Nonetheless, there are many steps in the development process designed to identify and prevent problems related to fairness issues.

Classroom assessment

Shepard (2006) defines formative assessment as "assessment carried out during the instructional process for the purpose of improving teaching or learning", while summative assessment "refers to the assessments carried out at the end of an instructional unit or course of study for the purpose of giving grades or otherwise certifying student proficiency" (p. 627). Any assessment that eventually affects a grade can be viewed as summative, and therefore many assessments, including standardized tests, can share both summative and formative purposes (Brookhart, 2003, 2004).

Classroom assessment is by far the most prevalent type of testing, yet most formal methods of test fairness are restricted to large-scale assessment. As a rule, classroom tests have a short life cycle, and it would not be feasible to techniques of differential measurement or prediction. Camilli (2006) suggested that a number of categories could be considered in evaluating fairness in classroom testing including clear and reasonable assessment criteria, the strength of the link between assessment and instruction, opportunity to learn, sensitivity of assessment procedures to cultural and religious differences, and the use of multiple measures. Moreover, because the instructor is the grading authority in the classroom, grading can be a type of modelling of both learning and self-assessment of students. When fair assessment procedures are internalized, they become a model process for the students' participation in their communities and a larger democratic culture.

Discussion

A number of current topics related to test fairness have been briefly sketched in this paper. First, a number of factors prevent DIF methods from being definitive including inexact group classification, cause–effect linkages, and the issues of sensitivity and specificity. The expectations that DIF analysis can lead to fairer tests should remain appropriately modest: It is but one step in a quality control procedure. The argument that DIF analysis alone is adequate for creating a fair test is not accepted within the psychometric community.

Second, significant limitations also exist with respect to differential selection. Even with a test composed of items that have equivalent measurement properties in two groups, differential prediction occurs to some degree due to measurement error when two groups differ in average score on a qualification test. It is well known that in the presence of group separation on the predictor variable, a common prediction line typically gives, on average, a slight selection advantage to members of lower scoring groups.

Third, according to the legal perspective, an extant selection test sets a baseline for evaluating whether other tests exist that have less disparate impact. Statistical analysis may have a role to play in the comparison of two alternative tests, but if the tests contain different amounts of measurement error, such an analysis cannot be definitive. Likewise, analyses are limited by the suitability of the criteria to be predicted. The choice of selection criteria is instead determined in a proceeding in which various types of validity information are offered and challenged. It is at this stage that an expert investigation of test content may be undertaken to determine whether a test is appropriately targeted to job-necessary behaviours, and whether the test accurately represents the indicators relevant to such behaviours.

Should there be frameworks for considering fairness issues such as Toulmin's argument structure (2003), or test validation? The approach taken in this paper is informed by the potential outcomes model (Holland, 1986) in which a counterfactual question is proposed: Would the assessment outcome have been different under other circumstances – including different tests, accommodations, or other altered conditions of testing? It is a question easily asked, but answered with much difficulty, if at all. Empirical investigation may provide clues for this purpose, if not useful evidence, but the fairness argument often takes place on procedural grounds due to unavoidable constraints in establishing cause–effect relationships and identification of a consensual criterion. According to Kane (2010)

> *procedural fairness* can be said to require that all test takers be treated in essentially the same way, that they take the same test or equivalent tests, under the same conditions or equivalent conditions, and that their performances be evaluated using the same (or essentially the same) rules and procedures. (p. 178)

Procedural fairness, especially as procedural due process, should also be extended to how tests are developed and how testing is aligned to other features within an educational system. This is especially evident in the case of classroom assessment.

On the other hand, Kane (2010) describes *substantive due process* as requiring that procedures to be applied are "reasonable in general and in the context in which they are applied" (p. 178). He extends this notion to *substantive fairness* as requiring that the "score interpretation and any test-based decision rule be reasonable and appropriate, and in particular, that they be equally appropriate for all test takers (at least roughly)" (p. 178–179). There is no doubt that the purpose of a cognitive test should be to assess some valuable aspect of cognitive behaviour, but as a whole this definition is a narrower framing of substantive due process than the counterfactual question "Is it reasonable to believe that with an alternative procedure an individual or group of individuals may have fared better?" The word *reasonable* can refer to a conclusion drawn by a "prudent and cautious" person. While the lower standard of reasonable suspicion is often applied in test development and accommodations, a choice between reasonable cause and suspicion is required. But these standards are considerably lower than that of scientific evidence, which is difficult to establish outside the realm of randomized experiments. In any case, there should be a structure, if not a theory, for a fairness argument, and it should be recognized that warrants for linking evidence to potential causes are not exclusively scientific.

References

Alexander v. Sandoval, 121 S. Ct. 1511 (2001).

American Educational Research Association, American Psychological Association, & National Council on Measurement in Education. (1999). *Standards for educational and psychological testing* (2nd ed.). Washington, DC: American Educational Research Association.

Barrett, G. V., Miguel, R. F., & Doverspike, D. (2011). The uniform guidelines: Better the devil you know. *Industrial And Organizational Psychology, 4*, 534–536.

Borsboom, D., Romeijn, J. W., & Wicherts, J. M. (2008). Measurement invariance versus selection invariance: Is fair selection possible? *Psychological Methods, 13*, 75–98.

Bouville, M. (2008). *The obsession with exam fairness.* Retrieved from http://www.mathieu.bouville. name/education-ethics/Bouville-exam-fairness.pdf

Brink, K. E., & Crenshaw, J. L. (2011). The affronting of the uniform guidelines: From propaganda to discourse. *Industrial and Organizational Psychology, 4*, 547–533.

Bronfenbrenner, U. (1986). Ecology of the family as a context for human development: Research perspectives. *Developmental Psychology, 22*, 723–742.

Bronfenbrenner, U., & Crouter, A. C. (1983). The evolution of environmental models in developmental research. In P. H. Mussen (Series Ed.) & W. Kessen (Vol. Ed.), *Handbook of child psychology: Vol. 1. History, theories, and methods* (4th ed., pp. 357–413). New York, NY: Wiley.

Brookhart, S. M. (2003). Developing measurement theory for classroom assessment purposes and uses. *Educational Measurement: Issues and Practice, 22*, 5–12.

Brookhart, S. M. (2004). *Grading.* Upper Saddle River, NJ: Pearson Education.

Camilli, G. (1993). The case against item bias techniques based on internal criteria: Do item bias procedures obscure test fairness issues? In P. W. Holland & H. Wainer (Eds.), *Differential item functioning: Theory and practice* (pp. 397–417). Hillsdale, NJ: Lawrence Erlbaum Associates.

Camilli, G. (2006). Test fairness. In R. L. Brennan (Ed.), *Educational measurement* (4th ed., pp. 221–256). Westport, CT: American Council on Education/Praeger.

Camilli, G., Briggs, D. C., Sloane, F. C., & Chiu, T.-W. (2013). Psychometric perspectives on test fairness: Shrinkage estimation. In K.F. Geisinger (Ed.-in-Chief), B. A. Bracken, J. F. Carlson, J. C. Hansen, N. R. Kuncel, S. P. Reise, & M. C. Rodriguez (Assoc. Eds.), *APA handbooks in psychology: APA handbook of testing and assessment in psychology: Volume 3. Testing and assessment in school psychology and education.* Washington, DC: American Psychological Association.

Camilli, G., & Shepard, L.A. (1994). *Methods for identifying biased test items.* Hollywood, CA: Sage.

Civil Rights Act of 1964, 42 U.S.C. § 2000e-2(k)(1)(A)(i). (1964).

Civil Rights Act of 1991, S. 611, 102nd Cong. (1991).

Cleary, T. A. (1968). Test bias: Prediction of grades of Negro and White students in integrated colleges. *Journal of Educational Measurement, 5*, 115–124.

College Board. (2012). *Accommodations.* Retrieved from http://professionals.collegeboard.com/ testing/ssd/accommodations

Congressional Research Service. (2006, January 30). *Probable cause, reasonable suspicion, and reasonableness standards in the context of the fourth amendment and the foreign intelligence surveillance act* (Memorandum to the Senate Select Committee on Intelligence). Retrieved from http://www.fas.org/sgp/crs/intel/m013006.pdf

Cronbach, L. J., Rogosa, D. R., Floden, R. E., & Price, G. G. (1977). *Analysis of covariance in non-randomized experiments: Parameters affecting bias* (Occasional Paper). Stanford, CA: Stanford Evaluation Consortium, Stanford University.

De Graaf, J. W. (1999). *Relating new to old: A classic controversy in developmental psychology* (Doctoral dissertation). Groningen, The Netherlands: Regenboog.

Equal Employment Opportunity Commission, Civil Service Commission, Department of Labor, & Department of Justice. (1978). Uniform guidelines on employee selection procedures. *Federal Register, 43*, 38290–39315.

Equal Employment Opportunity Commission. (1979). Adoption of questions and answers to clarify and provide a common interpretation of the uniform guidelines on employee selection procedures. *Federal Register, 44*, 11996.

Equal Employment Opportunity Commission. (1980). Adoption of additional questions and answers to clarify and provide a common interpretation of the uniform guidelines on employee selection procedures. *Federal Register, 45*, 29530.

Equal Employment Opportunity Commission. (2010). *Title VII of the Civil Rights Act of 1964 Charges.* Retrieved from http://www.eeoc.gov/eeoc/statistics/enforcement/titlevii.cfm

Ferdman, B. M. (1989). Affirmative action and the challenge of the color-blind perspective. In F. A. Blanchard & F. J. Crosby (Eds.), *Affirmative action in perspective* (pp. 169–176). New York, NY: Springer-Verlag.

Gregory v. Litton Industries, 472 F.2d 631 (9th Cir., 1972).

Griggs v. Duke Power Company, 401 U.S. 424 (1971).

Grover, S. (1996). *The business necessity defense in disparate impact discrimination cases* (Faculty Publications, Paper 19). Retrieved from http://scholarship.law.wm.edu/facpubs/19

Hanges, P. J., Aiken, J. R., & Salmon, E. D. (2011). The devil is in the details (and the context): A call for care in discussing the uniform guidelines. *Industrial and Organizational Psychology, 4,* 562–565.

Hartigan, J. A., & Wigdor, A. K. (1989). *Fairness in employment testing: Validity generalization, minority issues and the General Aptitude Test Battery.* Washington, DC: National Academy Press.

Helwig, R., & Tindal, G. (2003). An experimental analysis of accommodation decisions on large-scale mathematics tests. *Exceptional Children, 69,* 211–225.

Holland, P. W. (1986). Statistics and causal inference. *Journal of the American Statistical Association, 81,* 945–960.

Holland, P. W., & Thayer, D. T. (1988). Differential item performance and the Mantel-Haenszel procedure. In H. Wainer & H. I. Braun (Eds.), *Test validity* (pp. 129–145). Hillsdale, NJ: Lawrence Erlbaum.

Jacobs, R., Deckert, P. J., & Silva, J. (2011). Adverse impact is far more complicated than the uniform guidelines indicate. *Industrial and Organizational Psychology, 4,* 558–561.

Kane, M. (2010). Validity and fairness. *Language Testing, 27,* 177–182.

Kieffer, M. J., Lesaux, N. K., Rivera, M., & Francis, D.J. (2009). Effectiveness of accommodations for English Language Learners taking large-scale assessments. *Review of Educational Research, 79,* 1168–1201.

Levin, S. (2003). Social psychological evidence on race and racism. In M. Chang, D. Witt, K. Haikuta, & J. Jones (Eds.), *Compelling interest: Examining the evidence on racial dynamics in higher education in colleges and universities* (pp. 97–125). Stanford, CA: Stanford University Press.

Lord, F. M. (1960). Large-scale covariance analysis when the control variable is fallible. *Journal of the American Statistical Association, 55,* 307–321.

McDaniel, M. A., Kepes, S., & Banks, G. C. (2011a). Encouraging debate on the uniform guidelines and the disparate impact theory of discrimination. *Industrial and Organizational Psychology, 4,* 566–570.

McDaniel, M. A., Kepes, S., & Banks, G. C. (2011b). The *Uniform Guidelines* are a detriment to the field of personnel selection. *Industrial and Organizational Psychology, 4,* 494–514.

Mead, A. D., & Morris, S. B. (2011). About babies and bathwater: Retaining core principles of the uniform guidelines. *Industrial and Organizational Psychology, 4,* 554–557.

Messick, S. (1989). Validity. In R. L. Linn (Ed.), *Educational measurement* (3rd ed., pp. 13–103). New York, NY: American Council on Education and Macmillan.

Milkovich, G., & Newman, J. (2007). *Compensation* (9th ed.). New York, NY: McGraw-Hill.

Millsap, R. E. (1998). Group difference in intercepts: Implications for factorial invariance. *Multivariate Behavioral Research, 33,* 403–424.

Millsap, R. E. (2007). Invariance in measurement and prediction revisited. *Psychometrika, 72,* 461–473.

Office of Management and Budget. (1997, October 30). *Revisions to the Standards for the Classification of Federal Data on Race and Ethnicity* (Federal Register Notice 62FR58782-89). Washington, DC: Author.

Outtz, J. L. (2011). Abolishing the uniform guidelines: Be careful what you wish for. *Industrial and Organizational Psychology, 4,* 526–533.

Penfield, R., & Camilli, G. (2007). Test fairness and differential item functioning. In C. R. Rao (Ed.), *Handbook of statistics: Volume 26. Psychometrics* (pp. 125–167). Amsterdam, The Netherlands: Elsevier.

Reese, L., Balzano, S., Gallimore, R., & Goldenberg, C. (1995). The concept of educación: Latino family values and American schooling. *International Journal of Educational Research, 23,* 57–81.

Reynolds, D. H, & Knapp, D. J. (2011). SIOP as advocate: Developing a platform for action. *Industrial and Organizational Psychology, 4,* 540–544.

Russell, C. J. (2010). Better at what? *Industrial and Organizational Psychology, 3,* 340–343.

Sackett, P. R. (2011). The uniform guidelines is not a scientific document: Implications for expert testimony. *Industrial and Organizational Psychology, 4,* 545–546.

Schmitt, A. P., Holland, P. W., & Dorans, N. J. (1993). Evaluating hypotheses about differential item functioning. In P. W. Holland & H. Wainer (Eds.), *Differential item functioning* (pp. 281–315). Hillsdale, NJ: Lawrence Erlbaum Associates.

Sharf, J. C. (2011). Equal employment versus equal opportunity: A naked political agenda covered by a scientific fig leaf. *Industrial and Organizational Psychology, 4,* 537–539.

Shepard, L. A. (2006). Classroom assessment. In R. L. Brennan (Ed.), *Educational measurement* (pp. 623–646). Westport, CT: Praeger.

Society for Industrial and Organizational Psychology. (2003). *Principles for the validation and use of personnel selection procedures* (4th ed.). Bowling Green, OH: Author.

Tonowski, R. F. (2011). The uniform guidelines and personnel selection: Identify and fix the right problem. *Industrial and Organizational Psychology, 4,* 521–525.

Toulmin, S. (2003). *The uses of argument* (2nd ed.). Cambridge, UK: Cambridge University Press.

Welner, K. (2001). Alexander v. Sandoval: A setback for civil rights. *Educational Policy Analysis Archives, 9*(24). Retrieved from http://epaa.asu.edu/epaa/v9n24.html

Washington v. Davis, 426 U.S. 229 (1976).

A "conditional" sense of fairness in assessment

Robert J. Mislevy[a], Geneva Haertel[b], Britte H. Cheng[b], Liliana Ructtinger[b], Angela DeBarger[b], Elizabeth Murray[c], David Rose[c], Jenna Gravel[d], Alexis M. Colker[e], Daisy Rutstein[b] and Terry Vendlinski[b]

[a]Educational Testing Service, Princeton, NJ, USA; [b]Center for Technology in Learning, SRI International, Menlo Park, CA, USA; [c]CAST, Wakefield, MA, USA; [d]Graduate School of Education, Harvard University, Cambridge, MA, USA; [e]Independent Consultant, San Mateo, CA, USA

Standardizing aspects of assessments has long been recognized as a tactic to help make evaluations of examinees fair. It reduces variation in irrelevant aspects of testing procedures that could advantage some examinees and disadvantage others. However, recent attention to making assessment accessible to a more diverse population of students highlights situations in which making tests identical for all examinees can make a testing procedure less fair: Equivalent surface conditions may not provide equivalent evidence about examinees. Although testing accommodations are by now standard practice in most large-scale testing programmes, for the most part these practices lie outside formal educational measurement theory. This article builds on recent research in universal design for learning (UDL), assessment design, and psychometrics to lay out the rationale for inference that is conditional on matching examinees with principled variations of an assessment so as to reduce construct-irrelevant demands. The present focus is assessment for special populations, but it is argued that the principles apply more broadly.

Introduction

Standardizing aspects of an examination process across examinees can reduce variations that would advantage some examinees and disadvantage others. Scores on exams under which, unbeknown to the score user, some examinees had more time than others or had their work rated by different criteria, for example, are patently unfair. *Unidentified nonequivalent surface conditions provide nonequivalent evidence about learners.* Ensuring that test materials and procedures are the same for all examinees epitomizes one sense of "fairness": All examinees run the same race, so to speak. Some particular remaining aspects, such as the content of specific test items, may favour some students and other aspects may favour other students, but the idea is that these are random differences which tend to average out (Green, 1978). We refer to this strategy as *marginal inference.* Marginal is a statistical term that means "averaging over".

Efforts to extend educational experiences to a more diverse population of students reveal that the same situation need not provide the same learning opportunities to all students. Similarly, the same assessment tasks may not produce the same information about what they know and can do. If we want to assess students' proficiency with arithmetic word problems, the same printed test may serve the purpose for a sighted student but not one with limited vision. *Equivalent surface conditions may not provide equivalent evidence about learners.*

Alternative forms of assessment such as accommodated tests, customized tests, and examinee-choice of tasks suggest a different sense of fairness: Tests can differ in their surface characteristics in such ways that equivalent evidence about examinees' proficiencies can be obtained (Rose, Murray, & Gravel, 2012). We refer to this as *conditional inference*. Conditional is also a statistical term, which means taking certain information into account specifically rather than averaging over the ways it might vary. In assessment, conditional inference means deliberately varying aspects of an assessment for students to enable each student to access, interact with, and provide responses to tasks in ways that present minimal difficulty, so the primary challenge is the proficiency meant to be assessed. Thus, *surface conditions that differ in principled ways for different learners can provide equivalent evidence.*

Assessment that is tailored in some form has become widespread, such as the accommodations spurred by the Americans with Disabilities Act. However, the methodologies of educational assessment and educational measurement (psychometrics) evolved in the environment of standardized assessment procedures and marginal statistical inference. Currently, much applied work with testing accommodations is after-the-fact: Unitary forms of tasks from standardized tests are first created, then retro-fitted in an ad hoc manner. We describe a prospective framework for coordinated design and analysis that supports conditional inference across tailored forms of tasks. We build on developments in three distinct areas that are required jointly, namely, assessment design theory, universal design for learning (UDL; Rose & Meyer, 2002; Rose, Meyer, & Hitchcock, 2005), and psychometric modelling.

The following section reviews the assessment-argument structure in which assessment design takes place, using an "evidence centered design" framework (ECD; Mislevy & Haertel, 2006; Mislevy, Steinberg, & Almond, 2003). The interplay among construct-relevant and construct-irrelevant knowledge, skills, and abilities (KSAs) with task features and work products, and implications for validity, are examined.

Building on research and experience with UDL, the third section discusses key categories of construct-irrelevant KSAs that can hamper students' learning and performance in assessments. It notes strategies to circumvent them, provide support, or mitigate their effects.

An integration of the ECD and UDL frameworks is then proposed. A support tool for test developers, called a design pattern, which integrates validity principles with UDL principles, is described (Haertel, DeBarger, Villalba, Hamel, & Colker, 2010). The design pattern provides support for the matching strategies described in Hansen, Mislevy, and Steinberg (2007), Hansen, Mislevy, Steinberg, Lee, and Forer (2005), and Kopriva (2008). The ideas are illustrated with examples from the Principled Science Assessment Designs for Students with Disabilities project (Haertel et al., 2010), supported by the Institute of Educational Sciences, U.S. Department of Education.

A more technical section then discusses psychometric foundations for conditional inference, using von Davier's (2008) General Diagnostic Model (GDM).[1] This psychometric framework is used to describe and compare the logic of four paradigmatic assessment situations:

- Marginal inference when the testing population is homogeneous with respect to having all the necessary construct-irrelevant KSAs the tasks require.

- Marginal inference when needed accommodations have not been used and the resulting mismatches are unknown to the score user.
- Conditional inference when task features and student construct-irrelevant capabilities are ascertained after testing occurs.
- Conditional inference when tasks are matched to students a priori.

The article focuses on assessment of special populations, but the principles can be applied more broadly. The closing section is a more general discussion of the theoretical and practical advantages of the approach.

Assessment arguments

ECD is a framework that makes explicit, and provides tools for, building assessment arguments and assessments around the arguments (Mislevy & Riconscente, 2006; Mislevy, Steinberg, & Almond, 2003). ECD casts assessment as an argument from imperfect evidence. It aims to make explicit the claims, or the inferences one intends to make based on scores, and the nature of the evidence that supports those claims. It distinguishes layers at which different kinds of activities and structures appear in assessment design and operation, and provides tools and representations to support work at various layers.

This section describes ECD enough to coordinate the ideas that are central to the article: the roles of construct-relevant and irrelevant KSAs in validity, their relation to design choices about task features, UDL-infused design patterns that support task designers, and the connection to psychometric models.

ECD layers

ECD sees the design process as first crafting an assessment argument, then embodying it in tasks, rubrics, scores, and procedures. Messick (1994) gives the essence of an assessment argument: "A construct-centered approach would begin by asking what complex of knowledge, skills, or other attribute should be assessed... Next, what behaviors or performances should reveal those constructs, and what tasks or situations should elicit those behaviors?" (p. 17).

The layers in ECD are Domain Analysis, Domain Modelling, the Conceptual Assessment Framework (CAF), Assessment Implementation, and Assessment Delivery (Table 1). They address, respectively, the substantive domain; the assessment argument; the structure of assessment elements such as tasks, rubrics, and psychometric models; the implementation of these elements; and their functioning in an operational assessment.

This article centres on the Domain Modelling and CAF layers. Domain Modelling is where assessment arguments are constructed; we will analyse the way that tailoring task features to learners impacts validity. The CAF is where the corresponding psychometric modelling takes place and particular task features are linked to learners' needs.

The structure of assessment arguments

Messick's (1994) quote is a good start, but we need more machinery to examine the interplay of task design choices and validity. Figure 1 shows Toulmin's (1958) general schema for reasoning from particular data (D) to claims (C). A warrant (W; usually multifaceted, with backing (B) in research or experience) justifies this inference. In practice, we reason inductively, back up through the warrant, as indicated by the bold arrow from data to

Table 1. ECD layers.

Layer	Focus of attention	Activities and Representations
Domain Analysis	The substantive domain	Determining what is important in the domain; i.e., what kinds of things do people need to know and do, in what kinds of situations.
Domain Modelling	The assessment argument	Arranging products of the Domain Analysis into the structure of assessment arguments. (Assessment arguments; Design Patterns)
Conceptual Assessment Framework	The structure of assessment elements	More formal & technical specifications for the elements of operational assessments. (Student, Evidence, and Task Models)
Assessment Implementation	Implementing the elements	Task and test assembly, fitting psychometric models, tuning scoring procedures.
Assessment Delivery	The functioning of the elements in an operational assessment	Architecture for assessment delivery (Almond, Steinberg, & Mislevy, 2002).

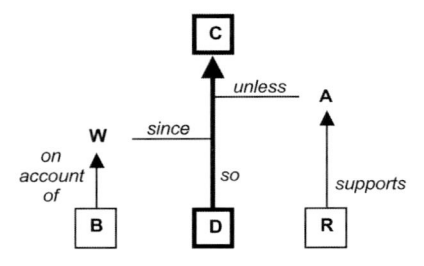

Figure 1. Toulmin's argument structure.

claim. Because data are rarely perfect or conclusive, we must usually qualify an inference in light of alternative explanations (A), which further "rebuttal" data (R) might support or weaken. Alternative explanations play a central role in validity and tailored task design.

Figure 2 applies the argument structure to assessment (Mislevy, 2006). We will focus on a single task, where "task" could range from a familiar multiple-choice item or an essay question to a language-proficiency interview or an open-ended problem in a computerized simulation. The claim is what we would like to say about some aspect of what a learner knows or can do. At the bottom of the diagram is a student's action in a situation: The student says, does, or makes something. The data is not the action itself, but our interpretations of the action and situation. There are three kinds of data:

- aspects of the person's actions;
- aspects of the situation; and
- additional information about the person's history or relationship to the observational situation.

The first of these is usually thought of as "the data" in assessment, but the second, the features of the situation, are equally necessary. The task must have features that engage the KSAs we are interested in. And if other task features present irrelevant impediments to a

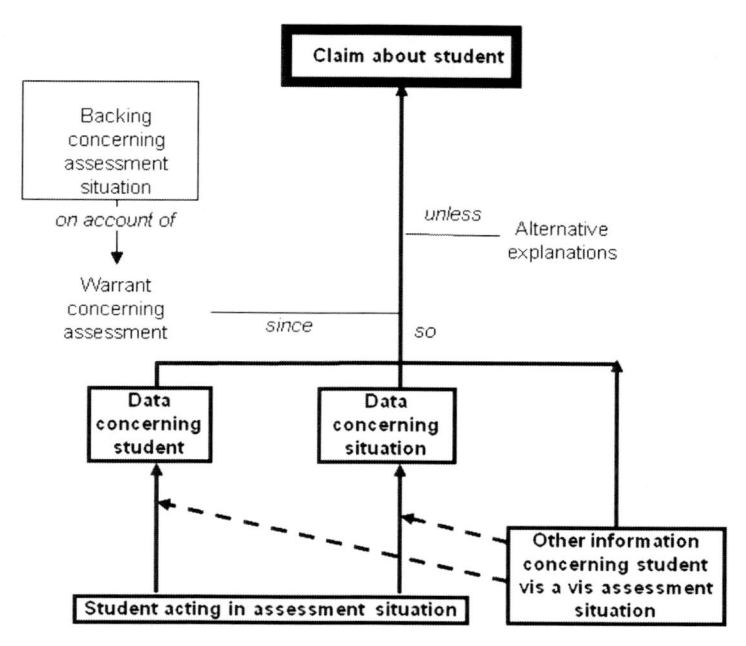

Figure 2.   Extended Toulmin diagram for an assessment argument.

student's performance, we may not get meaningful evidence about what we are interested in. The third kind of data – what we know about the student with respect to the construct-irrelevant KSAs needed to access, interact with, and respond to tasks – helps us design tasks to minimize these obstacles.

A warrant about the targeted, or construct-relevant, KSAs comes with assumptions about access, interaction, and response capabilities. A warrant in genetics test might be,

> If a student understands how to form an inheritance-mode model to account for the coat colors of mice resulting from a crossing of two parents, then she will probably be able to fill in the cells of a Punnett square with the revised model.

The features of a corresponding task might include a diagram and text about a crossing and a computer tool to drag and drop genetics symbols into the Punnett square. A student might understand the required genetics, but perform poorly on the task because she is unfamiliar with the interface, or cannot distinguish colours that are associated with different alleles, or cannot physically manipulate the drag-and-drop device, or does not read English well enough to know what to do. All of these are alternative explanations for poor performance on the standard form of the task, other than the claim that she does not understand the genetics. The knowledge, skills, and abilities represented in the alternative explanations are construct irrelevant. A student needs them to succeed on the task, but they are not what the task is meant to assess. Presenting the identical task to all students derails those who are unable to perform due to construct-irrelevant KSAs, whether or not they have the genetics proficiencies.

Validity

To get good evidence about the KSAs we care about, then, there are two things we need to do. First, we need to make sure that a task has features that are likely to elicit the targeted

KSAs, to the extent a student has them. A simulation task meant to probe understanding of Newton's laws that can be solved by trial and error gives "false positive" misleading information. Second, we need to make sure that the task does not require undue knowledge or skills that are unrelated to the targeted KSAs. A student who can work with Newton's laws but cannot figure out the simulation tool gives "false negative" misleading information. In both cases, alternative explanations are at play. Messick (1989) calls these threats to validity "construct under-representation" and "construct irrelevant sources of variance". They hold critical implications for task design.

Assessment design patterns

A design pattern addresses a recurring design problem and the core of its solution. Alexander, Ishikawa, and Silverstein (1977) introduced design patterns in architecture, and they have been widely adapted in software engineering (Gamma, Helm, Johnson, & Vlissides, 1994). They capture experience and provide guidance, in a structure that builds in deep principles of a domain. They can be applied to resolve a problem in many situations even though the particulars are never exactly the same.

The Principled Assessment Design for Inquiry (PADI) project developed design patterns for assessment to provide a practical yet theory-based approach to develop high-quality assessments of science inquiry (Mislevy, Chudowsky, et al., 2003). PADI assessment design patterns conceptualize the elements of assessment arguments and their interrelationships as they apply to some targeted aspect of learning. They bridge the knowledge of content experts and measurement experts who need to work together to design complex assessment tasks. They help designers think through the mechanics of tasks in a way that leads to a coherent assessment argument (Table 2).

Each design pattern details three essential elements around which all assessments revolve: the student's knowledge, skills, and abilities about which one wants to make

Table 2. Attributes of a PADI assessment design pattern.

Attribute	Definition
Title	Short name for the design pattern
Summary	Overview of the kinds of assessment situations students encounter in tasks supported by this design pattern.
Rationale	How tasks this design pattern supports provide evidence about the Focal KSAs.
Focal KSAs	Primary knowledge/skill/abilities of students that one wants to know about.
Additional KSAs	Other KSAs that may be required in tasks.
Potential observations	Features of performance that would provide evidence about the KSAs.
Potential work products	Different modes or formats in which students might produce the evidence.
Potential rubrics	Scoring rubrics that might be useful.
Characteristic features	Features of situations that are likely to evoke the desired evidence.
Variable features	Kinds of task features that can be varied in order to shift the difficulty or focus of tasks, or that require, circumvent, or support particular Additional KSAs.
Educational standards	Links to the related national, state, or professional standards.
Exemplar tasks	Links to sample assessment tasks that are instances of this design pattern.
References	Pointers to research and other literature that illustrate or provide backing for the design pattern.

claims (*Focal KSAs*); the salient characteristics of what students say, do, or make that would provide evidence about acquisition of the Focal KSAs (*Potential observations*); and features of task environment that are needed to evoke the desired evidence (*Characteristic features*). (The last two concern data both as to what we would want to see students do and the situations they act in.)

Rationale articulates the warrant that justifies the targeted inferences and the kinds of task and evidence that support them. *Additional KSAs* may be required in a task that addresses the focal KSAs. Since Additional KSAs are not what is intended to be assessed, they can introduce threats to test validity. They need to be identified and minimized or avoided in order not to introduce construct-irrelevant variance. Alternatively, if it is known that the examinees possess a sufficient level of a given Additional KSA, that Additional KSA can be incorporated in the assessment tasks along with the intended KSAs. *Variable features* of tasks enable task developers to adjust the difficulty of tasks or focus their evidentiary value on different aspects of the Focal KSA, or to incorporate or circumvent particular additional KSAs.

Potential work products are students' responses or performances that are the source of Observations; different work products might require different combinations of Additional KSAs to produce. *Potential rubrics* are links to rules and instructions for evaluating work products. A design pattern also links to standards, other design patterns, task templates, and sample tasks to illustrate the connections in the design pattern.

The next section briefly reviews UDL. The section following that shows how design patterns can be used to integrate UDL with assessment arguments and validity.

Universal design principles

The dialogue around student assessment now encompasses *all* students, as compared to past practices that excluded students with disabilities from accountability metrics. Beginning with the No Child Left Behind Act in 2001, states in the United States must include students with disabilities in reports of performance and progress. Developing assessment design frameworks that can produce tasks that are appropriate and accessible for a wide range of students requires new tools and approaches, including ones that can interface with frameworks for instructional and assessment materials (i.e., UDL) that are specifically designed to meet the needs of students with disabilities.

Rationale

UDL helps to meet the challenge of diversity by suggesting flexible assessment materials, techniques, and strategies (Dolan, Rose, Burling, Harris, & Way, 2007). The flexibility of UDL empowers assessors to meet the varied needs of students and to accurately measure student progress. The UDL framework includes three overarching principles that address three critical aspects of any learning activity, including its assessment. *Multiple means of representation* addresses the ways in which information is presented. *Multiple means of action and expression* focuses on the ways in which students can interact with content and express what they are learning. *Multiple means of engagement* addresses the ways in which students are engaged in learning (Rose & Meyer, 2002, 2006; Rose et al., 2005).

Principle I: provide multiple means of representation (the "what" of learning)

Students differ in the ways they perceive and comprehend information that is presented to them. For example, those with sensory disabilities (e.g., blindness or deafness), learning disabilities (e.g., dyslexia), and language or cultural differences may all require different ways of approaching content. Some may grasp information best when presented visually or through auditory means rather than printed text alone. Others may benefit from multiple representations of the content – a print passage presented with illustrative photographs or line drawings and an audio recording of the print passage.

Principle II: provide multiple means of action and expression (the "how" of learning)

Students differ in the ways they can interact with materials and express what they know. For example, individuals with significant motor disabilities (e.g., cerebral palsy), those who struggle with strategic and organizational abilities (executive function disorders, ADHD), and those who have language barriers, approach learning tasks differently, and will demonstrate their mastery differently. Some may be able to express themselves well in text but not in speech, and vice versa.

Principle III: provide multiple means of engagement (the "why" of learning)

Affect represents a crucial component to learning. Students differ in the ways in which they can be engaged or motivated to learn. Some enjoy spontaneity and novelty, while others prefer strict routine. Some persist with challenging tasks, while others give up quickly.

There is no one means of representation, expression, or engagement that will be optimal for all students in all assessment situations; providing multiple options for students is essential (CAST, 2012).

Categories of UDL

In addition to the three principles that provide general guidance for infusing UDL into assessment design, we identify particular categories of student abilities (perceptual, expressive, language and symbols, cognitive, executive functioning, and affective) that are required for successful performance on assessment tasks but are usually not the assessment target. We want to use task features that support students who lack such construct-irrelevant abilities, or select features that minimize demand for them.

Integrating ECD and UDL

A design pattern that integrates the principles of ECD and UDL can be used to create different versions of the kind of item that often appears on statewide science assessments, targeting the same construct-relevant KSAs but varying with respect to construct-irrelevant KSAs. An item called "Bicycle Rider"[2] illustrates the points.

Version A of Bicycle Rider

The multiple-choice Bicycle Rider item was designed to test both middle-school science content and inquiry practices. The content is forces and motion. The inquiry practice is the ability to use appropriate tools and technologies to gather, analyse, and interpret data. The item describes how a person rides a bike at changing or constant speeds over time. It then asks the student to indicate which of four graphs, each illustrating a different relationship between speed and time, best characterizes the bicycle rider's travel.

Version A of the item presents students with a stem that reads "Which graph **best** represents the motion of a cyclist speeding up and then continuing at a constant speed?"

Under the stem, an image of four small graphs depicting possible speed (y-axis) over time (x-axis) relationships is presented, each labelled with a letter in the upper left corner. A link to enlarge the image in a separate window is provided underneath. Under the text and images, four radio buttons, labelled simply A through D, appear in a vertical array. A student is to choose the button that matches the letter of the graph she thinks is the best answer.

Version A appeared on a practice test from one state's large-scale middle-school science assessment. This assessment was developed and delivered by CAL Testing. Many features of the online testing platform were developed with UDL concerns in mind and included the following (Shaftel, Yang, Glasnapp, & Poggio, 2005):

- Progress monitoring on the screen ("breadcrumbs" across top of screen).
- Variable font size, magnifier, contrast.
- Text to speech.
- Radio buttons for multiple choice response capture.
- Testing environment tools: highlighter, striker, eraser, ruler, calculator.

The point is not that either version is UDL infused or not, but an examination through the UDL/validity perspective of two variants from a potential family of tasks that tap the same construct but with features that require different combinations of Additional KSAs.

A UDL-infused design pattern

Version A of Bicycle Rider is aligned with a design pattern entitled "Interpreting Data in Tables, Charts, and Graphs". This design pattern was developed in collaboration with a state department of education in the *Principled Science Assessment Design for Students with Disabilities* project (Haertel et al., 2010; Rose et al., 2012; Zhang et al., 2010). The complete design pattern can be accessed at http://design-se.padi.sri.com/padi/AddNodeAction.do?NODE_ID = 2140&state = viewNode. This design pattern supports creating items that involve understanding and interpreting data and data-variable relationships as represented in tables, charts, or graphic forms. Since every science content area involves data, it supports item development in all areas.

This design pattern also integrates principles of universal design for learning (UDL) into specific design pattern attributes. Haertel et al. (2010) provide a more detailed discussion, but the key ideas are these:

- Focal KSAs are knowledge, skills, or other attributes that are the focus of the design pattern, and are usually construct relevant in a task the design pattern supports. They are intimately connected with the characteristic task features. For example, the focal KSAs to be assessed in Bicycle Rider are:
  - o ability to compare and /or contrast multiple representations and the data represented therein;
  - o ability to describe simple mathematical relationships or trends among data;
  - o ability to draw conclusions or make predictions based on data.

- Additional KSAs identify other knowledge and skills that may or may not be construct relevant but are required to successfully answer the item; the assessment designer determines whether the Additional KSAs will be supported through the use of variable features in the assessment or whether they will remain unaddressed.

Examples of two Additional KSAs that are prerequisite knowledge for successfully completing an item like Bicycle Rider are:

o awareness of different representational forms;
o knowledge of what data are.

Additional KSAs that represent learner needs (UDL) for successful performance on an item also appear in Additional KSAs, organized in the six categories listed in the UDL section. We will see examples when we compare the two versions of the item.

- Characteristic features of tasks must be present if the task is to provide evidence about the construct. Making sure the task embodies all of the characteristic features ensures that the construct-relevant KSAs will be assessed. For items like Bicycle Rider, characteristic features include:

  o the presentation contains numeric data;
  o the presentation includes at least one representational form;
  o the presented data are in a scientific context.

- Variable task features include ones that allow a designer to adjust the difficulty, the scope, and the focus of a task while obtaining evidence about the construct. UDL-infused design patterns, in particular, detail features that can be varied to support, bypass, or appropriately target demands for construct-irrelevant KSAs. They are linked to the relevant Additional KSAs, so that clicking on a particular Additional KSA highlights variable task features that can be manipulated to increase, decease, or support demands for that KSA. Variable features a designer can consider when writing an item like Bicycle Rider are given below. The next section shows how some of these Variable Features were used to change demands for particular Additional KSAs in Version B of Bicycle Rider.

  o Number of representations.
  o Complexity of representational form(s).
  o Number of variables represented in the table, graph, or chart.
  o Perceptual features: visual information (e.g., automatic text to speech).
  o Language and symbols: supports for syntactic skills and underlying structure (e.g., highlighted syntactical elements).
  o Cognitive features: supports for critical features, big ideas, and relationships (e.g., examples to emphasize critical concepts).
  o Executive features: supports for managing information (e.g., locate radio buttons near relevant images).
  o Affect features: supports for intrinsic motivation (e.g., enhanced relevance with real world context).

- Potential observations are suggested to gather evidence about the focal KSAs. For example, if a task is intended to assess the focal KSA "the ability to compare and contrast multiple representations and the data represented therein", then one potential observation would involve having the student read a description of a data relationship and select from among several graphical representations the one that most accurately depicts it. In the design pattern, the relevant potential observation is:

  o identification of representational forms of data that communicate the same mathematical relationships among data (or trends in data).

- Potential work products indicate a form in which students can produce responses. Work products can vary in ways that are sensitive to resource constraints and logistical considerations. In UDL-infused design patterns, students with varying profiles of needs (e.g., visually impaired, limited dexterity) may require different work product options. The entries in Potential Work Product and Additional KSA are linked to help task designers see the connections. An example of a work product is:

  o selection of a representation to match a data relationship.

Version B of Bicycle Rider

Both versions of Bicycle Rider address UDL concerns at the level of the testing platform. We introduced variations motivated by the design pattern in the specifics of Version B. Possible sources of construct-irrelevant variance were identified related to individual students' learning needs in terms of perception, expression, language and symbols, cognition, executive functioning, and engagement (affective). These categories of needs appear as Additional KSAs in the design pattern. These Additional KSAs are linked to variable task features in the design pattern that could be used to support students' needs for construct-irrelevant KSAs. These variable features were used to identify revisions that would reduce particular construct-irrelevant demands, while maintaining the characteristic features and thus the construct-relevant demands. These UDL-motivated variations were thus constrained by the essential focus of the assessment argument.

The item stem of Version B reads (with bolding): "A student rides her bike to school. She first **speeds up for 1 minute.** She then **continues at a constant speed for 5 minutes.** [line break.] Which graph best represents her motion over this time?" Under the stem, four time-by-speed graph answer options appear. They show the same relationships as the graphs in Version A, but they are visually improved through enlargement and clearer labelling. Furthermore, a radio button appears directly to the top left of each y axis, obviating a letter-based choice, and thus eliminating a set of correspondences to identify and the associated demand for working memory. For students above these hurdles, the variant would differ negligibly; its difficulty would be driven by their understanding of the graph-motion representation. For students challenged by the construct-irrelevant KSAs, Variant B poses less demand for these KSAs. They might still answer incorrectly if they do not understand the representation, but the same response would provide more valid information since the alteration reduces the force of alternative explanations for missing the item because of demands for construct-irrelevant KSAs.

Note that this logic reveals a shortcoming of using "differential boost" (Fuchs, Fuchs, Eaton, Hamlett, & Karns, 2000) to evaluate the effectiveness of UDL-motivated item revisions. It can be that a revision reduces a need for a construct-irrelevant KSA for many students, and for more students *without* disabilities who have the focal skill than students *with* disabilities who have the skill. The group without disabilities now has even fewer false-negative wrong answers. Validity has increased, yet the pattern in percents-correct is the opposite of differential boost.

Table 3 summarizes the UDL variations implemented in Version B. The Interpreting Data in Tables, Charts, and Graphs design pattern (http://design-se.padi.sri.com/padi/AddNodeAction.do?NODE_ID = 2140&state = viewNode) shows how the extended UDL features are represented in the design pattern template.

Two examples of principled changes between the Version A and B items illustrate the UDL design logic. First, note that in the stem in Version A, no context is given for the ride

Table 3.   UDL principles (categories of students' needs) supported by variable features in Version B of Bicycle Rider

UDL Principle (Category of Student Need)	Task Model Variables Implemented to Address UDL Principles in Version B of Bicycle Rider
Perceptual Features	-Flexible size of text and images
	-Flexible amplitude of speech and sound
	-Adjustable contrast
	-Flexible layout
	-Visual graphics
	-Verbal descriptors (spoken equivalents for text and images)
	-Automatic text to speech
Skill and Fluency	-Alternative to written response (radio buttons)
Language and Symbols	-Embedded support for key terms,
	-Alternate syntactic levels (simplified text)
	-Support for decoding (digital text and automatic text to speed)
Cognitive Features	-Using explicit examples to emphasize critical concept (minutes cyclist accelerating and at constant speed)
	-Presentation of graphical representation simultaneously as compared to one at a time (reduce cognitive load)
Executive Features	-Reduced working memory
	-Locate radio buttons near relevant images on-screen
	-Progress monitoring
Affect Features	-Real-world context to heighten engagement
	-Age-appropriate materials

or the amount of time it takes. The stem in Version B says who is riding the bike and the amount of time the ride takes. This second version was guided by the Cognitive and Affective UDL categories, providing a real-world context and explicit designation of time. There is a tradeoff: Version A has fewer words and does not introduce a potentially distracting context, whereas Version B may increase engagement. There will be some students for whom Version A better matches their profile of construct-irrelevant KSAs, and other students for whom Version B does.

Second, the graphs in Version A are assigned a letter (A through D) that must be referenced in the array underneath to make the radio-button answer choice. In Version B, the radio buttons appear directly adjacent to the graphs, eliminating the letter choice translation. Minimizing steps speaks directly to the Skill and Fluency, Cognitive, and Executive Functioning UDL categories. These UDL-motivated variations of task features were facilitated by the technology platform that supports both versions, illustrating how computer delivery can produce tailored forms from an item family to individual students.

A psychometric framework

The previous sections showed how the UDL and ECD frameworks could be integrated, so one can construct tasks that evoke comparable evidence even though surface features vary to tap combinations of construct-irrelevant KSAs that match the capabilities of different students. This section provides a psychometric framework for inference in an assessment designed according to these principles. It expresses the argument structures can be expressed in terms of von Davier's (2008) general diagnostic model (GDM). The GDM is a member of a class of models called cognitive diagnosis models

(Leighton & Gierl, 2007) or diagnostic classification models (Rupp, Templin, & Henson, 2010).

Key ideas

A cognitive diagnosis model gives probabilities of task responses as functions of features of tasks and student proficiencies associated with those features. The analyst indicates which "attributes" are involved in each task; students are similarly characterized in terms of their proficiency with respect to the same set of attributes.

The simplest cognitive diagnostic models have dichotomous attributes: Tasks do or do not require them, students do or do not have them. For example, Tatsuoka's (1983) mixed-number subtraction example characterized students in terms of which algebraic procedures a student has mastered, and tasks in terms of which procedures they require. Probabilities of success are modelled in terms of how a student's profile of proficiencies on the attributes matches up with the profile of attributes an item requires. The ideas extend to more complicated response variables, such as counts and ordered category responses, and to more complicated attributes of people, such as ordered categorical states (such as level on a learning progression) and continuous variables (such as decoding skill).

Cognitive diagnosis models allow a range of ways to combine student proficiencies to model item response probabilities. They support compensatory combinations (being high in some proficiencies can make up for being low in others), and combinations such as disjunctions, when different proficiencies can be employed to succeed on a task, and conjunctions, for when certain proficiencies are necessary jointly. We can use conjunctive combinations to model the effect of necessary but construct-irrelevant KSAs. We can posit, for example, that a task requires a conjunctive combination of several construct-irrelevant KSAs and a set of construct-relevant KSAs, which are effective only given a sufficient value on the conjunction of construct-irrelevant KSAs.

Taking advantage of these combination properties, we will lay out a quantitative model for the logic of four testing situations that can also be described as qualitative assessment argument structures. We use the vector of attribute values to describe which construct-irrelevant and construct-relevant demands are designed into a task variant. We use the vector of attribute variables to describe students' profiles of construct-irrelevant and construct-relevant KSAs. We use the structure of the model to express what is likely to happen when a particular student is presented a particular variant of a task. We show how this conceptualization fits the strategy of administering task variants for each student to give them the best chance to show what they know and can do.

A general diagnostic model

The key elements of a cognitive diagnosis model are contained in the general form $p(\mathbf{X} = \mathbf{x} | \boldsymbol{\theta}, \mathbf{Q}, \boldsymbol{\eta})$, where $\mathbf{X} = (X_1, ..., X_n)$ represents n task response variables and $\mathbf{x} = (x_1, ..., x_n)$ values they can take; $\boldsymbol{\theta} = (\theta_1, ..., \theta_K)$ is a vector of K proficiency variables (KSAs) that categorize a student ("attributes" in cognitive diagnosis terminology); $\mathbf{Q}$ is a matrix with n rows, one per task, with the jth row a vector $\mathbf{q}_j = (q_{j1}, ..., q_{jK})$ indicating the qualitative association of Task j to the K attributes; and $\boldsymbol{\eta}$ is a vector of parameters that gives the quantitative relationship between task features and students' probabilities of success. This expression indicates that there are multiple aspects of students' knowledge and skill; that tasks have features we can relate to these proficiencies in known ways, by virtue of the tasks' construction; and in a manner to be specified, how they interact cognitively determines how students are likely to respond.

Particular forms of these variables and functions must be specified. The following basic specifications allow us to make observations about conditional inference:

- Assume all items are dichotomous, where $x_j = 1$ indicates a correct response and 0 indicates incorrect.
- Partition θ into $(\phi_1, ..., \phi_K, \theta)$, where the ϕ_ks are construct-irrelevant KSAs and θ is the construct that is the target of measurement. Eliciting evidence about θ necessarily requires some construct-irrelevant KSAs to access, interact with, and respond to a task.
- Define the task-attribute vectors $\mathbf{q}_j$ such that q_{jk} indicates the demand for construct-irrelevant KSA k required by Task j. Some of the elements of $\mathbf{q}_j$ may also be defined in terms of the presence of supports or accommodations, as might be found in students' Individualized Education Programs (IEPs). In this case, the corresponding ϕs indicate a student's need for such supports or accommodations. *All* tasks are constructed to have some level of demand on θ. They can differ as to which ϕ_ks they require and what amounts. We can define families of tasks that are equivalent as to their construct-relevant demands, but differ as to construct-irrelevant demands (Kopriva, 2008).
- Define the combination functions $h_k(q_{jk}, \phi_k)$ to take the value 1 if a student's value of ϕ_k equals or exceeds the level of demand for KSA k that is required in Task j, and 0 if not. That is, $h_k(q_{jk}, \phi_k) = 1$ means that the student is *above the hurdle* with respect to the demands for KSA ϕ_k posed by Task j; for example, whether a student's visual acuity makes it possible for her to read the font-size of Task j. If a task has no demand for a ϕ_k, then $h_k(q_{jk}, \phi_k) = 1$. When an element of $\mathbf{q}_j$ is defined in terms of the presence of a support or accommodation, $h(q_{jk}, \phi_k) = 1$ if either the student does not need the support of accommodation or if she needs it and it is present. Here $h(q_{jk}, \phi_k) = 0$ means the student needs the support or accommodation but Task j does not provide it. Again $h_k(q_{jk}, \phi_k) = 1$ means the student is *above the hurdle*.
- Define the construct-relevant combination function $f(\theta, \beta_j)$ as a standard psychometric model, such as an item response theory (IRT) model in which the probability of a correct response is a function of a student's θ and characteristics of Task j such as its difficulty with respect to θ.
- Let π_j be the (chance) probability of a student getting Task j right even if he is not above the hurdle on one or more construct-irrelevant KSAs, that is, ϕ_ks. (Together, the π_j s and ϕ_ks constitute $\mathbf{\eta}$ in the GDM.)

The form of the probability model that accommodates conditional-inference is then

$$\Pr\left(x_j = 1 \middle| \phi_1, ..., \phi_K, \theta, \mathbf{q}_j, \beta_j, \pi_j\right) = \pi_j + \left(1 - \pi_j\right) \prod_k \left[h_k\left(\phi_k, q_{jk}\right)\right] f\left(\theta, \beta_j\right). \quad (1)$$

By the way that the q_{jk}s, ϕ_ks, and $h(q_{jk}, \phi_k)$s are defined)s are defined, $\prod \left[h_k\left(\phi_k, q_{jk}\right)\right] = 0$ if there is at least one k for which Task j's demand with respect to construct-irrelevant KSA ϕ_k exceeds the student's capabilities. In this case, the entire second addend is 0; the probability of getting the item right is just π_j, and the response does not depend on θ at all. If, on the other hand, for every ϕ_k there is either no demand or the demand is within the student's capabilities (i.e., she is "above the hurdle" for those construct-irrelevant

KSAs), then $\prod \left[h_k(\phi_k, q_{jk}) \right] = 1$ and the probability of a correct response depends on θ. It may be a high probability or a low probability, but it depends on the targeted KSAs. This is a mathematical expression to say that valid inference about the construct is *conditional* on the task's necessary construct-irrelevant KSA demands being satisfied.

This model can be extended in many ways, such as alternative response types and multivariate θs. Another extension is more gradual h functions. Instead of all or nothing, over the hurdle or not, one can model performance that gradually degrades as a student falls farther below a task's demand for some ϕ_ks.

Putting these ideas into practice requires specifying the structure of $\mathbf{Q}$ and the forms of the h_ss and f. Strategies and tools for doing so are appearing in the cognitive diagnosis literature (e.g., Kunina-Habenicht, Rupp, & Wilhelm, 2012; Rupp et al., 2010). We note that this research concludes that it is much better to start with strong hypotheses from theory and experience, to build tasks and accommodation options around these frameworks, then fine-tune specifications, rather than write tasks and try to come up with ϕs and $\mathbf{Q}$s post hoc.

The conditional framework introduces a responsibility to test designers and test users to demonstrate that alternative, not-surface-equivalent, forms of tasks do in fact provide equivalent evidence about students. Some instances will not be straightforward. When students can choose items, for example, they may make choices that disadvantage them (Wainer & Thissen, 1994). When variants differ in terms of the language in which they are presented, literal translation need not result in equivalence with respect to construct-relevant demands; more thoughtful adaption with respect to cultural as well as linguistic matters is required (Hambleton, Merenda, & Spielberger, 2004). Experiments with different forms of tasks can shed light on the interacting demands of construct-relevant and -irrelevant task features (Abedi, Lord, Hofstetter, & Baker, 2005). Design strategies and analytical tools developed in these specific areas can be adapted to implementation of the conditional assessment paradigm more generally.

Four inferential situations

We can use the GDM for conditional inference to examine four paradigmatic assessment situations, under the assumption that Equation (1) is the correct model.

Marginal inference when all students are above all construct-irrelevant KSA hurdles

The traditional standardized testing situation, before the introduction of supports or accommodations, assumed a homogeneous population, in the following sense: All students were assumed to have sufficient capabilities in all construct-irrelevant KSAs required by all the items in the test. If this were so, $\prod \left[h_k(\phi_k, q_{jk}) \right] = 1$ for all students, their performance is direct evidence about θ through $f(\theta, \beta_j)$; and, since the everyone-over-all-ϕ hurdles is correct, it is not necessary to include the ϕs and the $\mathbf{q}$s in the operational model. All of the systematic variation among students' performances is assumed to be due to variation in their θs. When this case holds, familiar scores, whether through classical test theory or IRT, support valid inferences about the construct. Under these conditions, equivalent surface conditions do indeed help provide equivalent evidence about students.

Marginal inference when, unbeknown to the score user, some students are not above construct-irrelevant hurdles

This is the case we want to avoid: All students are administered the standard form of the test, with its items' varying $\mathbf{q}$ features and their consequent ϕ demands, and some students are not above all the hurdles on all the items. That is, there are at least some items and students for which $h(q_{jk}, \phi_k) = 0$. If tests are scored in the usual way, assuming that the preceding case holds, then inferences about students' θs are obtained through $f(\theta, \beta_j)$ for any such item. The student's performance on such items, however, is spuriously low, at π_j, and because $\prod\left[h_k(\phi_k, q_{jk})\right] = 0$, the response contains no information about her θ.

Even if a student is above all the hurdles, so $\prod\left[h_k(\phi_k, q_{jk})\right] = 1$, she still might not have a high probability of answering correctly if her θ is low. This is what we want scores to tell us. Getting an item wrong due to lack of ϕ and getting it wrong due to a low θ have identical observed data, an incorrect response. It is misleading as evidence about θ in the first case, while it is relevant in the second.

An interesting situation arises when we do not know whether students are above the hurdles for construct-irrelevant KSAs, but it just so happens that they all are. Their responses depend on only θ. Had we ensured beforehand that all were above the hurdle, we would see exactly the same data, analyse it with the same model $f(\theta, \beta_j)$, and get exactly the same scores – but inferences from them would be more valid, because we rule out alternative explanations for poor performance due to construct-irrelevant demands.

Conditional inference when task features and student construct-irrelevant capabilities are inferred after testing occurs

Here students are tested with surface-equivalent forms, but we use a full model like Equation (1). It is sometimes possible, using the statistical machinery of cognitive diagnosis, to infer students' patterns of ϕs from the patterns of their responses (Rupp et al., 2010). Doing so requires careful construction of items and tests so the **q**s are known and properly balanced. It is then possible to obtain inferences about students' θs from their response patterns, carrying out *conditional inference by analysis*. The assessment situation is the same as the second case described above, but now we are using an appropriate psychometric model to try to sort out the influence of construct-relevant and construct-irrelevant demands.

This approach is usually unsatisfying, because the added uncertainty that comes from trying to estimate the ϕs jointly with θs renders the estimates unreliable. The lessons for this case are that (a) it may be possible to carry out valid conditional inference using an appropriate model, (b) the appropriate model is not the standard model for marginal inference, and (c) doing this is generally not practical.

Conditional inference when tasks are matched to students a priori

This situation obtains when (a) students vary meaningfully with respect to the construct-irrelevant KSAs that are necessary to access, interact with, or respond to assessment tasks; (b) we know how they vary, such as by having their IEPs or knowing what prerequisite knowledge they have; (c) we have or can construct items such that their demands for construct-irrelevant KSAs are known; and (d) we assign to each student, for each item, a variant for which $\prod\left[h_k(\phi_k, q_{jk})\right] = 1$. Now scores depend on θ, not ϕs. Inference about θ from the assessment is more valid, because we have weakened alternative explanations for poor performance due to lack of necessary ϕs. Because we have done the required work in matching students with task variants, we can again use the simple test scoring models $f(\theta, \beta_j)$ and carry out *conditional inference by design*. Compared to the previous case, the modelling demands are lower and the reliability as well as the validity of scores is higher.

Conclusion

Both theoretical and practical benefits accrue from integrating UDL and ECD in the assessment design process.

The central benefit of fairness

Increasing fairness in assessment by integration of ECD and UDL principles from the start has been the goal of our work. The *Standards for Educational and Psychological Testing* (American Educational Research Association, American Psychological Association, & National Council of Measurement in Education, 1999) sees fairness as fundamental to test validity, and specifically addresses incorporating UDL to help develop tests that are fair to all examinees. Our goal to build "fair" assessments is expressed in thoughtfully applying the ideas of ECD to provide all students with an opportunity to perform at their best in assessment situations. Infusing UDL into the design process from the very beginning is a principled, proactive way to reduce accessibility barriers of assessment tasks, in contrast to retrofitting them individually.

Much of the practice of ECD is focused on the identification of sources of construct-irrelevant variance that can result in flawed inferences from scores. Unexamined design choices can lead to tasks that use unnecessarily unfamiliar language and syntax, poorly understood social and cultural item contexts and task stimuli, or modes of representations (visual, aural, behavioural) that may be systematically biased against subgroups with limited access to requisite background knowledge or use of sensory modalities. Fairness requires that task contexts be sufficiently familiar, appropriate, and accessible to all students. Articulation of task models from the beginning of the process reduces the incidence of tasks that disadvantage particular students.

Theoretical benefits

There is a growing body of research and practical experience with assessments meant to serve more diverse student populations. Educative, moral, and legal imperatives motivate the work. Various projects investigate problems from perspectives of special education, educational technology, and domain learning, but there are gaps and conceptual mismatches across experts from different backgrounds. This article provides a unified theoretical framework for assessment design and analysis.

A unified framework helps bring together principles from different fields. A UDL-infused design pattern, for example, not only brings in insights from educational technology, science learning research, and special education, it does so in a form that makes the connections for test designers and helps them build tasks with valid assessment arguments from the outset.

The extension to a psychometric framework further aides practice, since there has been little connection between the psychometric community and the UDL community. The work articulates the vision of fairness arising from the UDL and special needs communities with the models of performance and formal statistical inference from the psychometric world. The framework makes it possible to take advantage in a principled way of the opportunities that computer-administered testing affords. Test delivery systems are now available that can adapt in real time to student needs and provide choices to students to support construct-irrelevant KSAs (Shaftel et al., 2005). Given prior information about students such as their IEPs, it becomes feasible to assemble instances of task models that vary in their surface characteristics but provide equivalent evidence about the targeted construct (Hansen et al., 2005).

Practical benefits

Increased engagement

State-of-the-art assessment design now includes the use of context-rich, situated tasks often presented in online or computer-based environments. These tasks often involve story narratives to increase student engagement and motivation and present students with conceptual links previously unavailable in paper-and-pencil testing. Technology-enhanced tasks also support the use of open-ended, interactive contexts that focus on student reasoning processes, permit multiple solution paths, and present varied stimuli and concepts that were impossible in paper-pencil assessment.

The same characteristics of technology-enhanced tasks that help assess students' extended reasoning may present accessibility barriers to students with disabilities. Students with cognitive disabilities, for example, may be overwhelmed with extended reasoning tasks due to cognitive load and memory or executive functioning demands. Research has shown that some combinations of stimuli can overwhelm students' working memory. Chandler and Sweller (1992) documented a split attention effect where students' learning was hampered by the combination of animation, narration and on-screen text, as compared to just animation and narration.

An ECD process can guide designers in the application of UDL principles as they consider ways to recruit interest, sustain effort, and provide options for self-regulation. For example, designers might consider ways that students can monitor their progress as they work through a task. Variable task features that could help students monitor their progress include a progress bar, intermittent messages to the student about their progress, and interactive navigation through an extended task.

Linking instructional practices to student needs

In ECD's domain modelling layer, design elements reflect the assessment of that domain but also reflect aspects of learning. Designers specify Focal KSAs for assessment, which are also key learning goals (Krajcik, McNeill, & Reiser, 2008). Work products that provide evidence of proficiency in a domain also characterize the activities that students engage in for learning. Because the ECD process has required identifying Additional KSAs, students' learning needs have also been identified as well. The linkage among the additional KSAs and the variable features applies not only to assessment but to day-to-day instruction.

A student's performance on a prerequisite learning goal can also provide information about an Additional KSA, to be supported or built on accordingly by the classroom teacher. Additional KSAs thus provide teachers with information about whether a student has the knowledge needed to acquire the new learning target. Assessment tasks and associated instructional activities can be designed to support the cognitive load that students encounter in multi-step, complex learning goals and problem situations. Teachers can use the design patterns and the specification of additional KSAs associated with Focal KSAs to create instructional activities that support student's learning needs.

Variable task features articulated in design patterns thus correspond to the very same scaffolds that are the critical features of instruction, to ensure that instructional content is accessible to students. For example, using multiple representations in instruction can help make instructional concepts salient (Ainsworth, 2006), and can be used analogously in assessment design to ensure that target KSAs are presented in multiple ways and remain the primary focus of a task. Similarly, vocabulary support, demonstrations of skills, and contrasting cases can be used in both instruction and assessment. While the present article focuses on large-scale assessment, these ideas apply equally to classroom testing.

Acknowledgements

Research findings and assessment tasks described in this article were supported by the Principled Assessment Science Assessment Designs for Students with Disabilities (Institute of Education Sciences, US Department of Education, R324A070035). Any opinions, findings, and conclusions or recommendations expressed in this material are those of the authors and do not necessarily reflect the views of the funding agencies. We are grateful to the guest editor Hossein Karami, Heather Buzick, Eric Hansen, Shelby Haberman, and two anonymous reviewers for helpful suggestions, to John Poggio (University of Kansas), Richard Vineyard (Nevada State Department of Education), and Abel Leon (CAL Testing) for their generous support during the implementation of assessment tasks at schools and school districts, to Robert Dolan as co-PI at the start of the project and advisor thereafter, and to Eric Hansen for advice on evidence-centered design and task accommodations.

Notes

1. Hansen et al. (2007) and Hansen et al. (2005) give an alternative specification using Bayes nets.
2. Released item in the "7th Grade Science Formative Test" by CAL Testing (formerly Kansas Computerized Assessments). Retrieved April, 2009 from http://kca.cete.us, Center for Educational Testing and Evaluation.

References

Abedi, J., Lord, C., Hofstetter, C., & Baker, E. (2005). Impact of accommodation strategies on English language learners' test performance. *Educational Measurement: Issues and Practice, 19*(3), 16–26.

Ainsworth, S. (2006). DeFT: A conceptual framework for considering learning with multiple representations. *Learning and Instruction, 16*, 183–198.

Alexander, C., Ishikawa, S., & Silverstein, M. (1977). *A pattern language: Towns, buildings, construction.* New York, NY: Oxford University Press.

Almond, R. G., Steinberg, L. S., & Mislevy, R. J. (2002). Enhancing the design and delivery of assessment systems: A four-process architecture. *Journal of Technology, Learning, and Assessment, 1*(5). Retrieved from http://www.bc.edu/research/intasc/jtla/journal/v1n5.shtml

American Educational Research Association, American Psychological Association, & National Council of Measurement in Education. (1999). *Standards for educational and psychological testing.* Washington, DC: AERA.

CAST. (2012). *Universal design for learning guidelines Version 2.0.* Wakefield, MA: Author.

Chandler, P., & Sweller, J. (1992). The split-attention effect as a factor in the design of instruction. *British Journal of Educational Psychology, 62*, 233–246.

Dolan, R. P., Rose, D. H., Burling, K., Harris, M., & Way, D. (2007, April). *The universal design for computer-based testing framework: A structure for developing guidelines for constructing innovative computer-administered tests.* Paper presented at the National Council on Measurement in Education Annual Meeting, Chicago, IL.

Fuchs, L. S., Fuchs, D., Eaton, S. B., Hamlett, C., & Karns, K. (2000). Supplementing teacher judgments about test accommodations with objective data sources. *School Psychology Review, 29*, 65–85.

Gamma, E., Helm, R., Johnson, R., & Vlissides, J. (1994). *Design patterns.* Reading, MA: Addison-Wesley.

Green, B. (1978). In defense of measurement. *American Psychologist, 33*, 664–670.

Haertel, G., DeBarger, A. H., Villalba, S., Hamel, L., & Colker, A. M. (2010). *Integration of evidence-centered design and universal design principles using PADI, an online assessment design system* (Technical Report 3). Menlo Park, CA: SRI International.

Hambleton, R. K., Merenda, P. F., & Spielberger, C. D. (Eds.). (2004). *Adapting educational and psychological tests for cross-cultural assessment.* Mahwah, NJ: Erlbaum.

Hansen, E. G., Mislevy, R. J., & Steinberg, L. S. (2007). *Accessibility of testing within a validity framework* (U.S. Patent # 7217134). Washington, DC: U.S. Patent and Trademark Office.

Hansen, E. G., Mislevy, R. J., Steinberg, L. S., Lee, M. J., & Forer, D. C. (2005). Accessibility of tests within a validity framework. *System: An International Journal of Educational Technology and Applied Linguistics, 33,* 107–133.

Kopriva, R. J. (2008). *Improving testing for English language learners.* Philadelphia, PA: Psychology Press.

Krajcik, J., McNeill, K. L. & Reiser, B. J. (2008), Learning-goals-driven design model: Developing curriculum materials that align with national standards and incorporate project-based pedagogy. *Science Education, 92,* 1–32.

Kunina-Habenicht, O., Rupp, A. A., & Wilhelm, O. (2012). The impact of model misspecification on parameter estimation and item-fit assessment in log-linear diagnostic classification models. *Journal of Educational Measurement, 49,* 59–81.

Leighton, J., & Gierl, M. (Eds). (2007). *Cognitive diagnostic assessment for education: Theory and applications.* New York, NY: Cambridge University Press.

Messick, S. (1989). Validity. In R. L. Linn (Ed.), *Educational measurement* (3rd ed., pp. 13–103). New York, NY: Macmillan.

Messick, S. (1994). The interplay of evidence and consequences in the validation of performance assessments. *Educational Researcher, 23*(2), 13–23.

Mislevy, R. J. (2006). Cognitive psychology and educational assessment. In R. L. Brennan (Ed.), *Educational measurement* (4th ed., pp. 257–305). Phoenix, AZ: Greenwood.

Mislevy, R. J., Chudowsky, N., Draney, K., Fried, R., Gaffney, T., Haertel, G., … Wilson, M. (2003). *Design patterns for assessing science inquiry* (PADI Technical Report 1). Menlo Park, CA: SRI International.

Mislevy, R. J., & Haertel, G. D. (2006). Implications of evidence-centered design for educational testing. *Educational Measurement: Issues and Practice, 25,* 6–20.

Mislevy, R. J., & Riconscente, M. M. (2006). Evidence-centered assessment design: Layers, structures, and terminology. In S. Downing & T. Haladyna (Eds.), *Handbook of test development* (pp. 61–90). Mahwah, NJ: Erlbaum.

Mislevy, R. J., Steinberg, L. S., & Almond, R. G. (2003). On the structure of educational assessments. *Measurement: Interdisciplinary Research and Perspectives, 1,* 3–62.

Rose, D. H., & Meyer, A. (2002). *Teaching every student in the digital age: Universal design for learning.* Alexandria, VA: ASCD.

Rose, D. H., & Meyer, A. (Eds.). (2006). *A practical reader in universal design for learning.* Cambridge, MA: Harvard Education Publishing Group.

Rose, D., Meyer, A., & Hitchcock, C. (Eds.). (2005). *The universally designed classroom.* Cambridge, MA: Harvard Education Press.

Rose, D., Murray, E., & Gravel, J. (2012). *UDL and the PADI process: The foundation* (Technical Report 4). Menlo Park, CA: SRI International.

Rupp, A. A., Templin, J., & Henson, R. A. (2010). *Diagnostic measurement: Theory, methods, and applications.* New York, NY: Guilford Press.

Shaftel, J., Yang, X., Glasnapp, D., & Poggio, J. (2005). Improving assessment validity for students with disabilities in large-scale assessment programs. *Educational Assessment, 10,* 357–375.

Tatsuoka, K. K. (1983). Rule space: An approach for dealing with misconceptions based on item response theory. *Journal of Educational Measurement, 20,* 345–354.

Toulmin, S. (1958). *The use of argument.* Cambridge, UK: Cambridge University Press.

von Davier, M. (2008). A general diagnostic model applied to language testing data. *British Journal of Mathematical and Statistical Psychology, 61,* 287–307.

Wainer, H., & Thissen, D. (1994). On examinee choice in educational testing. *Review of Educational Research, 64,* 159–195.

Zhang, T., Mislevy, R. J., Haertel, G., Javitz, H., Murray, E., Gravel, J., & Hansen, E. G. (2010). *A design pattern for a spelling assessment for students with disabilities* (Technical Report 2). Menlo Park, CA: SRI International.

The unfairness of equal treatment: objectivity in L2 testing and dynamic assessment

James P. Lantolf and Matthew E. Poehner

The Pennsylvania State University, University Park, PA, USA

This paper considers dynamic assessment (DA) as it relates to second language (L2) development. DA is grounded in Vygotsky's (1987) sociocultural theory of mind, which holds that human consciousness emerges as a result of participation in culturally organized social activities where mediation plays a key role in guiding development. In DA, the evidential basis for diagnosing and promoting development includes independent as well as mediated performance. Unlike in conventional testing, objectivity derives not from standardization, which treats everyone in precisely the same manner; rather, objectivity is argued on the grounds that mediation is guided by a viable theory of mind. Fairness in assessment is thus reframed with the understanding that the quality of support offered may vary across individuals. The paper illustrates how this transpires in the case of classroom-based and formal testing applications of DA with L2 learners.

Introduction

The most recent guidelines for fairness review of assessments produced by the Educational Testing Service (ETS), located in Princeton, NJ, recognize "fair and valid assessments" as essential to helping "advance quality and equity in education" (ETS, 2009, p. 1). The view of fairness described by ETS is intended to ensure that tests "show respect for diverse groups of people, are sensitive to the needs and feelings of the intended test takers, avoid images and content that are insulting or demeaning, and are free of unnecessary barriers to the success of all test takers" (p. 2). Fairness is closely linked with validity as both are threatened by construct-irrelevant variance. That is, variance in scores that do not pertain to the knowledge, skills, and other attributes that the test is intended to measure reduces the confidence one can have in interpretations of test performance as some individuals may perform better or worse as a result of some other factors. As validity is concerned with the appropriateness of interpretations of test scores and their use in decision-making (Messick, 1989), every effort must be made to minimize construct-irrelevant variance. To the extent that certain groups (e.g., ethnic or racial minorities, members of a particular sex or sexual orientation, immigrants, speakers of another language, individuals of certain socioeconomic backgrounds) within a population of test takers are more affected by such variance than other groups, the fairness of the test is undermined (ETS, 2009, pp. 3–4). A *fairness review* of a test functions "by removing identifiable construct-irrelevant sources of variance that may affect different groups in different ways" (ETS, 2009, pp. 3–4).

Fairness, of course, is a perennial concern in educational measurement, and with good reason. With the increased dominance of standardized testing over the past century, it has become commonplace in many educational systems for test scores to be the primary, if not sole, form of evidence used in decision-making. As tests have become more high stakes, critiques of testing and the misuses of test scores – and in particular the disadvantaging of certain populations – have become more strident (e.g., Hanson, 1993; Shohamy, 2007). Responses from testing specialists have primarily focused on the quality of test instruments, standardization of administration procedures, and transparency in linking assessment evidence and its interpretation (Kane, 1992; Mislevy, 1996). In short, fairness has been addressed through adherence to objective and rigorous methods of testing modelled after practices adopted from the natural sciences.

The present paper considers fairness from a different perspective on assessment, that of dynamic assessment (DA). DA emerges from the sociocultural theory of the human psyche (SCT) as originally proposed by the Russian psychologist L. S. Vygotsky (1987), and elaborated by his contemporaries and scholars working within the theory today. SCT begins from the premise that psychological functions arise through participation in activities in which we are mediated by others and by artefacts made available through culture. While the dominant view in psychology has restricted mental functioning to what occurs "in the heads" of individuals, Vygotsky distinguished between *intermental* plane of psychological functioning, established through joint activity, and the *intramental* plane, where individuals assume control (i.e., regulation) over what was originally collaborative activity and make it their own. Vygotsky's description of the Zone of Proximal Development (ZPD) offers a conceptual and practical link between these planes, as an individual's self-regulation during independent task performance reveals abilities that are already formed and under the person's control; in contrast, participation in mediated activity reveals abilities that have not yet fully formed but are in the process of emerging (Vygotsky, 1998). From this perspective, varying mediation to understand the full range of an individual's development is a requisite feature of diagnosis. In fact, it is restricting access to the mediational means of development that poses a threat to the validity and fairness of assessment because one cannot assume that all individuals will require the same quality and quantity or even that a given individual will require similar mediation at different points in time (Poehner, 2011a). Thus, while standardizing every aspect of the testing process has been prioritized in most approaches to assessment, DA addresses fairness through what at first blush appears to be "unequal treatment".

As we explain below, unequal treatment in DA does not imply simply helping individuals improve their test scores as may occur in coaching programmes. The variability inherent in DA procedures is driven by a commitment to arrive at fine-grained diagnoses of learner functioning, and as such rigor, objectivity, and systematicity are as much a concern as they are in other assessment traditions. DA differs, however, in terms of the theoretical basis that drives its practice, drawing specifically on Vygotsky's conceptualization of mediation and the ZPD. Vygotsky's colleague, A. R. Luria (1961), captured this idea in one of the earliest presentations of DA research by advocating that validity and fairness may be derived not from the "statistical approaches" that had already gained dominance in psychology in the West but through adherence to theoretical principles. In what follows, we elaborate Luria's proposal of fairness through unequal treatment and provide examples of recent DA research involving second language (L2) reading and listening comprehension that illustrate how the approach functions.

As should be clear from this description, DA permits much greater flexibility than is generally accepted in assessment procedures. Indeed, while some approaches to DA carefully script mediation and follow a standardized administration procedure (e.g., Brown & Ferrara, 1985; Guthke & Beckmann, 2000), others advocate allowing mediation to emerge through mediator–learner dialoguing (Feuerstein, Rand, & Hoffman, 2003). As Lantolf and Poehner (2004) explain, such open-ended *interactionist* forms of DA would likely appear to some as a form of teaching and learning activity rather than assessment, and even the scripted *interventionist* DA approaches showcase substantial variability in their administrations as individuals will receive different levels of mediation for each assessment task or item depending upon their needs (Haywood & Lidz, 2007). However, the principle of varying the assessment procedure according to learner needs as these become apparent is not considered an obstacle to fairness in DA but is crucial to establishing it.

Scientism: objectivity, measurement, and rigor

Polkinghorne (1983) traces the roots of the struggle for an adequate methodology in the human (later referred to as the social) sciences to the Enlightenment, when scholars faced the methodological dilemma of whether to study humans and the human condition on the model of hermeneutics, grounded in biblical exegesis, or on the model of the natural sciences, wherein humans are construed as material objects (Van Langenhove, 1995, pp. 13–14). In the former, humans would be approached as texts whose meanings were to be uncovered; in the latter, focus would be on uncovering the causes of material events (Van Langenhove, 1995, p. 14).

According to Cole (1996, p. 32), the successes attained in the natural sciences through implementation of experimentation, quantification, and measurement was an irresistible allure for psychologists wishing to uncover "universal mechanisms" of the human mind. Consequently, "scientism" – "the view that the methods actually used in natural science constitute all the intellectual equipment we need in order to achieve cognitive results of any value" (Kolakowski, 1978, p. 1064) – took control of psychology. Through quantification and measurement, under proper experimental conditions, psychology could legitimately lay claim to being a rational, rigorous, and objective science.[1] As it entered the 20th century, psychology redefined most of its central constructs (e.g., intelligence, motivation, memory, attention) in ways that could then be represented mathematically according to the intensity of an individual's response to stimuli (Danziger, 1997).

Eventually, psychologists shifted their gaze from the psychology of individuals to the psychology of aggregates. This of course increased the reliability of the statistical procedures deployed to interpret the results of experiments. As Danziger (1997) points out, however, while experimental participants could be grouped according to categories found in the social world (e.g., age, gender, social class, etc.), new cohorts without social parallels were also formed. People were aggregated on the basis of performance on pre-treatment tests, measures such as IQ, or whether they were to function as controls or experimental participants. Moreover, psychologists also encountered the problem that "many experiments are simply not possible for practical or ethical reasons" (Van Langenhove, 1995, p. 16).

Through the efforts of researchers such as Cronbach (1957), psychometrics was proposed as a solution to this state of affairs. With its roots in the work of 19th-century statistician and eugenicist Francis Galton, psychometric psychology foregoes causal inference and instead uses tests and other measurements to link behaviour in one circumstance with behaviour in another, as, for instance, performance on an intelligence test with success in school (Van Langenhove, 1995, p. 16). To establish the connections with validity and reliability, Cronbach argued that it was necessary to abandon traditional *impressionistic* testing in favour of scientific, psychometric testing, which insists on standardization and formal validation, instead of placing faith in the assessor's ability to synthesize evidence according to what appears most salient or relevant and to do so in a manner that is fair to all.[2] It is in this respect, Cronbach (1990) concludes, that psychometric and impressionistic styles of testing differ most sharply: "Advocates of rigor regard the tester as an erratic instrument whose unregulated interpretations entangle truth with speculation. Impressionists view the observer as a sensitive and even indispensable instrument" (pp. 36–37). He continues, "the impressionistic interpreter aspires to be an artist, sensitive in observing and skilful in conveying impressions" (p. 36). The matter of interpretation is perhaps the heart of the distinction Cronbach wishes to convey and the superiority of psychometric testing. As he puts it, "some testers aim to 'measure' the individual, some to 'characterize' him" (p. 34).

Measurement, of course, falls within the parameters of scientific methodology and would therefore appear to be in a strong position with regard to questions of validity and fairness. As Cronbach (1990) explains, "the psychometric style is marked by definiteness of task, objectivity of recording, rigor in scoring and combining data, and stress on validation" (p. 35). To be sure, adherence to a scientific methodology is not without its price, as Cronbach himself acknowledges. While impressionistic approaches to assessment allow for the investigation of errors and the processes underlying performance, the psychometrician must remain squarely focused on the products of assessment performance, that is, the behaviours that are "unambiguously observable" and amenable to measurement (p. 36).

The choice to delimit the object of study to phenomena that may be examined through methods borrowed from the natural sciences – or to define the phenomena in those terms – is not unique to psychology. The field of linguistics has been dealing with the effects of a similar move by Chomsky, himself following in the footsteps of de Saussure, to restrict the scope of linguistic research to features of language that could be studied scientifically (Chomsky, 1966). In both cases, there can be little doubt that the selected framing has generated important insights. The question to be considered is what understandings might be possible through other framings. While Cronbach is clearly confident in the soundness of psychometric testing and its advantages over other methods, Vygotsky (1997) was concerned with the question of how psychology might be rendered scientific, which he sought to answer without compromising what he understood to be the ontological status of the object of interest – the human psyche.

Ontology of mediation

With the ascendency of scientism, psychology showed greater interest in its epistemology than it did in the ontological status of its object of study, which in our view, with the exception of work at its margins (e.g., Danziger, 1997), continues to the present day. Vygotsky (1997), in developing his theory of the human psyche, however, began by laying a new ontological foundation and went on to argue that it was important to develop a research methodology that was appropriate for the object of analysis rather than to borrow a potentially problematic methodology from other scientific disciplines regardless of its success in those disciplines (see Van der Veer & Valsiner, 1991). Given his theoretical position that humans are fundamentally social beings, whose consciousness is always and everywhere mediated as a consequence of participation in social activity-embedded cultural institutions (e.g., family, politics, education, religion, work, leisure, etc.), Vygotsky (1978) proposed that psychology required a methodology that reflected this new ontological perspective. Indeed, he cautioned that the task of psychology was not to measure individuals but to interpret them (Vygotsky, 1998, p. 204). This does not mean that sociocultural psychology does not use statistical analysis in their research; it does mean, however, that statistical procedures, when used, are subordinated to the overarching goal of interpretation.

The approach to research that Vygotsky proposed to investigate his theoretical claims has been termed the *genetic method*. In brief, it advocates understanding mental behaviour not through inferences drawn on the basis of observations of independent performance of tasks under experimental conditions but rather through tracing and intervening in mental processes as they are being formed (Vygotsky, 1987). Given that mediation fulfils a central role in Vygotsky's theory of consciousness, it is not surprising that it also plays a central role in the research methodology proposed to study mental behaviour. Following Vygotsky's genetic method, the degree of change brought about during a procedure and the social conditions required – in particular, the forms of mediation – are essential to understanding development. It is in this regard that Vygotsky (1998) emphasized the value of the ZPD for education. He explained that for instruction to optimally impact the development of new abilities, it must be neither too far beyond an individual's current level of functioning nor should it be aimed at what the individual can already do independently. The cooperative nature of ZPD activity involves identifying abilities – through learner participation and responsiveness to mediation – that are emerging and therefore most susceptible to instructional intervention. At the same time, the quality of this interaction might bring about changes in learner functioning during the diagnostic process itself as new insights suddenly emerge, ideas are synthesized, and connections are made during the course of joint activity. Within SCT, this phenomenon is referred to as *microgenesis* (Wertsch, 1985).

Microgenesis undoubtedly poses challenges within a psychometric framework, where it is assumed that abilities are more or less stable during assessment (Büchel & Scharnhorst, 1993). Indeed, exclusively observing an individual's independent performance of tasks helps ensure that the possibility of microgenesis is minimized. In DA, however, microgenesis is interpreted as one form of evidence that mediation was appropriately attuned to emergent abilities (Poehner, 2011a). A common feature of DA studies is the inclusion of *transfer tasks*, that is, tasks that target the same constructs as the rest of the test but that are designed to be more difficult. Analysis of transfer task performance, including mediation required, can provide powerful evidence of microgenesis (Brown & Ferrara, 1985).

Finally, mediation itself is not construed as haphazard or random "help" in DA but is carefully calibrated to learner needs and responsiveness so that learners assume as much responsibility as possible for the task. Tension between learner capabilities and the demands of assessment tasks is required for the procedure to go beyond an individual's present level of development and to take account of emerging abilities. The systematicity with which mediation is provided during DA, whether in the form of scripted prompts or dialogic interaction, allows for the determination of the precise level of explicitness that an individual requires during the procedure. Typically, the reporting of DA outcomes include either a learner profile that indicates the problematic items along with the kinds of mediation required to overcome the problems or a set of scores that compares independent and mediated performance (see Haywood & Lidz, 2007).

DA and validity

Any discussion of outcomes must address the question of validity. As research on validity has evolved, the concept itself has shifted from a property of test instruments established through correlating scores (Cronbach & Meehl, 1955) to an understanding that test performance itself is not the focus of validation but rather what that performance may reveal about underlying abilities, or constructs (Cronbach, 1990). Perhaps the most important contribution to current conceptualizations of validity comes from Messick (1989), who proposed a multi-faceted model that approaches validation as a process wherein test developers and others wishing to use assessment results must develop careful arguments regarding the appropriateness of their decisions. Specifically, Messick was concerned with the consequences of test misuse for individuals, education systems, and society. He argued that testers have an ethical responsibility to carefully model the abilities they wish to measure, develop measurement instruments and procedures based on those models, and explicitly connect the information gained through the test to any particular interpretation of individuals' abilities as well as any possible decisions that might be made on the basis of the test. The more recent influential validity models of Kane (1992) and Mislevy (1996) are in fact sometimes described as argument-based validity frameworks and are very much in line with Messick's position.

Although DA proceeds from a perspective that is in stark contrast to the view underlying most psychometric assessments, it nevertheless must still address the matter of validity. As Poehner (2011b) proposes, however, the manner in which validity arguments may be developed must be aligned with the theoretical framework that guides DA. Given its commitment to understanding learner abilities through intervening in, and guiding, their development, Poehner maintains that this must be taken as the chief criterion for establishing the validity of any DA procedure. He outlines two interrelated foci for DA validation studies, *micro* and *macro validity*, which he notes in some ways parallel validation concerned with particular test items versus the validity of an entire procedure. Micro validity examines particular moves made by a mediator during DA, whether these are dialogic or scripted prompts, and asks how they functioned in the interaction between mediator and learner. That is, did the mediating move in question appear appropriate to the learner's performance or response that immediately preceded it? In addition, how did the learner respond to that particular mediating move? These questions offer a guide to DA validation by underscoring that the overall success of DA is tied to the mediator's skill in preparing and, in some models, negotiating mediation with learners according to their needs. Macro validity, then, broadens the analytical focus to the entire DA procedure and asks how successful the interaction was in revealing and guiding learner development.

Poehner's (2011b) discussion of DA validation reveals several important areas of overlap with validity studies more generally. As with any assessment, DA must begin with a clearly articulated conceptualization of the abilities or knowledge that the procedure aims to understand. This is particularly important where that same understanding of abilities is used to guide the design of mediation intended to support development, both during the procedure as well as through enrichment sessions. In addition, just as validity is associated not with an assessment instrument but with interpretations of performance and the use of these interpretations in decision-making, a given DA procedure may have more or less validity for some learners than others (Poehner, 2011b). That is, the same mediating moves may be better aligned with the needs of some learners than others, with the result that a given procedure could more effectively support the development of certain individuals than others. As we explain below, it is for this reason that much L2 DA research has favoured a more individualized approach over standardization, although of course this does not obfuscate the need to carefully examine the quality of mediation and how it functions during interaction. Finally, just as macro validity is dependent upon the appropriateness of mediating moves throughout the procedure, the overall effect of particular moves may not be fully understood without considering the procedure as a whole. In other words, micro and macro validity are interdependent as both ultimately revolve around the procedure's success in revealing and promoting learner development. Viewed in this light, validation is not only a concern for assessors but also for teachers seeking to organize classroom activities to meet the needs of all learners.

Summary

To summarize the discussion to this point, the defining feature of DA is its commitment to go beyond observations of a test taker's independent performance of assessment tasks to include performance that is undertaken collaboratively with the assessor, often referred to as a mediator. The kind and amount of support individuals require, as well as their responsiveness during interaction, enriches assessments by identifying both the underlying causes of poor performance and how near individuals are to successful independent functioning. At the level of implementation, what marks a procedure as dynamic is the intentional inclusion of *mediation* during the assessment itself. DA approaches vary widely regarding how mediation is conceived of and delivered, but most involve some combination of hints, prompts, leading questions, examples, feedback, and explanations of relevant principles (Poehner, 2008b). The point of mediation is not simply to help individuals complete tasks but to determine the minimum level of support they require to perform successfully. For this reason, mediation is usually offered first in an implicit form, such as telling the test taker that there is a problem or suggesting that s/he re-attempt the task; when this is insufficient, mediation becomes more explicit. The picture that emerges of an individual's abilities goes beyond noting whether s/he can perform the task correctly and includes the point at which s/he was able to take over responsibility for completing it.

L2 DA research

Our intent in this section is to review the major studies that have been carried out to date on DA and L2 assessment in order to illustrate the advantages and disadvantages of implementing this approach to assessment. By and large, the psychological and educational literatures reflect two general orientations to the implementation of DA, with some variation on the basic theme in each orientation. The L2 literature has followed suit. The first approach, and in our view the one that most directly adheres to Vygotsky's understanding of mediation in the ZPD, as mentioned, is referred to as *interactionist* DA, while the second, *interventionist* DA, represents an attempt to implement mediation in a more standardized format that better lends itself to quantification and statistical analysis.[3] We will describe each approach more specifically as we address the relevant L2 research.

Interactionist L2 DA

In interactionist DA, mediation is specifically tailored to the ability of individual learners as it emerges in their interaction with a mediator during the assessment process. In keeping with the principles of Vygotsky's developmental theory, the goal of interaction is to shift control over performance from mediator to learner as efficiently and as effectively as possible. In L2 contexts, this usually means gaining control over a specific feature of the target language. This shift requires that the mediator must consistently explore a learner's readiness to take responsibility and make adjustments in mediation accordingly, until the point is reached where the learner shows signs of ability to function independently. Thus, mediation may need to be quite explicit at the beginning of the process and may entail stating specifically where a learner has made a mistake, modelling overtly how a task can be carried out, or explaining in detail how a particular feature is normally used in the L2. Over time, which may be a few minutes to several weeks, mediation can be expected to evolve to implicit forms of assistance where a learner need only be reminded through an implicit statement (e.g., "are you sure?") or non-verbal behaviour, such as a gesture or raising an eyebrow, that something may be amiss. In DA, when a learner moves toward only requiring implicit forms of mediation it is interpreted as evidence of development, even though s/he may not yet be able to function completely independently.

Perhaps the first L2 study that incorporated mediation meeting interactionist expectations was Aljaafreh and Lantolf's (1994) investigation of an English language writing tutor's efforts to negotiate support with learners that was attuned to their ZPD. Although carried out before DA came into its own in the L2 field, the study nevertheless was organized around the principle of providing mediation at varying levels of explicitness depending upon learner responsiveness and tracing changes to the level of mediation learners required over time. Three of the important conclusions arrived at in the study are that different learners can manifest the same apparent learning difficulties when performing independently, but they require different types of mediation to overcome the problems; the same learner is likely to require different forms of mediation for the same problem at different points in time; development is not only a matter of changes in independent learner performance but it may also manifest as changes in responsiveness to mediation. In other words, as Aljaafreh and Lantolf showed, while a learner may produce the same mistake at different points in time, the quality of mediation required to overcome the difficulty may shift from more explicit to more implicit as the learner gains greater control over a particular feature of the L2.

In one of the two earliest L2 studies overtly framed as DA, Antón (2009)[4] discusses how the procedure was implemented as a placement test for advanced language study in a university Spanish programme. The purpose of the test is to make better informed, and more fine-grained, decisions with regard to pedagogical treatment of students wishing to major in Spanish. The test comprises a written and oral component, which the students first complete independently without mediation. This is followed immediately by "a mediated learning experience geared toward gaining insight into the potential language development" of the students (Antón, 2009, p. 582). Here, we will describe one section of the four-section speaking test. The section under consideration consists of a picture narrative and is conducted in three phases. In the first, a student narrates in Spanish the picture story without intervention from the assessor; in the second phase, the student is given a second opportunity to narrate the story, but this time the assessor provides hints intended to improve the student's performance. If the mediation does not result in better performance, a third phase is introduced in which the assessor narrates the entire story and asks the student to imitate the assessor's narration on the assumption that s/he should be able to "imitate what is in the process of being acquired"; that is, what is in the ZPD (Antón, 2009, p. 583).

Antón (2009) reports the outcome on the speaking test of two students whose relative independent performances in the first phase of the assessment, among other things, reflected problems sustaining use of the past tense and in distinguishing between the two temporal aspects of Spanish (preterit and imperfect). However, when provided with mediation in the second phase, one of the students was able to correct the tense problems fairly easily and then given the chance to retell the story showed the ability to sustain the past tense throughout and was even able to makes some distinctions in aspect use. The other student, even under direct and extensive mediation, was unable to overcome the tense difficulties. The assessor determined that the first student did not require extensive instruction and recommended some work on vocabulary and participation in weekly "conversation hours" to improve control over the language (p. 588). With regard to the second student, the assessor recommended minimally enrollment in a "conversation course and/or a study abroad option" as well as "weekly sessions with a mentor" (p. 591). The learners' respective responses to mediation revealed their differential developmental levels and subsequent pedagogical support that was needed to move the learning process forward in each case.

The second early L2 DA study was conducted by Kozulin and Garb (2002). It differs from Antón's (2009) study in that the procedure actually occurs over multiple sessions that include focused instruction, an approach inspired by the work of Reuven Feuerstein, a leading proponent of DA (Feuerstein, Rand, & Hoffman, 1979). The researchers administered a DA version of an EFL test in reading for academic purposes. Using the pre-test-mediation-re-test approach, Kozulin and Garb administered the reading test independently (i.e., without mediation) to a group of 18- to 25-year-old immigrants to Israel. They then carried out an analysis of test items to determine the information needed to answer the items as well as the strategies that would be useful for "successful completion" of the test (Kozulin & Garb, 2002, p. 119). Based on analysis of the test, guidelines were designed for teachers to use as they next mediated the students. This included an information page focusing on grammatical constructions (e.g., question words, auxiliary constructions, complement structure) and basic lexical knowledge (not described in the article) that students had to learn for homework and that would be needed during mediation. In mediation, the students were engaged in a series of questions designed to help them understand the text structure, cohesive properties, and background knowledge of a set of four texts of increasing length and complexity. The teachers were guided in their mediation by the students' performance on the pre-test. Each mediation session (one for learning grammar and basic vocabulary and one for text comprehension) lasted 50 min. A second test was then administered that matched the pre-test in terms of length, difficulty, and reading strategies required.

Perhaps not too surprisingly, the students' performance as a group improved significantly from the pre- to the re-test, indicating that mediation made a difference. However, and this is the important point, while the pre-test scores correlated with the re-test scores (r = .80), the gain scores for individual students could not be predicted on the basis of their pre-test performance. That is, while some students shared the same score on the pre-test, their respective performances differed significantly on the re-test, with some showing slight (e.g., 3% to 10%) improvement following mediation and others manifesting a marked increase in their re-test scores (e.g., 17% to 30%).

Such results support Vygotsky's (1978) essential argument that independent performance, or actual level of development, cannot predict future performance (that is, how an individual will respond to mediation). In fact, another difference from Antón's (2009) work is that Kozulin and Garb (2002) make explicit reference to the construct of *learning potential,* or the capacity to benefit from mediation. Following a scoring procedure pioneered by Budoff and his colleagues (e.g., Budoff & Friedman, 1964), the authors classified students into three categories reflecting their initial test performance and their degree of improvement: high gainers, modest gainers, and low gainers. We will return to a discussion of learning potential scores in more detail when we consider an on-line DA that we recently developed for reading and listening comprehension.

Poehner (2008b) also reports on a DA programme with L2 learners that makes specific reference to the work of Feuerstein. Unlike the approach followed by Kozulin and Garb (2002), wherein information about student test performance was provided to classroom teachers for the purpose of guiding their efforts to mediate student learning, in Poehner's study an individualized enrichment programme was designed for each learner according to an analysis of responsiveness to mediation during an initial DA session. Specifically, the programme began with an oral narration task in which learners viewed clips from popular films and were asked to recount events from the story in the L2. As an assessment, the choice to focus on oral abilities in the language and the use of an open-ended task meant that it was not possible to predict beforehand the kinds of difficulties learners would encounter, and the mediator needed to detect difficulties as these emerged over the course of the narration and begin a process of offering mediating hints, prompts, and feedback. Despite these challenges, the design allowed for an investigation into the development of L2 oral proficiency as well as intervention into that process. Among the challenges learners faced was to appropriately control verbal tense and aspect in order to establish relations among events, states of being, and actions that occurred in the narrative and to foreground some of these over others. This involved understanding tense and aspect as linguistic concepts that may be drawn upon to construct particular meanings and frame narratives as well as control over the forms through which these features of language are realized in French. The focus of enrichment therefore became to help learners develop a conceptual understanding of tense and aspect that they could draw upon to mediate their communication in the language. This, too, was accomplished through the construction of oral narratives, a task in which their efforts were mediated by charts, diagrams, and verbal explanations of the concepts as well as through dialogic interaction with a mediator. In fact, Poehner (2008b) reports that an outside observer would likely be unable to distinguish sessions intended to serve a diagnostic function from those that constituted enrichment to support learner development because all sessions were marked by open-ended dialogue between a mediator and a learner as they jointly engaged in the L2 narration tasks.

An important feature that emerged from the qualitative analysis of DA interactions in Poehner's (2008b) study concerns forms of learner participation. Through close analysis of mediator–learner dialoguing, Poehner (2008a) identified learner contributions to interaction that went far beyond simply "responding" to mediation. Building on the notion of *learner reciprocity*, first proposed by Feuerstein (Feuerstein et al., 1979) and elaborated by Lidz (1991), Poehner argued that learner cooperation is essential for DA to fulfil its diagnostic and instructional functions. Learners in Poehner's study exhibited behaviours that included actively soliciting specific forms of support from the mediator, negotiating mediation offered by asking clarifying questions and thinking through with the mediator how a principle might be extended to a hypothetical situation, turning to the mediator for approval after completing a task, and even refusing a mediator's attempt to provide support in order to attempt a task independently. According to Poehner (2008a), these forms of reciprocating behaviour offer additional insights into learners' emerging capabilities that are lost when attention is only given to the mediator's efforts and whether these prompt a successful response from the learner.

A final feature of Poehner's L2 DA programme worth mentioning is that the multi-session approach created the possibility to incorporate Brown's and Ferrara's notion of transfer (Brown & Ferrara, 1985), discussed earlier, by rendering the oral narration tasks increasingly difficult for individual learners as they came to function more autonomously. While the video clips participants watched and narrated early in the programme depicted everyday contexts and events that unfolded in a relatively straightforward manner, subsequent prompts included videos and excerpts from literature that were less conventional and predictable. Inclusion of such tasks allowed for ongoing diagnosis, as it was possible to determine participants' capacity to recontextualize learning rather than to simply carry out variation of the same kind of task. Feuerstein, Rand, and Rynders (1988) describe this capacity as *transcendence* and argue that it offers powerful evidence concerning whether observed changes in learner functioning constitute task-specific training or in fact indicate new understandings that may be generalized beyond a particular task. As with Brown and Ferrara's research on the related notion of transfer, Feuerstein maintains that even individuals who come to function independently on a given set of tasks may still vary widely when presented with more demanding ones. An additional advantage to including progressively more difficult tasks in a DA programme, according to Poehner (2008b), is that it allowed for ongoing ZPD activity regardless of learner development, as tasks could continue to be made more demanding in order to sustain a level of challenge that would require learner interaction with a mediator.

Following the procedure developed by Poehner (2008b) for speaking ability, Ableeva (2010) carried out a DA project to diagnose and promote listening ability in a second language. Participants were intermediate-level learners of French as a foreign language at the university level. As with Poehner's (2008b) study, Ableeva used a multi-assessment procedure whereby participants were presented with a series of listening tasks carried out independently and in mediated format. The participants were asked to listen to and recall in English a series of passages produced by native speakers of French visiting the US where the general topic was French and American dining customs.

As with Poehner's (2008b) study, after the initial round of independent and mediated performances, the students in Ableeva's (2010) study took part in an enrichment programme designed on the basis of the initial assessment sessions. During these sessions, Ableeva was able to identify the source of various problems that learners experienced when listening to authentic aural texts in the target language. Included among these, according to Ableeva, were phonological, lexical, grammatical, and cultural difficulties. The mediated sessions were able to tease out what otherwise would have been ambiguous origins of learner problems. To give one example (see Ableeva & Lantolf, 2011, for details): One of the participants had misheard a verb form as an imperfect construction; but, in fact, the item was a conditional form. The initial quandary presented to the mediator was whether the source of the problem was phonological in that the student had failed to correctly perceive the form as a conditional or whether the student had no knowledge of conditional aspect in French to begin with. Under mediation, the researcher was able to determine that the student indeed was familiar with the conditional and could identify it in written form, but had misheard it as an imperfect in the passage. Uncovering the source of the problem made a difference with regard to the design of the enrichment programme, where the learner needed help with phonological rather than grammatical knowledge.

Following enrichment, the students were given a second series of assessments, which increased in complexity both in terms of topic and language (e.g., French TV programme that addressed smoking in French restaurants) and an increase of articulation rate (e.g., a 20-second radio commercial). These assessments were administered in an independent as well as mediated format to determine the extent to which the students were able to transfer the knowledge gained in the enrichment programme to novel circumstances. In general, the students were able to transfer their knowledge to some though not all of the new more complex passages. In particular, most of them had difficulties coping with the articulation rate of the radio commercial. This represents an important finding of the study and shows that there are limits to what individuals are capable of even under mediation. As Vygotsky (1987) reminds the reader, mediation in the ZPD does not imply that development is not without boundaries. In other words, borrowing the example given by Vygotsky, someone who can only do basic arithmetic is not likely to be successful at mastering calculus.

One must first learn algebra. Mediation, nevertheless, is far more likely to allow individuals to achieve their full potential at any given point in time; but that potential changes over time as the individual develops.

Interventionist DA

This approach to DA represents an attempt to standardize the quality and quantity of mediation available during an assessment activity. In some respects, it is individualized while in others it is not. Unlike in interactionist DA, mediation does not emerge from the interaction between a mediator and the person under assessment; instead, it is scripted beforehand and is hierarchically arranged from most implicit to most explicit. The extent to which the individual moves through the hierarchy of mediation can vary across individuals. Some may require only one or two hints, while others may need the most explicit form of mediation available in the hierarchy. Learners requiring only implicit mediation retain primary responsibility for assessment performance, and this is interpreted as an indication that they are relatively close to successfully executing the relevant tasks on their own. In contrast, learners in need of more explicit mediation have further to go before they may be expected to function independently.

The standardization of hints and clues in interventionist DA limits the extent to which mediation can be fully tailored to an individual's needs; however, it does allow for psychometric comparison across performances. One of the first interventionist approaches to L2 DA was the *Lerntest* (learning test) devised by Jürgen Guthke and his colleagues (Guthke, Heinrich, & Caruso, 1986) at Leipzig University (see Lantolf & Poehner, 2004). The *Lerntest* concept was used for a variety of assessment tasks, including general cognitive performance as well as language aptitude. The language aptitude test (see Guthke et al., 1986) was designed to predict learning outcomes of international students required to study German before enrolling in universities in the then German Democratic Republic. Based on an invented language, the test reflected the rubrics traditionally included in language aptitude tests (ability to decipher word meanings, analyse grammatical features, etc.). The scores were weighted depending on the level of mediation required for the test taker to produce a correct response to each test item. Based on the scores generated, predictions could be made as to the length of time learners would require to reach an acceptable level of proficiency in German prior to the start of their university studies.

A classroom-based approach to interventionist DA was implemented by an elementary school Spanish instructor, as reported on in Lantolf and Poehner (2011). The instructor devised an innovative approach to DA in which she established a set of six hierarchically organized hints and clues to be used to help her students during classroom practice activities. As with the *Lerntest*, the instructor assigned a weighted score to each level of mediation in the hierarchy, ranging from 0 (if no mediation was required) to 6 (if a student was unable to arrive at a correct response and the instructor was required to provide it along with an explanation). The instructor created a scoring grid for each class activity on which she inscribed the name of each student participating in a given activity and on which she entered a student's weighted score. The scoring grid enabled the teacher to compare performances across students as well as to keep track of the performances of individual students over time. In this way, she was able to compare and track the development of students synchronically and diachronically.

Lantolf and Poehner (2011) traced the ability of one student to mark nominal concord over time based on the level of mediation provided by the instructor. During the initial oral activity, the student made several failed attempts to produce the correct number and gender agreements between a modifier and a noun despite a series of increasingly explicit hints from the instructor. The student was only able to produce a correct utterance when the instructor presented him with an option question (i.e., is it this or is it that?). At that point, the student was able to select the correct option. A week later, the same student participated in a similar, though not identical, activity calling for use of different vocabulary. This time, the student was able to produce a correct utterance on his initial attempt, although he paused for a few seconds prior to speaking, an indication that he was most likely thinking about how to mark the appropriate agreements. Lantolf and Poehner (2011) argue that the learner's earlier struggle, during which he was supported by the instructor, compelled him to think about the grammatical feature and positioned him to be able to recall what he had apparently learned during that task. On the teacher's scoring grid, the student progressed from a Level 5 to a Level 0, an indication of development.

The final example of interventionist DA comes from a recent project that developed an online instrument to diagnose and promote reading and listening ability in Chinese, French, and Russian. The project is reported on in detail in Poehner and Lantolf (in press).[5] The tests, aimed at intermediate proficiency, incorporate four levels of mediation arranged from most implicit to most explicit. At one end of the hierarchy, testees who produce an incorrect response are exposed to a focused chunk of relevant text, either in written or spoken form, and are provided with a second opportunity to select a correct response from a set of options. As they work through each item, the textual chunks are increasingly narrowed until the point at which only two response options are available. At that point, if an incorrect choice is still selected, the correct response is provided and a brief explanation is made available. In fact, at any point that a correct answer is selected, the option to view an explanation is made available. The rationale for this is that it maintains DA's emphasis on learning – and potential microgenesis – during the procedure.

The tests generate three quantitative scores along with an overall graphically displayed profile for each testee or, if so desired, by a teacher, for an entire class. The first score represents an individual's independent performance and is generated on the basis of the initial response attempt for each test item. The second, mediated score is the sum of the total number of mediated correct responses weighted from high to low. The more mediation required to produce a correct response, the lower the overall mediated score will be and vice versa. The third score is generated using the learning potential formula reported in Kozulin and Garb (2002) that takes account of the difference between the independent and mediated scores. It also reflects Budoff and Friedman's (1964) notion of high, modest, and low gainers. Thus, as the analysis in Poehner and Lantolf (in press) shows, two individuals might produce equivalent independent scores but quite different mediated scores – an indication that the individuals are not developmentally at the same ability level, given that one responds more favourably to mediation than the other. In addition, again as Poehner and Lantolf document, individuals with higher independent scores do not necessarily receive higher learning potential scores than individuals with lower independent scores. Furthermore, individuals with low learning potential scores are predicated to require more instruction than individuals with high learning potential scores, even if the independent scores are equivalent. The crucial factor then is the degree to which testees respond to mediation as reflected in their respective learning potential score.

Finally, the test also generates a graphic profile, which arranges test items by construct sub-domains (i.e., grammar, phonology, vocabulary, discourse knowledge, and cultural knowledge) and displays the score (independent or mediated) that an individual received for each item within each sub-domain. In this way, it is easy to discern which aspects of comprehension posed the most difficulty for individual learners, information that may be relevant to placement decisions as well as determining the focus of subsequent instruction. The test can also display graphic profiles of the same information for groups of learners, as when an entire class takes the test. This allows, for instance, an instructor or programme director to make determinations concerning the achievement or progress of large groups of learners.

Conclusion

A statement that is frequently attributed to Albert Einstein asserts that all individuals possess genius, but that judging a fish by its ability to climb will leave the fish forever believing that it is a failure. While Einstein's statement may be read as a critique of holding all individuals to the same standard, presumably on the assumption that they have different abilities, a Vygotskian perspective maintains that all individuals are capable of developing but may follow different trajectories and require different resources. A social ontology of abilities brings into focus the question of how an individual's social environment may be arranged to optimally reveal their capabilities and support ongoing development. With regard to formal education, this means that the conditions under which assessment and instruction activities are carried out need to be varied if they are to align with an individual's developmental needs at any given point. That is, if abilities are understood to emerge through a history of participation in various activities with others, there is no reason to assume that all individuals will manifest their abilities in the same way or on the same time schedule.

In DA, aligning the social environment with learner needs occurs through the provision of mediation. The diagnostic value of tracking forms of mediation required during DA is that shifts from explicit to implicit support are taken as an indication that a particular ability, or control over a linguistic feature of an L2, is developing. In particular, as mediation becomes more implicit, learners are assuming greater responsibility for executing the task and are therefore moving closer to independent performance. This process means that each individual is treated differently during DA and that the same individual will be treated differently over time. From a psychometric testing perspective, this variation would likely be construed as unequal, and perhaps unfair, treatment. It should be clear that from a DA perspective the expressed intent is to fully diagnose learner ability and over- come limitations in that ability in order to move the developmental process forward, and this is accomplished through "unequal" treatment. It should also be clear, however, that unequal treatment in this sense does not threaten the fairness of the procedure because all individuals are offered the forms of mediation to which they appear most responsive during a given interaction. Moreover, mediation is determined through joint engagement with learners and sensitivity to their needs as these are made manifest. That the entire orien- tation to interaction is guided by principles derived from a robust theory of mind is a notable strength of DA and sets it apart from most conventional assessments.

From the perspective of psychometric assessment, one might conclude that DA intro- duces an additional source of error measurement into scoring, as interaction with a mediator may move an individual's observed score further from his/her true score. In our view, it is important to keep in mind that the purpose of DA is not to artificially inflate test scores for certain individuals or for all individuals. A more appropriate depiction of what occurs in DA might be that every individual has two true scores, one revealing abilities that have fully formed and one pertaining to abilities that are still emerging, that is, their ZPD. The process of mediation is intended then to yield a secondary observed score indicative of the ZPD. In the online language comprehension DA tests we described in this paper, we described these two types of observed scores as a learner's independent and mediated score, respectively. Given Vygotsky's (1987) prediction that two sets of scores may vary independently of one another (i.e., individuals with similar independent scores may have very different mediated scores), a prediction that has been substantiated by our own DA research as well as that of others, DA's expansion of the evidential basis upon which assessment decisions may be made offers considerable potential for determining, among other things, appropriate levels of study and forms of instructional support for individuals. As Lidz (1991) puts it, success in DA derives from gaining insights into learner "modifiability … [and] facilitating improved learner performance" (p. 6). In this way, DA offers a means of addressing not only fairness in assessment practices but also fairness in educational opportunities more generally.

Notes

1. The hermeneutic approach to social science research managed to survive the hegemony of scientism largely through the philosophical studies of Dilthey, Gadamer, and Husserl and can be observed in the current research of discursive psychologists such as Harré and Gillett (1994) and Harré and Stearns (1995).
2. Researchers investigating classroom-based assessments undertaken for formative purposes might well object to Cronbach's (1990) depiction of non-psychometric frameworks as an oversimplification or even "straw man" characterization. Indeed, a good deal of work has been devoted precisely to establishing theoretical bases for formative assessment and rigorous requirements for validation studies and use arguments (see, e.g., Moss, Pullin, Gee, Haertel, & Young, 2008) that go well beyond the sort of haphazard, anecdotal observation implied by Cronbach.
3. For a discussion of how both approaches have been implemented in the psychological and educational literature, see the following publications: Haywood and Lidz (2007), Lidz (1991), and Sternberg and Grigorenko (2002).
4. Although Antón's (2009) study carries a fairly recent publication date, she reported on the project much earlier in a paper delivered at the annual conference of the American Association of Applied Linguistics in 2002.
5. This project was funded by a grant from the United States Department of Education (Grant Award P017A080071). However, the contents of this article do not necessarily represent the policy of the Department of Education, and one should not assume endorsement by the Federal Government. Although we served as official co-PIs for the project, we want to acknowledge the indispensible contributions of co-researchers, Rumia Ableeva, Ekaterina Arshevskaya, Xiaofei Lu, Adam van Compernolle, Mei-Hsing Tsai, and Jie Zhang. We also acknowledge the contribution of Arlo Besinger, who developed the computer platform for the administration and scoring of the tests. The tests are available on the webpage of CALPER (Center for Advanced Language Proficiency Education and Research) at The Pennsylvania State University. They may be accessed free of charge for non-commercial users; however, they are password protected. The URL is http://calper.la.psu.edu/dyna_assess.php?page = exams

References

Ableeva, R. (2010). *Dynamic assessment of listening comprehension in L2 French* (Unpublished PhD dissertation). The Pennsylvania State University, University Park, PA.

Ableeva, R., & Lantolf, J. P. (2011). Mediated dialogue and the microgenesis of second language listening comprehension. *Assessment in Education, 18*, 133–149.

Aljaafreh, A., & Lantolf, J. P. (1994). Negative feedback as regulation and second language learning in the Zone of Proximal Development. *The Modern Language Journal, 78*, 465–483.

Antón, M. (2009). Dynamic assessment of advanced language learners. *Foreign Language Annals, 42*, 576–598.

Brown, A., & Ferrara, R. A. (1985). Diagnosing "zones of proximal development". In J. V. Wertsch (Ed.), *Culture, communication and cognition. Vygotskian perspectives* (pp. 273–305). Cambridge, UK: Cambridge University Press.

Büchel, F. P., & Scharnhorst, U. (1993). The learning potential assessment device (LPAD): Discussion of theoretical and methodological problems. In J. H. M. Hamers, K. Sijtsma, & A. J. J. M. Ruijssenaars (Eds.), *Learning potential assessment: Theoretical, methodological and practical issues* (pp. 83–111). Amsterdam, The Netherlands: Swets & Zeitlinger.

Budoff, M., & Friedman, M. (1964). "Learning potential" as an assessment approach to the adolescent mentally retarded. *Journal of Consulting Psychology, 28*, 434–439.

Chomsky, N. (1966). *Cartesian linguistics. A chapter in the history of rationalist thought*. New York, NY: Harper & Row.

Cole, M. (1996). *Cultural psychology. A once and future discipline*. New York, NY: Bradford Books.

Cronbach, L. J. (1957). Two disciplines of scientific psychology. *American Psychologist, 12*, 671–684.

Cronbach, L. J. (1990). *Essentials of psychological testing* (5th ed.). New York, NY: Harper & Row.

Cronbach, L. J., & Meehl, P. E. (1955). Construct validity in psychological tests. *Psychological Bulletin, 52*, 281–302.

Danziger, K. (1997). *Naming the mind. How psychology found its language*. London, UK: Sage.

Educational Testing Service. (2009). *ETS guidelines for fairness review of assessments*. Retrieved from www.**ets**.org/Media/About_**ETS**/pdf/overview.pdf

Feuerstein, R., Rand, Y., & Hoffman, M. B. (1979). *The dynamic assessment of retarded performers: The learning potential assessment device, theory, instruments, and techniques*. Baltimore, MD: University Park Press.

Feuerstein, R., Rand, Y., & Rynders, J. E. (1988). *Don't accept me as I am. Helping retarded performers excel*. New York, NY: Plenum.

Guthke, J., & Beckmann, J. F. (2000). The learning test concept and its applications in practice. In C. S. Lidz & J. G. Elliott (Eds.), *Dynamic assessment: prevailing models and applications* (pp. 17–69). Amsterdam, The Netherlands: Elsevier.

Guthke, J., Heinrich, A., & Caruso, M. (1986). The diagnostic program of "syntactical rule and vocabulary acquisition" – A contribution to the psychodiagnosis of foreign language learning ability. In F. Klix & H. Hagendorf (Eds.), *Human memory and cognitive capabilities. Mechanisms and performances* (pp. 903–911). Amsterdam, The Netherlands: Elsevier.

Hanson, F. A. (1993). *Testing testing: Social consequences of the examined life*. Berkeley, CA: University of California Press.

Harré, R., & Gillett, G. (1994). *The discursive mind*. Thousand Oaks, CA: Sage.

Harré, R., & Stearns, P. (Eds.). (1995). *Discursive psychology in practice (research and practice)*. Thousand Oaks, CA: Sage.

Haywood, H. C., & Lidz, C. S. (2007). *Dynamic assessment in practice. Clinical and educational applications*. New York, NY: Cambridge University Press.

Kane, M. T. (1992). An argument-based approach to validity. *Psychological Bulletin, 112*, 527–535.

Kolakowski, L. (1978). *Main currents of Marxism. The founders, the golden age, the breakdown*. Oxford, UK: Oxford University Press.

Kozulin, A., & Garb, E. (2002). Dynamic assessment of EFL text comprehension of at-risk students. *School Psychology International, 23*, 112–127.

Lantolf, J. P., & Poehner, M. E. (2004). Dynamic assessment: Bringing the past into the future. *Journal of Applied Linguistics, 1*, 49–74.

Lantolf, J. P., & Poehner, M. E. (2011). Dynamic assessment in the classroom: Vygotskian praxis for L2 development. *Language Teaching Research, 15*, 11–33.

Lidz, C. S. (1991). *Practitioner's guide to dynamic assessment*. New York, NY: Guilford.

Luria, A. R. (1961). Study of the abnormal child. *American Journal of Orthopsychiatry. A Journal of Human Behavior, 31*, 1–16.

Messick, S. A. (1989). Validity. In R. L. Linn (Ed.), *Educational measurement* (3rd ed., pp. 13–103). New York, NY: American Council on Education.

Mislevy, R. J. (1996). Test theory reconceived. *Journal of Educational Measurement, 33*, 379–416.

Moss, P. A., Pullin, D. C., Gee, J. P., Haertel, E. H., & Young, L. J. (Eds.). (2008). *Assessment, equity, and opportunity to learn*. Cambridge, UK: Cambridge University Press.

Poehner, M. E. (2008a). Both sides of the conversation: The interplay between mediation and learner reciprocity in dynamic assessment. In J. P. Lantolf & M. E. Poehner (Eds.), *Sociocultural theory and the teaching of second languages* (pp. 33–56). London, UK: Equinox.

Poehner, M. E. (2008b). *Dynamic assessment. A Vygotskian approach to understanding and promoting L2 development*. Berlin, Germany: Springer.

Poehner, M. E. (2011a). Dynamic assessment: Fairness through the prism of mediation. *Assessment in Education: Principles, Policy and Practice, 18,* 99–112.

Poehner, M. E. (2011b). Validity and interaction in the ZPD: Interpreting learner development through L2 Dynamic assessment. *International Journal of Applied Linguistics, 21,* 244–263.

Poehner, M. E., & J. P. Lantolf (in press). Bringing the ZPD into the equation: Capturing L2 development during computerized dynamic assessment (C-DA). *Language Teaching Research.*

Polkinghorne, D. (1983). *Methodology for the human sciences. Systems of inquiry.* Albany, NY: State University of New York Press.

Shohamy, E. (2007). Language tests as language policy tools. *Assessment in Education: Principles, Policy & Practice, 14,* 117–130.

Sternberg, R. J., & Grigorenko, E. L. (2002). *Dynamic testing. The nature and measurement of learning potential.* Cambridge, UK: Cambridge University Press.

Van der Veer, R., & Valsiner, J. (1991). *Understanding Vygotsky.* Oxford, UK: Blackwell.

Van Langenhove, L. (1995). The theoretical foundations of experimental psychology and its alternatives. In J. A. Smith, R. Harre, & L. van Langenhove (Eds.), *Rethinking psychology* (pp. 10–24). London, UK: Sage.

Vygotsky, L. S. (1978). *Mind in society. The development of higher psychological processes.* Cambridge, MA: Harvard University Press.

Vygotsky, L. S. (1987). *The collected works of L. S. Vygotsky. Volume 1. Problems of general psychology. Including the volume thinking and speech.* New York, NY: Plenum.

Vygotsky, L. S. (1997). The historical meaning of the crisis in psychology: A methodological investigation. In R. W. Rieber & J. Wollock (Eds.), *The collected works of L. S. Vygotsky. Vol. 3. Problems of the theory and history of psychology* (pp. 233–344). New York, NY: Plenum.

Vygotsky, L. S. (1998). The problem of age. In R. W. Rieber (Ed.), *The collected works of L. S. Vygotsky. Volume 5. Child psychology* (pp. 187–206). New York, NY: Plenum.

Wertsch, J. V. (1985). *Vygotsky and the social formation of mind.* Cambridge, MA: Harvard University Press.

The quest for fairness in language testing

Hossein Karami

English Department, Faculty of Foreign Languages and Literature, University of Tehran, Tehran, Iran

The search for fairness in language testing is distinct from other areas of educational measurement as the object of measurement, that is, language, is part of the identity of the test takers. So, a host of issues enter the scene when one starts to reflect on how to assess people's language abilities. As the quest for fairness in language testing is still in its infancy, even the need for such a research has been controversial, with some (e.g., Davies, 2010) arguing that such research is entirely in vain. This paper will provide an overview of some of the issues involved. Special attention will be given to critical language testing (CLT) as it has had a large impact on language testing research. It will be argued that although CLT has been very effective in revealing the ideological and value implications of the constructs of focus in language testing, extremism in this direction is not justified.

Introduction

The quest for fairness in educational assessment has begun since at least the 1960s (Angoff, 1993). Although language testing has largely drawn on educational measurement and psychometrics for much of its methodological part, language testing researchers have only recently started to explicitly include fairness issues in their discussions of the requirements of an appropriate test development and use policy. The search for fairness in the use of language tests may be distinct from other areas of educational measurement as the object of measurement, that is, language, is part of the identity of the test takers. Language tests have at times even been used for identification purposes with grave consequences for the examinees. McNamara (2005) provides various examples of the so-called shibboleth tests. The consequences of such tests have been more serious than any other measures because the failure on these tests could mean the end of an examinee's life (see below).

Early discussions of fairness in language testing started during the 1990s (Kunnan, 2000). Much work has been done ever since. However, as the research on fairness is still in its infancy, even the fundamental aspects of fairness still remain controversial. On the one hand, some researchers (e.g., Kunnan, 2000, 2004) have interpreted fairness in a very broad way and have proposed fairness frameworks that encompass almost all other considerations including validity. Others (e.g., Xi, 2010) have interpreted fairness to be an aspect of validity. Still others (e.g., Davies, 2010) have argued that the search for fairness in language testing is entirely in vain.

In this paper, we discuss some of the most significant work done so far. The discussion is roughly divided into two parts. In the first part, we will focus on the psychometric aspects of fairness. The consequential aspects of test use and interpretation and the related fairness issues are then discussed. Special attention will be given to critical language testing and some of its implications for research.

Fairness

The Cambridge Advanced Learners' Dictionary defines fairness as "the quality of treating people equally or in a way that is right or reasonable". Similarly, the Merriam Webster Dictionary defines the term "fairness" as "marked by impartiality and honesty: free from self-interest, prejudice, or favoritism". By implication, a test may be said to be fair if it is "free of bias" or "favoritism". Specifically, a test is said to be fair if it does not unduly advantage any groups. This is indeed the traditional definition of fairness in educational measurement (Kane, 2010). This is also evident in Cole and Moss's (1989) definition of bias as the "*differential validity of a given test score for any definable, relevant subgroup of test takers*" (p. 205, italics in original). As will be explained below, this is a very basic notion of fairness and leaves out many issues related to consequences and value implications of test use and interpretation.

McNamara and Ryan (2011) differentiate between fairness and justice. They conceptualize fairness as being related to the technical (mostly psychometric) qualities of the test. Akin to the traditional definition of fairness alluded to earlier, they define fairness as "the extent to which the test quality, especially its psychometric quality, ensures procedural equality for individual and subgroups of test-takers and the adequacy of the representation of the construct in test materials and procedures" (p. 163). Justice, on the other hand, pertains to the social consequences of test use along with the value implications and the sociopolitical ideologies underlying the test constructs. They go on to map their model onto Messick's (1989) progressive matrix of validity (see Table 1). Fairness relates to the evidential basis of test use and interpretation, the top row in Messick's matrix. Justice, on the other hand, pertains to the consequential basis, encompassing the value implications and social consequences of test use and interpretation. This dichotomy is similar to the distinction Shohamy (1997) makes between two major sources of bias in language tests: "those associated with the test itself, such as method effects and those associated with the consequences and uses of language tests" (p. 341).

The research in language testing has mostly focused on fairness rather than justice. A variety of techniques have been utilized to investigate various aspects of fairness. This research has been mainly concerned with sources of construct-irrelevant variance and the effects of various learner-related variables on test performance. The variables investigated so far include such factors as gender (e.g., Aryadoust, Goh, & Lee, 2011; Karami, 2011; Ryan & Bachman, 1992; Takala & Kaftandjieva, 2000), language background (Brown, 1999; Chen & Henning, 1985; Elder, 1996; Kim, 2001; Ryan & Bachman, 1992), and academic background or content knowledge (Alderson & Urquhart, 1985; Hale, 1988; Pae, 2004).[1] Justice, on the other hand, has not received equal attention from language testers. Justice-related research has mostly focused on the social consequences of the test

Table 1. Messick's (1989) validity matrix.

	Test Interpretation	Test Use
Evidential Basis	Construct Validity	Construct validity + Utility/Relevance
Consequential Basis	Value Implications	Social Consequences

use (the fourth cell in Messick's matrix) with less attention to the value implications (the third cell), at least as far as empirical research is concerned.

Any scientific research is based on some theory (even if it is only a rough sketch) of the factors and variables playing a role in a particular area. The search for fairness in language testing is no exception. Various test fairness frameworks have been proposed mainly during the last 2 decades. The next section will provide an overview of the fairness frameworks proposed by language testers.[2]

Fairness models in language testing

An early attempt to develop a fairness framework in the context of language testing was Kunnan (2000). Fairness in Kunnan's model was a cover term including three other qualities: validity, access, and justice. Justice in turn includes two components: societal equity and legal challenges. With respect to societal equity, he argues that "the notion of societal equity goes beyond equal validity and access and focuses on the social consequences of testing in terms of whether testing programs contribute to societal equity or not and in general, whether there are any pernicious effects due to them or not" (p. 4). As he explicitly states, Kunnan's model of fairness goes beyond comparable validity and includes social consequences of test use. He also formally includes legal considerations within justice. Kunnan's delineation of the terms here is a bit vague because he puts the concerns with the social consequences of test use under the term justice. It is not clear how these differ from the social aspects of test use that is part of validity. Whether he intends another definition of validity is not clear either.

Kunnan (2004) revised his earlier framework. Two major fairness principles are introduced: *justice* and *beneficence*. This time, justice is defined differently:

> *The Principle of Justice*: The test ought to be fair to all test takers; that is, there is a presumption of treating each person with equal respect.
>
> Sub-principle 1: A test ought to have comparable construct validity in terms of its test-score interpretation for all test-takers.
>
> Sub-principle 2: A test ought not to be biased against any test-taker groups, in particular by assessing construct-irrelevant matters. (p. 33)

It is evident that Kunnan (2004) has restricted the meaning of justice to a consideration of the role construct-irrelevant factors play in test administration and interpretation. His definition of justice is highly similar to McNamara and Ryan's (2011) fairness. Kunnan addresses the role of social consequences in another principle:

> *The Principle of Beneficence*: A test ought to bring about good in society; that is, it should not be harmful or detrimental to society.
>
> Sub-principle 1: A test ought not to inflict harm by providing test-score information or social impacts that are inaccurate or misleading. (pp. 33–34)

This latter principle is also similar to McNamara and Ryan's definition of justice. However, Kunnan does not include issues related to the value implications of test constructs in his principle of beneficence. He goes on to elaborate five "main qualities": validity, absence of bias, access, administration, and social consequences. Each of these qualities in turn has its own subcomponents.

Kunnan (2010) later admits that his earlier frameworks have been "micro-analytic" in the sense of being limited in scope. Therefore, he revised his earlier models. He declares that the evaluation of fairness should be seen within the wider context in which it is used. Specifically, in Kunnan (2005), four sets of contexts are recognized: political and economic; educational, social, and cultural; technological and infrastructure; and the legal and ethical contexts. He then further elaborates on each category explaining the kinds of issues that can be addressed within each context. He is of course cautious enough to note that the list is not exhaustive and may be extended. We agree with Kunnan that any evaluation of test use and interpretation should be seen within the wider sociopolitical context. However, we also believe that any model of test fairness evaluation should also suggest a mechanism for laying priorities and possibly offer tangible directions for practitioners. Needless to say, the social context of test use is extremely complex with many factors playing a role. Modelling such a context is no simple task. Any model of the social context will be indeed very complicated. We are actually facing a dilemma here: By broadening the scope of the fairness frameworks, many of the factors that play a role can be given due attention; on the other hand, the more broadened they get, the less manageable they may be in practical contexts. Therefore, a choice is always to be made between relative degrees of theoretical plausibility and practicality. It appears that Kunnan is not much concerned with laying priorities for validation research. This is indeed evident from Kunnan (2010), where he argues that "priorities are best identified within a specific test context" (p. 186).

A more recent attempt at elucidating fairness issues can be found in Xi (2010), who aims to develop a framework that provides "a principled way to anticipate potential threats to fairness, to identify and prioritize research needs, and to gauge the progress of fairness investigations" (p. 148). The building block of her framework is Toulmin's (2003) argument structure. It is clear that, unlike Kunnan (2010), Xi is concerned with priorities in fairness research. She bases her framework on "comparable validity" and defines fairness as "comparable validity for *identifiable* and *relevant* groups across all stages of assessment" (p. 154). It is evident that, unlike Kunnan (2005), Xi has opted for a "micro-analytic" approach (i.e., focusing largely on fairness rather than justice). She goes on to elaborate on this definition, saying "fairness requires that construct-irrelevant factors, construct under-representation, inconsistent test administration practices, inappropriate decision-making procedures or use of test results have no *systematic* and *appreciable* effects on test scores, test score interpretations, score-based decisions and consequences for *relevant* groups of examinees" (p.154). It is evident that Xi is also concerned with consequences though there is little talk of value implications. In addition, this conceptualization does not consider any issues that do not differentially affect different groups as relevant to fairness. This is also evident in the example rebuttals in her analysis of the validity argument for the Test of English as a Foreign Language (TOEFL). This may make Xi's model fall short of resolving the problems she set for. Such a model cannot deal with the cases where all examinees are uniformly, and unfairly, treated. As an example, consider a high-stakes university entrance exam that is annually administered to hundreds of thousands of students. The crucial impact of such a test on the stakeholders', and particularly the examinees', lives is undeniable. Now, suppose further that the testing agency does not inform the examinees as to the materials to be tested, the number of questions to be included, and the amount of time to be allotted to each section and to the entire test. Such practice is clearly unfair. But there may be no easily identifiable "relevant groups". Xi may argue that such practices clearly undermine the validity of the test and will be easily handled within the validation process. Such an argument will not do because in that case, the majority of the fairness rebuttals she has included in her framework will also be dealt with in validation. Indeed, defining fairness this way has led Davies (2010) to argue that, "the pursuit of fairness in language testing is in vain" (p. 171).

Another problem with Xi's (2010) conceptualization of fairness comes from a failure to address a plethora of issues related to the ideologies and value implications underlying test use and interpretation (Kunnan, 2010; McNamara & Ryan, 2011). As stated earlier, Xi makes a reference to test consequences in her definition of fairness; however, the issue of values implications is not considered. Testing does not occur in a "value-free psychometric test-tube" (Bachman, 1990, p. 279). A whole array of sociopolitical issues are at play. Limiting fairness research to an evaluation of the psychometric aspects of the measuring instruments is to ignore the specific context of use.

Bachman and Palmer (2010) go a step further and include explicit criteria for fairness in their Assessment Use Argument (AUA). The inclusion of explicit fairness criteria within a validity framework is clearly a step forward. It makes explicit what aspects of fairness should be evaluated at each step along the AUA. However, it seems that, as was the case with Xi (2010), Bachman and Palmer's model is mainly focused on fairness, and many issues related to justice are not included. This is not to say that their model totally ignores justice. Their model, for example, requires that tests are developed with beneficial consequences in mind. What is missing in Bachman and Palmer is a discussion of the ideological and value implications of test constructs and how these issues can be integrated into their AUA. After all, it may turn out that such issues, by their very nature, cannot be included within the boundaries of such frameworks as AUA (Kunnan, 2010).

Among other frameworks that have been proposed so far, the works by Lynch (2001) and Lynch and Shaw (2005) may be notable in that their approach draws on a different theoretical foundation. Their framework has been in keeping with the developments in critical language testing (CLT), and the elements of their framework are assumed to respond to the concerns raised in CLT. A detailed explanation of their model is not provided here though, due to space limitation and the fact that their framework has not been as influential as the ones cited above.

Justice

As discussed earlier, McNamara and Ryan (2011) defined justice as the consequential basis of test use and interpretation. This encompasses both the value implications inherent in the constructs of focus and the social consequences of test use (the third and fourth cells in Messick's (1989) progressive validity matrix). It was also pointed out that language testers have been mainly concerned with test consequences (often discussed in the form of impact or washback).[3] The issues related to the value implications of the constructs have not been given equal attention.

An awareness of the impact of language tests on the society and the value implications of test constructs has led to two major trends in language testing (see McNamara, 2000). A group of language testers (e.g., Davies, 1997a, 1997b, 2008; Stansfield, 1993) have emphasized the importance of creating an "ethical milieu" mainly through professional standards, codes of conduct, and codes of ethics. The other trend has been CLT. The latter trend is more controversial and has greatly impacted the research in language testing during the last decade. Therefore, the next section will provide a detailed discussion of CLT.

Critical language testing

Drawing on the work on critical theory (e.g., Foucault, 1979) and critical applied linguistics (e.g., Pennycook, 2001), the proponents of CLT frequently cite examples of the abuses of language tests to support their position that tests are tools for discrimination and "means for control" (Shohamy, 2001a, 2001b). They further argue that "the content and knowledge contained in tests represent the interests of those in power, who are often interested in perpetuating their domination and in excluding unwanted groups" (Shohamy, 2001a, p. 375). Similarly, Spolsky (1995) has argued that:

> From its beginnings, testing has been exploited also as a method of control and power – as a way to select, to motivate, to punish. The so-called objective test, by virtue of its claim of scientific backing for its impartiality, and especially when it operates under the aegis and with the efficiency of big business, is even more brutally effective in exercising this authority. (p. 1)

Perhaps the most outstanding example of the use of tests for discrimination and control is the case of the shibboleth tests. The story of shibboleth tests is described in the *Book of Judges* and narrated by McNamara (2008) this way:

> Defeated soldiers of the tribe of Ephraim tried to pass as conquering Gileadites, but were outed as they tried to escape by being forced to pronounce the word *shibolet*, meaning "an ear of wheat", or possibly "a stream", which as Ephraimites they pronounced *sibolet*. An Ephraimite identity was thus "uncovered" through a language test; the Ephraimite soldiers so revealed were put to death in their tens of thousands. (p. 416–417)

Much of the problem with the shibboleth tests lies in the purpose or aim of the assessment rather than the assessment tool. That is, even if we were to allocate unlimited time and resources to the development of a psychometrically sound test, the purpose of the test would still be unjustified. More specifically, the decision itself is unethical regardless of the appropriateness of the measurement instrument used. The use of a psychometrically sound measurement tool does not justify the use to which the test is put. This is why a definition of fairness limited to an appraisal of the psychometric qualities of the test is inadequate. Note that the distinction between the fairness of the measuring instrument itself and the fairness of the intentions behind the use of the test (i.e., justice) often emphasized by CLT is different from the discussions appearing in the mainstream language testing research where it is assumed that the "intended aim" of the assessment process is "beneficial" (Bachman, 2005). For example, in his "assessment utilization argument", Bachman (2005) includes a warrant he calls "utility", defining it as the requirement that "the score-based interpretation is actually *useful* for making the intended decision" (p. 19). Bachman further elaborates on *utility* saying it refers to the extent to which the information provided by the scores and the relevant interpretations are conducive to more appropriate decisions. He includes three other warrants in his utilization argument: *relevance*, *sufficiency*, and *intended consequences*. The first two warrants require that the test be relevant to the decision to be made and that the information provided by the test be sufficient respectively. By *intended consequences*, Bachman (2005) stipulates that the decisions made on the basis of the assessment will be beneficial to the stakeholders and the society at large. He elaborates further that the "intended consequences pertain to the beneficial outcomes that the test user expects to achieve by using the assessment" (p. 19). It is clear that Bachman assumes that the test users have good intentions and that they struggle to bring about good to the test takers and the society.

It appears that the difference between CLT and the classical psychometric tradition lies mainly in their starting points. The psychometric tradition starts from the premise that all test use and interpretation is done with good intentions. This is explicitly acknowledged in Bachman and Palmer (2010): "We begin with the premise that people generally use language assessments in order to bring about some beneficial outcomes or consequences for stakeholders" (p. 86). They go on to argue that "decision makers use language assessments to help them make decisions that *they believe will help bring about some specific beneficial consequence*" (p. 89, emphasis added). Bachman and Palmer (2010) of course recognize that the use of a particular test may not always bring about the intended *beneficial* consequences and may lead to some unwanted, unintended, detrimental consequences. Being aware of the possible discrepancies between the *intended* and *actual* consequences, they contend that the *intended* consequences, decisions, and interpretations should be taken into account at the time of test development. However, the *actual* consequences and interpretations should be considered when the validity of the test is examined. Therefore, Bachman and Palmer are also fully aware of the negative social consequences that the use of tests may bring about. However, their assumption all along their argument is that test developers start with good intentions and that any negative consequences are unintended.

Such an assumption is also evident in Messick's (1980) discussion of the importance of a consideration of the consequential aspects of test use:

> [O]ne of the key questions to be posed whenever a test is suggested for a specific purpose is 'Should it be used for that purpose?' Answers to that question require an evaluation of the potential consequences of the testing in terms of social values, but that is no trivial enterprise. There is no guarantee that at any point in time we will identify all of the critical possibilities, especially those *unintended side effects that are distal to the manifest testing aims*. (p. 1020, emphasis added)

It seems that Messick does not consider "manifest testing aims" as ill intended and is concerned mainly with the "side effects" that are "unintended". So, it appears that, unlike critical language testers, Messick is less concerned with the *intentional abuse* of the tests for a purpose other than it is declared for. Whenever a test is used, Messick assumes, as Bachman and Palmer (2010) do, it is used with beneficial consequences in mind. They appear to assume that any negative social consequences are unintended. This is also apparent in Messick's reference to Kaplan's declaration that "not all value concerns are unscientific, that indeed some of them are called for by the scientific enterprise itself, and that [in scientific enquiry] *those which run counter to scientific ideas can be brought under control*" (as cited in Messick, 1989, p. 58, emphasis added).

At times, CLT proponents' arguments seem to be in keeping with the classic psychometric tradition. For example, Shohamy (2007) frequently refers to Messick's works in her discussion and credits Messick with pushing the view that tests are not "naïve tools aimed at measuring progress and carrying out exclusively pedagogical goals" (p. 522). Shohamy's (2007) discussion of the power of the language tests and especially English language tests appears to be in keeping with Messick's view. However, at other places she explicitly argues that CLT "signifies a paradigm shift in language testing in that it introduces new criteria for the validity of language tests" (Shohamy, 1998, p. 333).

Therefore, it appears that while the psychometric tradition starts from the premise that tests are developed and used with good intentions, the CLT proponents take the opposite stance, namely that tests are tools of social control. Furthermore, the critical language testers differ on the extent of distrust in the use of tests. As McNamara (2000) puts it, critical language testing at its extreme rejects the entire psychometric tradition.

We do not believe that the extreme position is a plausible direction for language testers to take. Simply because language tests have been misused in some contexts does not necessarily mean that we have to abandon language tests altogether. Such abuses are not specific to language tests. Take the human rights as an example. There have been many cases where human rights have been misleadingly exploited to achieve political goals and sometimes even justify violations of human rights! What are we to make of such abuses? Are we to abandon our pursuit of human rights simply because it is sometimes abused? Definitely not. We believe that the same applies to language testing. Simply because language tests are sometimes abused does not necessarily mean that we ought to quit language testing and psychometrics, and specifically the use of language tests, altogether. In fact, the reverse conclusion is more plausible. We need a principled basis to hold the users of language tests accountable for the decisions they make. Language testing and psychometrics can provide us with such a principled basis.

A reviewer has suggested that testing agencies, such as the Educational Testing Service, usually invite, and offer grants to, independent researchers to appraise the quality of the tests they develop. Studies such as the one by Chapelle, Enright, and Jamieson (2008) on the validity of the TOEFL iBT (i.e., the internet-based version of TOEFL) provide more transparency regarding the kind of interpretations that can be justifiably drawn from the test scores and is clearly an important step towards accountability. While the reviewer is correct on this, it should be noted that few studies have been concerned with issues of concern to CLT (i.e., the issues related to the value implications), and the majority of the research conducted so far has been limited to an evaluation of the psychometric characteristics of the tests. For example, there is little talk of fairness in Chapelle et al. (2008), and a consideration of the consequential basis of the TOEFL is generally missing.

The implications of critical language testing for practitioners have also been at times rather far reaching. Shohamy (2007), for example, has argued that "English language teachers need to develop critical strategies to examine the uses and consequences of English language tests, to control the power of tests and minimize their detrimental impact" (p. 530). However, such a task is much easier said than done. The policies toward tests are a reflection of the larger political philosophies of the nations (Fulcher, 2009). We cannot expect "democratic assessment" in a country that does not value democracy. Kunnan (2010) appears to have recognized this and argues that his fairness framework has been designed for "a well-ordered society in which there is social cooperation between citizens who are free and equal and the primary goal is social and political justice" (p. 184). Ironically, the examinees in less democratic countries are most affected by the abuses of the tests, and they are largely unaware of their own rights. In such contexts, the situation is no better for teachers. They do not have much power themselves. Expecting the teachers to stand up to defend the rights of their students is to expect too much from people who have little power. The following excerpt from a teacher educator is a clear testimony to the problem just described:

> Teachers in many contexts are not different from factory workers in terms of their working hours; in many countries, a typical language teacher works for 8 hours per day, 5 or even 6 days per week. Most of these teachers are poorly paid and "putting bread on the table for my family," as one such teacher put it, is their main priority. The financial and occupational constraints they work within do not leave them with the time or the willingness to act as iconoclasts and social transformers, roles that will jeopardize their often precarious means of subsistence. (Akbari, 2008, p. 646).

How can we expect these teachers to strive for controlling the power of tests? Do they ever think about such matters? How can such powerless people control the power of the tests? As stated earlier, this is to expect too much from people who have little power. We agree with Hamp-Lyons (2007) that the success of even teacher-based and classroom assessment is largely determined by the status of the teachers in the society. Teachers do not have the desired status in many countries. As long as they do not enjoy a high status, they cannot be of much help in controlling the power of tests.

In sum, we do believe that critical language testing has been very effective in bringing to our sight the disastrous consequences that the test uses/interpretations may have. Test use is not simply assumed to be beneficial. Much attention should be paid to ideological and value implications of our constructs. However, we do not think that the extreme critical testing perspective is a plausible stance to take because language testing and psychometrics can provide us with a mechanism to address many of the concerns voiced by CLT. The wholesale dismissal of psychometrics in favour of CLT would amount to throwing the baby out with the bathwater.

As stated earlier, a possibility for bringing fairness into language testing is to create an ethical milieu. One of the controversial issues so far has been the delineation of the responsibility of language testers in face of the consequences language tests may have for the stakeholders. Bachman and Palmer (2010) restrict the responsibility of the test developers/users to some *intended* consequences arguing that the aim of the AUA is to help the test developers and users to be held accountable for *intended* uses of tests. They justify their position by arguing that

> Given the almost infinite range of possible unintended consequences of using a particular assessment and making a decision based on this, even the most contentious and diligent test developer cannot possibly anticipate or guard against all the potential unintended consequences of using a particular assessment. (pp. 111–112).

Davies (2008) takes a similar stance, arguing that language testers cannot take the responsibility for all social consequences. What can be done instead is "the internal (technical) bias analysis and a willingness to be accountable for a test's 'fairness', or in other words, limited and predictable social consequences we can take account of and regard ourselves as responsible for" (p. 433). On the other hand, Hamp-Lyons (1997) broadens the scope of the responsibility of language testers, declaring that language testers should take responsibility for all test consequences.

It is necessary to limit the responsibility of language testers as they cannot be held accountable for all consequences. In contexts where test users and test developers are not the same people, much of the responsibility for the interpretation and use of the test lies with test users. So individual testers are not responsible for any abuses that are made of the tests they have developed with beneficial outcomes in mind. It is clear that the higher the stakes involved, the more the need for accountability in language assessment. The bottom line may be that test users and developers are not responsible for consequences that cannot be traced back to sources of construct-irrelevant variance or construct underrepresentation (Messick, 1989).

A possible way of ensuring accountability may be bringing to the courts those testing agencies that do not comply with professional standards (Fulcher & Bamford, 1996). In fact, the litigations of the 1970s and 1980s in the United States are considered as a landmark in bias studies because legal issues entered the scene (McNamara & Roever, 2006). A frequently quoted instance was the case of the Golden Rule Settlement in 1976. The Golden Rule Insurance Company filed a suit against the Educational Testing Service (ETS) and the Illinois Department of Insurance due to an alleged bias against Blacks in the tests they developed. The court issued a verdict in favour of the Golden Rule Insurance Company. The ETS was considered liable for the tests it developed and was legally ordered to make every effort to rule out bias in its tests. Holding the testing agencies and all those who develop/use tests accountable will be a serious step towards ensuring fairness. However, it should be noted here again that the testing policies usually reflect the general political vibes of the nations. In countries where there is little democracy, filing a suit against a particular testing agency for undemocratic testing policies may make little sense.

Conclusion

Bachman (1990) suggested that validity is the single most important consideration in language testing. After over two decades of research on validity and its scope, it seems that validity encompasses almost everything in language assessment. Bachman's declaration may have lost much of its initial sense as virtually everything is now included within validity or what Bachman and Palmer (2010) call *assessment justification*. The question of "what is the most important consideration in testing?" is irrelevant today. Rather, we are faced with the question "what are the priorities in validation?" The latter question does not have a simple answer. Each assessment context is unique with unique and varied demands on and stakes for test developers/users and the stakeholders, respectively. However, we do believe that fairness is a top priority in virtually all contexts.

Notes

1. See Ferne and Rupp (2007), for a comprehensive overview of DIF studies in language testing.
2. We will use the terms model and framework interchangeably here. For a discussion of the differences involved, see VanPatten and Williams (2007).
3. Due to space limitations, we will not discuss washback here and will focus on critical language testing that has been at the center of discussions on the value implications and the sociopolitical aspects of test use and interpretation (for extended discussions of washback, see Alderson & Hamp-Lyons, 1996; Alderson & Wall, 1993; Bailey, 1996; Cheng, 2005; Cheng, Watanabe, & Curtis, 2004; Hawkey, 2006; Messick, 1996; Wall, 1997, 2000, 2005).

References

Akbari, R. (2008). Postmethod and practice. *TESOL Quarterly, 42*, 641–652.

Alderson, J. C., & Hamp-Lyons, L. (1996). TOEFL preparation courses: A case study. *Language Testing, 13,* 280–297.

Alderson, J. C., & Urquhart, A. (1985). The effect of students' academic discipline on their performance on ESP reading tests. *Language Testing, 2,* 192–204.

Alderson, J. C., & Wall, D. (1993). Does washback exist? *Applied Linguistics 14*, 115–129.

Angoff, W. H. (1993). Perspectives on differential item functioning methodology. In P. W. Holland & H. Wainer (Eds.), *Differential item functioning* (pp. 3–24). Hillsdale, NJ: Lawrence Erlbaum Associates.

Aryadoust, V., Goh, C., & Lee, O. K. (2011). An investigation of differential item functioning in the MELAB listening test. *Language Assessment Quarterly, 8*, 361–385.

Bachman, L. F. (1990). *Fundamental considerations in language testing.* Oxford, UK: Oxford University Press.

Bachman, L. F. (2005). Building and supporting a case for test use. *Language Assessment Quarterly, 2*, 1–34.

Bachman, L. F., & Palmer, A. S. (2010). *Language assessment in practice.* Oxford, UK: Oxford University Press.

Bailey, K. M. (1996). Working for washback: A review of the washback concept in language testing. *Language Testing 13*, 257–279.

Brown, J. D. (1999). The relative importance of persons, items, subtests and languages to TOEFL test variance. *Language Testing, 16*, 217–238.

Chapelle, C. A., Enright, M. K., & Jamieson, J. M. (Eds.). (2008). *Building a validity argument for the test of English as a foreign language.* New York, NY: Routledge.

Chen, Z., & Henning, G. (1985). Linguistic and cultural bias in language proficiency tests. *Language Testing, 2,* 155–163.

Cheng, L. (2005). *Changing language teaching through language testing: A washback study.* Cambridge, UK: Cambridge University Press.

Cheng, L., Watanabe, Y., & Curtis, A. (2004). *Washback in language testing: Research contexts and methods.* Mahwah, NJ: Lawrence Erlbaum Associates.

Cole, N. S., & Moss, P. A. (1989). Bias in test use. In R. Linn (Ed.), *Educational measurement* (3rd ed., pp. 201–219). Washington, DC: American Council on Education & National Council on Measurement in Education.

Davies, A. (1997a). Demands of being professional in language testing. *Language Testing, 14,* 328–339.

Davies, A. (1997b). Introduction: The limits of ethics in language testing. *Language Testing, 14,* 235–241.

Davies, A. (2008). Ethics and professionalism. In E. Shohamy & N. H. Hornberger (Eds.), *Encyclopedia of language and education: Vol. 7. Language testing and assessment* (2nd ed., pp. 429–443). New York, NY: Springer.

Davies, A. (2010). Test fairness: A response. *Language Testing, 27,* 171–176.

Elder, C. (1996). The effect of language background on "foreign" language test performance: The case of Chinese, Italian, and Modern Greek. *Language Learning, 46,* 233–282.

Ferne, T., & Rupp, A. (2007). A synthesis of research on DIF in language testing: Methodological advances, challenges, and recommendations. *Language Assessment Quarterly, 4,* 113–148.

Foucault, M. (1979). *Discipline and punish.* New York, NY: Vintage Books.

Fulcher, G. (2009). Test use and political philosophy. *Annual Review of Applied Linguistics, 29,* 3–20.

Fulcher, G., & Bamford, R. (1996). I didn't get the grade I need. Where's my solicitor? *System, 24,* 437–448.

Hale, G. A. (1988). Student major field and text content: Interactive effects on reading comprehension in the Test of English as a Foreign Language. *Language Testing, 5,* 49–61.

Hamp-Lyons, L. (1997). Washback, impact and validity: Ethical concerns. *Language Testing, 14,* 295–303.

Hamp-Lyons, L. (2007). The impact of testing practices on teaching: Ideologies and alternatives. In J. Cummins & C. Davison (Eds.), *The international handbook of English language teaching* (Vol. 1, pp. 487–504). Norwell, MA: Springer.

Hawkey, R. (2006). *Impact theory and practice: Studies of the IELTS test and Progetto Lingue 2000.* Cambridge, UK: Cambridge University Press.

Kane, M. (2010). Validity and fairness. *Language Testing, 27,* 177–182.

Karami, H. (2011). Detecting gender bias in a language proficiency test. *International Journal of Language Studies, 5,* 167–178.

Kim, M. (2001). Detecting DIF across the different language groups in a speaking test. *Language Testing, 18,* 89–114.

Kunnan, A. J. (2000). Fairness and justice for all. In A. J. Kunnan (Ed.), *Fairness and validation in language assessment* (pp. 1–14). Cambridge, UK: Cambridge University Press.

Kunnan, A. J. (2004). Test fairness. In M. Milanovic & C. Weir (Eds.), *European language testing in a global context: Proceedings of the ALTE Barcelona Conference* (pp. 27–48). Cambridge, UK: Cambridge University Press.

Kunnan, A. J. (2005). Language assessment from a wider context. In E. Hinkel (Ed.), *Handbook of research in second language learning* (pp. 779–794). Mahwah, NJ: LEA.

Kunnan, A. J. (2010). Test fairness and Toulmin's argument structure. *Language Testing, 27,* 183–189.

Lynch, B. K. (2001). Rethinking assessment from a critical perspective. *Language Testing, 18,* 351–372.

Lynch, B., & Shaw, P. (2005). Portfolio, power and ethics. *TESOL Quarterly, 39,* 263–297.

McNamara, T. F. (2000). *Language testing.* Oxford, UK: Oxford University Press.

McNamara, T. (2005). 21st century Shibboleth: Language tests, identity and intergroup conflict. *Language Policy, 4,* 351–370.

McNamara, T. (2008). The socio-political and power dimensions of tests. In E. Shohamy & N. Hornberger (Eds.), *Encyclopedia of language and education: Vol. 7. Language testing and assessment* (2nd ed., pp. 415–427). New York, NY: Springer.

McNamara, T. F. & Roever, C. (2006). *Language testing: The social dimension*. Oxford, UK: Blackwell.

McNamara, T., & Ryan, K. (2011). Fairness versus justice in language testing: The place of English literacy in the Australian Citizenship Test. *Language Assessment Quarterly, 8*, 161–178.

Messick, S. (1980). Test validity and the ethics of assessment. *American psychologist, 35*, 1012–1027.

Messick, S. (1989). Validity. In R. L. Linn (Ed.), *Educational measurement* (3rd ed., pp. 13–103). New York. NY: American Council on Education and Macmillan.

Messick, S. (1996). Validity and washback in language testing. *Language Testing 13*, 243–256.

Pae, T. (2004). DIF for learners with different academic backgrounds. *Language Testing, 21*, 53–73.

Pennycook, A. (2001). *Critical applied linguistics*. Mahwah, NJ: Lawrence Erlbaum Associates.

Ryan, K., & Bachman, L. F. (1992). Differential item functioning on two tests of EFL proficiency. *Language Testing, 9*, 12–29.

Shohamy, E. (1997). Testing methods, testing consequences: Are they ethical? Are they fair? *Language Testing, 14*, 340–349.

Shohamy, E. (1998). Critical language testing and beyond. *Studies in Educational Evaluation, 24*, 331–345.

Shohamy, E. (2001a). Democratic assessment as an alternative. *Language Testing, 18*, 373–391.

Shohamy, E. (2001b). *The power of tests: A critical perspective of the uses of language tests*. London, UK: Longman.

Shohamy, E. (2007). The power of language tests: The power of the English language and the role of ELT. In J. Cummins & C. Davison (Eds.), *International handbook of English language teaching* (pp. 521–531). New York, NY: Springer.

Spolsky, B. (1995). *Measured words: The development of objective language testing*. Oxford, UK: Oxford University Press.

Stansfield, C. W. (1993). Some ethical issues and problems in language testing. *Issues in Applied Linguistics, 4*, 189–205.

Takala, S., & Kaftandjieva, F. (2000). Test fairness: A DIF analysis of an L2 vocabulary test. *Language Testing, 17*, 323–340.

Toulmin, S. (2003). *The uses of argument*. Cambridge, UK: Cambridge University Press.

VanPatten, B., & Williams, J. (2007). The nature of theories. In B. VanPatten & J. Williams (Eds.), *Theories in second language acquisition: An introduction* (pp. 1–16). Mahwah, NJ: Lawrence Erlbaum.

Wall, D. (1997). Impact and washback in language testing. In C. Clapham & D. Corson (Eds.), *Encyclopedia of language and education: Vol. 7. Language testing and assessment* (pp. 291–302). Dordrecht, The Netherlands: Kluwer Academic.

Wall, D. (2000). The impact of high-stakes testing on teaching and learning: Can this be predicted or controlled? *System, 28*, 499–509.

Wall, D. (2005). *The impact of high-stakes examinations on classroom teaching: A case study using insights from testing and innovation theory*. Cambridge, UK: Cambridge University Press.

Xi, X. (2010). How do we go about investigating test fairness? *Language Testing, 27*, 147–170.

Decisions that make a difference in detecting differential item functioning

Stephen G. Sireci and Joseph A. Rios

University of Massachusetts Amherst, Amherst, MA, USA

There are numerous statistical procedures for detecting items that function differently across subgroups of examinees that take a test or survey. However, in endeavouring to detect items that may function differentially, selection of the statistical method is only one of many important decisions. In this article, we discuss the important decisions that affect investigations of differential item functioning (DIF) such as choice of method, sample size, effect size criteria, conditioning variable, purification, DIF amplification, DIF cancellation, and research designs for evaluating DIF. Our review highlights the necessity of matching the DIF procedure to the nature of the data analysed, the need to include effect size criteria, the need to consider the direction and balance of items flagged for DIF, and the need to use replication to reduce Type I errors whenever possible. Directions for future research and practice in using DIF to enhance the validity of test scores are provided.

Introduction

Educational and psychological assessment in the 21st century is characterized by a concern for fairness to all examinees who take an assessment. We live in a diverse world where people differ with respect to ethnicity, culture, language, and a host of other variables. Assessments are designed to measure the same attributes (constructs) with the same precision across examinees regardless of differences with respect to irrelevant variables such as ethnicity, culture, sex, and other demographics. For this reason, test developers use several quality control procedures to ensure that test items are fair and appropriate for all examinees. Some of these procedures involve qualitative reviews of items by content experts and sensitivity reviewers (Ramsay, 1993; Sireci & Mullane, 1994), while other procedures are statistical. In this article, we review statistical procedures designed to identify items that appear to have different statistical properties across certain groups of examinees, which is referred to as *differential item functioning* (DIF). Such items are said to "function differentially" across groups, which is a potential indicator of item bias.

Our discussion of DIF centres on test fairness and validity. According to the *Standards for Educational and Psychological Testing* (American Educational Research Association (AERA), American Psychological Association, & National Council on Measurement in Education, 1999), "Validity refers to the degree to which evidence and theory support the interpretations of test scores entailed by proposed uses of tests" (p. 9). Fairness refers to an equal opportunity for all examinees to demonstrate their true proficiency on an assessment. Given that validity refers to appropriate test score interpretations, fairness is inherent within the concept. That is, if test score interpretations are valid, they are also fair to all examinees.

In this article, we describe how analysis of DIF can be used to promote validity. We discuss some of the most popular statistical methods for identifying items that exhibit DIF, and we discuss the major research design and practical issues that are involved in conducting DIF analyses. We conclude with a set of recommendations for using DIF to promote the validity of test score interpretations.

What is differential item functioning?

DIF refers to the situation where the statistical properties of an item are inconsistent across two or more groups of examinees. Statistical properties of an item typically refer to item difficulty or endorsement, and item discrimination. In educational testing where items have correct answers, item difficulty is generally defined as the proportion of examinees who answer the item correctly. In surveys and psychological assessments where there are no correct answers, the degree to which examinees select (endorse) a particular response replaces the concept of difficulty. In this article, we use the term "difficulty", but we use it generally to refer to the likelihood of examinees from a particular group making a specific response to an item. The concept of item discrimination refers to the degree to which an item differentiates between those who are high and low on the proficiency (construct) measured by the test. An item with high discrimination is one that examinees at one extreme of the continuum have a very different response pattern than those at the other end of the continuum, and this difference in response correlates with the overall test score. DIF refers to the situation where item difficulty or discrimination varies across specific groups of examinees, such as those defined by sex or ethnicity.

According to Clauser and Mazor (1998), "(DIF) is present when examinees from different groups have differing ... likelihoods of success on an item, *after they have been matched on the [proficiency] of interest*" (p. 31, emphasis added). The italicized phrase is key to understanding DIF, because it represents an *interaction* between group membership and the likelihood of a particular response on an item, conditional on the attribute measured. The conditioning or "matching" feature is essential to DIF analysis because if two groups differ with respect to their performance on an item, this difference could reflect a valid (true) difference between the groups on the construct measured. However, if individuals from the different groups are matched on the construct measured, then there should be no differences with respect to how they respond to the item. That is, individuals who are equal on the construct measured should have equal probabilities of specific responses to an item. If that property does not hold across groups, the item is said to exhibit DIF.

DIF, impact, and bias

The preceding paragraph described the distinction between DIF and item *impact*. Item impact refers to an overall difference in item performance across groups. For example, women may perform much better on a test item than men. That difference, or impact, may reflect a true difference between women and men on what the test is measuring; therefore, it may not reflect a problem with the item. However, if there is a difference in performance across men and women who are equal with respect to the construct measured (i.e., matched), it may be a signal that the item is biased in some way. Item *bias* is present when an item has been statistically flagged for DIF *and the reason for the DIF is traced to a factor irrelevant to the construct the test is intended to measure.* Therefore, for item bias to exist, a characteristic of the item that is unfair (construct irrelevant) to one or more groups must be identified. DIF is a statistical observation that is used to flag an item for further review of potential unfairness. Thus, it is a necessary, but insufficient, condition for item bias. However, in saying that, responsible test developers will rarely retain items, regardless of construct-irrelevant explanations, that display both statistical significance and large effect sizes supporting DIF.

A conclusion of item bias must contain both the statistical finding of DIF and a qualitative interpretation linking the source of DIF to a characteristic of the item that is irrelevant to the construct measured. Therefore, analysis of DIF is an important endeavour in promoting test score validity and fairness across subgroups of examinees. For item and test scores to have the same "meaning" across groups, the items should be functioning similarly, otherwise the meaning of what the item measures changes, depending on the group responding to the item. In broader terms, this is a matter of measurement invariance, which refers to the consistency of the assessment across specific subgroups of examinees. DIF analyses are a vital aspect of both test development and validation as they assist in ensuring that measures are unbiased and reflect the same underlying latent construct(s) for all examinees (Walker, 2011).

DIF terminology

Before proceeding, it is important to define a few terms associated with the DIF literature. For example, when conducting DIF analyses it is important to designate reference and focal group examinees. A *reference group* can be defined as the standard to which the focal group is compared, and tends to comprise examinees from a "majority" group (e.g., Caucasians, males, native language speakers, etc.). In contrast, the *focal group* is a special group of interest, and tends to comprise "minority" examinees (e.g., ethnic minorities, females, language minorities). Interest in determining whether there is possible item bias for focal group examinees is the essence of DIF analyses.

As mentioned earlier, to evaluate DIF, examinees from different groups must be matched on the attribute measured to make direct comparisons. The variable used to link similar examinees is referred to as the matching or *conditioning variable*. Total test score tends to be used as the conditioning variable within DIF analyses as it is a readily available and reliable means of matching examinees; however, some researchers have suggested using additional variables for conditioning purposes (Clauser, Nungester, & Swaminathan, 1996). Lastly, a distinction must be made concerning the different types of DIF. In general, there are two forms: (a) uniform DIF and (b) non-uniform DIF. Uniform DIF can be conceptualized as one group having a higher probability of correctly endorsing the studied item across the entire test score continuum (see Figure 1). Non-uniform DIF is distinctive in that the probability of correctly endorsing the studied item differs across the groups, but the direction and magnitude varies across the conditioning variable. One example of non-uniform DIF is presented in Figure 2. The distinction between uniform and non-uniform DIF is important because it could help explain why the item functions differentially across groups. As we explain in the next section, some DIF detection methods can identify non-uniform DIF, while others cannot.

DIF detection methods

Numerous statistical procedures have been developed to evaluate DIF. These procedures essentially fall into five categories: (a) descriptive statistical approaches (e.g., conditional

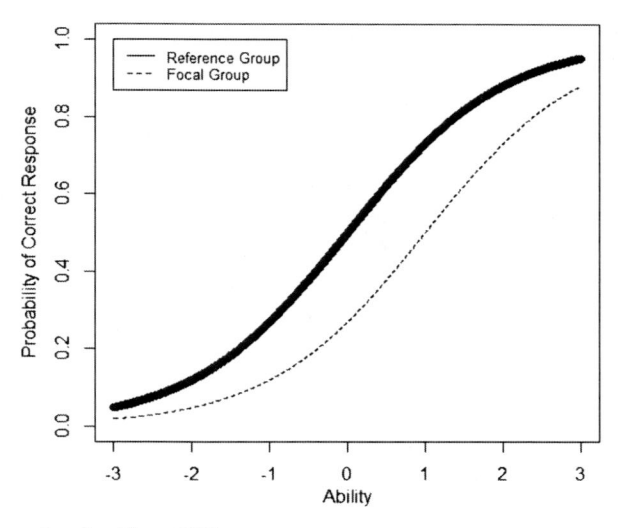

Figure 1.   An example of uniform DIF.

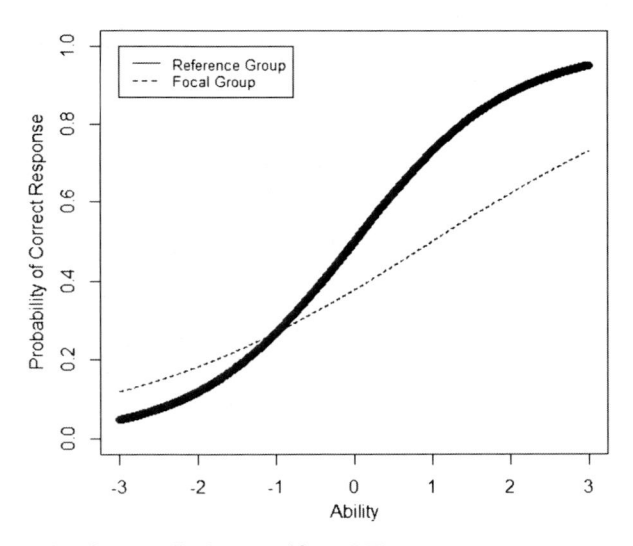

Figure 2.   An example of non-ordinal non-uniform DIF.

proportion correct), (b) graphical display, (c) contingency tables, (d) regression models, and (e) methods based on item response theory (IRT). Camilli (2006) differentiated among these methods using only two classifications – those based on observed scores and those based on IRT. We cannot describe all methods in this article, and so we focus on the most popular methods from each of the five categories. Specifically, we describe the standardization index (Dorans & Kulick, 1986), the Mantel-Haenszel method (Holland & Thayer, 1988), logistic regression (Swaminathan & Rogers, 1990; Zumbo, 1999), Lord's chi square (Lord, 1980), and the IRT likelihood ratio test (Thissen, Steinberg, & Wainer, 1988). Each of these methods has advantages and disadvantages related to practical considerations, such as sample size, item format (dichotomous vs. polytomous), type of DIF (uniform vs.

non-uniform), and ease of interpretation. These considerations, as well as a general description of each method, are described next.

Observed score methods

Standardization index

The standardization index was first introduced by Dorans and Kulick (1986). The index essentially computes an average difference across groups in the proportion of examinees selecting a particular response, conditional on the matching variable. There are both signed and unsigned indices, to distinguish between uniform and non-uniform DIF. The signed index is,

$$D_{\text{std}} = \frac{\sum_{s=1}^{S} K_s [P_{fs} - P_{rs}]}{\sum_{s=1}^{S} K_s}, \tag{1}$$

where S = score level, K_s = weight of the score level, P_{fs} = the proportion correct at score level s for the focal group, and P_{rs} = the proportion correct at score level s for the reference group. This equation is referred to as the signed version because positive differences across groups can be offset by negative differences. Thus, it will not pick up on non-uniform DIF (as illustrated in Figure 2). To evaluate non-uniform DIF, the unsigned version of the index is used:

$$D_{\text{std}} = \frac{\sum_{s=1}^{S} |K_s [P_{fs} - P_{rs}]|}{\sum_{s=1}^{S} K_s}. \tag{2}$$

The standardization index matches examinees at particular score levels, and compares the difference in p values (proportion correct) for individual items between the reference and focal groups. A score level can represent either a single total score or a grouping of scores. In deciding how to group examinees into different score levels, sample size and score distributions may play critical roles. Muñiz, Hambleton, and Xing (2001) noted that when dealing with small sample sizes, creating too many score levels or ability groupings will result in unstable p values that can lead to biased evaluations of DIF. Another issue with the standardization index is deciding on how to weight the score levels. The levels can be unweighted, or weighted by the size of the reference group, focal group, or both.

The signed version of the standardization index ranges from -1.0 to 1.0, while the signed version ranges from 0 to 1.0. Although there is not a statistical test, an effect size can be computed to assist with practical interpretations of DIF. Researchers have suggested a critical value of $+/- 0.10$ to flag items for DIF (Dorans & Kulick, 1986; Muñiz et al., 2001; Sireci, 2011; Sireci, Patsula, & Hambleton, 2005). The logic behind this effect size criterion is that if 10 items are deemed to possess DIF for one group, a 1-point (10 items x .10 = 1 point) total score disparity between groups would be apparent.

The advantages of the standardization index are (a) it is easy to calculate, (b) it allows for easy interpretation and explanation to stakeholders (DeMars, 2011), (c) the results can be easily graphed, and (d) it can be applied to small sample sizes (Muñiz et al., 2001). Calculation of the p values (proportion correct) for dichotomous items is equal to the sample mean for a particular item, while the p value for polytomous items is equal to the average of the observed score divided by the total number of possible points within an item. Such a calculation does not require specialized DIF software and can be calculated in Microsoft

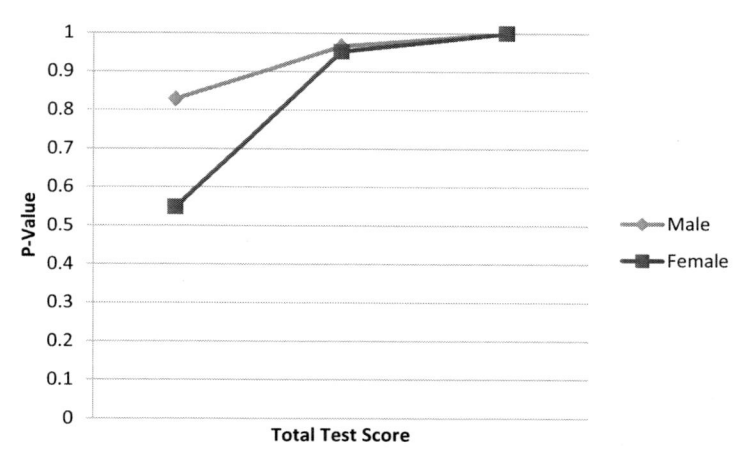

Figure 3. An example of a graph for the standardization index procedure.

Excel or in any general statistical software package. With respect to graphing the results for easy communication to lay audiences, Figure 3 provides an example of an item flagged for non-uniform DIF using the standardization index. It can be easily seen that women who score below average on the test did much worse on the item than men with the same total test score. These plots make interpretation and explanation of DIF straightforward for non-statistical audiences (DeMars, 2011). Software for conducting the standardization procedure is also available free of charge (Robin, 2001).

One must also consider some of the disadvantages associated with the standardization index. For one, p values, like all percentages, suffer from not being calibrated on an equal-interval scale. That is, a difference between .60 and .70 cannot be assumed to be equal to a difference between .40 and .50. This limitation makes for misjudgements in comparing across the item difficulty scale (Wood, 1988). Secondly, as mentioned earlier, if the sample sizes are too small within a grouping, unstable p estimates will be obtained, which could erroneously flag items for DIF (i.e., Type I errors) or mask the presence of DIF (i.e., Type II errors).

Mantel-Haenszel

The Mantel-Haenszel (MH) method can be viewed as an extension of the standardization index in that both procedures take examinees from two groups, match them on overall ability or proficiency, and then compare the groups on the likelihood of success for an item (Holland & Thayer, 1988). One of the major distinctions between these two methods is that instead of the proportion correct, MH uses the common odds ratio. This is accomplished by pooling information across levels of the matching variable (typically observed total test score) to evaluate how much greater the likelihood of success is on a particular item for the reference group when compared to the examinees in the focal group. The MH odds ratio is calculated as follows:

$$\hat{\alpha}_{MH} = \frac{\Sigma_j (A_j D_j)/T_j}{\Sigma_j (B_j C_j)/T_j} \tag{3}$$

The information necessary to calculate $\hat{\alpha}_{MH}$ can be represented in a 2 x 2 matrix for each level of the matching variable as demonstrated in Table 1.

Table 1. Information required to calculate the Mantel Haenszel odds ratio.

Group	Correct	Incorrect	Total
Reference	A_j	B_j	N_{rj}
Focal	C_j	D_j	N_{fj}
Total	M_{1j}	M_{0j}	T_j

For the $\hat{\alpha}_{MH}$ equation, A_j = the frequency of reference group members who correctly endorsed the item in level j, B_j = the frequency of reference group members who incorrectly endorsed the item in level j, C_j = the frequency of focal group members who correctly endorsed the item in level j, D_j = the frequency of focal group members who incorrectly endorsed the item in level j, and T_j = the total sample size in level j. The $\hat{\alpha}_{MH}$ value can be interpreted as the average exceeding factor of the odds that reference group examinees correctly endorse item i when contrasted to comparable focal group examinees. Values of $\hat{\alpha}_{MH} > 1$ suggest that the reference group performed better on average than comparable members of the focal group (Holland & Thayer, 1988). The significance in the deviation of likelihood of success between reference and focal groups is calculated in a one degree of freedom chi-square statistic as follows:

$$x^2_{MH} = \frac{\left[\left| \Sigma_j A_j - \Sigma_j [E(A)_j] \right| - 0.5 \right]^2}{\Sigma_j Var(A_j)} \tag{4}$$

where

$$E(A_j) = \frac{N_{rj} M_{1j}}{T_j} \tag{5}$$

and

$$Var(A_j) = \frac{N_{rj} N_{fj} M_{1j} M_{0j}}{T_j^2 - (T_j - 1)}. \tag{6}$$

In addition to the commons odds ratio scale, the Mantel-Haenszel statistic can be transformed onto the delta metric. Holland and Thayer (1988) suggested that reporting the Mantel-Haenszel statistic on the delta scale is more convenient as it puts the statistics on a symmetrical scale in which the null value (no DIF) is 0, allowing for easier interpretation. In comparison, the odds ratio metric ranges from 0 to ∞ with $\alpha = 1$ signifying no DIF. The conversion from the odds ratio to delta metric is,

$$\Delta_{MH} = -2.35 \times \ln(\hat{\alpha}_{MH}) \tag{7}$$

The value of Δ_{MH} can be interpreted as the average additional difficulty (in delta units) observed for the reference group when compared to similar (in ability) focal group members on the studied item. Negative values indicate the degree to which the reference group found the item to be easier than their focal group counterparts. Upon computing the Δ_{MH} statistic, effect size classifications can be applied to evaluate the magnitude of DIF. Zieky (1993) proposed that negligible or small DIF is indicated by a $|\Delta_{MH}| < 1.0$, medium DIF is indicated by a $1.0 < |\Delta_{MH}| < 1.5$, and large DIF is represented by $|\Delta_{MH}| \geq 1.5$.

Overall, the MH procedure provides a powerful means of evaluating uniform DIF as all focus is placed on the evaluation of one parameter. That is, this procedure assesses the degree to which the odds ratio differs from one across all levels of the matching variable (Sireci, 2011). In addition, MH can be easily computed using general statistical software, such as SAS or SPSS. For detailed syntax and practical examples of performing this procedure in SAS, the reader is referred to Stokes, Davis, and Koch (2000) or Camilli and Shepard (1994). Although the MH procedure was originally developed for analysis with dichotomously scored items, Zwick, Donoghue, and Grima (1993) extended it for use with polytomously scored items. MH effect size guidelines for polytomous items can be found in Zwick, Thayer, and Mazzeo (1997).

One must also consider the limitations associated with the MH procedure. For one, a major disadvantage is that it cannot detect non-uniform DIF. Furthermore, research has demonstrated that estimates of MH statistics are influenced by a number of factors. For example, Camilli and Penfield (1997) found that estimates of differential test functioning via the MH procedure were underestimated when guessing was a factor in estimating ability. Slight underestimates of MH statistics have also been reported for large sample sizes ($N > 500$), while small sample sizes ($N < 250$) have been found to provide overestimated estimates of MH statistics (Spray, 1989). Poor DIF detection results using small sample sizes ($N = 100$) have been reported across numerous studies (Fidalgo, Mellenbergh, & Muñiz, 1998; Mazor, Clauser, & Hambleton, 1992; Muñiz et al., 2001; Parshall & Miller, 1995). As a result, researchers have suggested that an adequate sample size for use with the MH procedure is around 250–500 in each group (Camilli & Shepard, 1994; Muñiz et al., 2001; Spray, 1989). In addition, determining the score levels in which to match examinees can influence DIF estimates, just as with the standardization index. Furthermore, most implementations of the MH procedure require complete 2 x 2 tables. If missing data are present, one can apply one of the following two strategies: (a) listwise deletion, which results in the loss of observed data, and (b) to avoid deleting missing cases, one can impute values (Emenogu, Falenchuk, & Childs, 2010). However, both of these strategies assume that the data are missing at random, which may be untenable.

Logistic regression

Although there are multiple techniques for assessing DIF, logistic regression has several advantages to other methods (Clauser & Mazor, 1998; Rogers & Swaminathan, 1993; Zumbo, 1999). Logistic regression models the probability of responding to an item correctly by group membership and a conditioning variable (usually the total test score). More specifically, an item response is the dependent variable, the independent variable is group membership, and total test score is the covariate. Analysis of DIF occurs in stepwise fashion, involving three distinctive stages for each item. First, total test score is entered into the logistic regression analysis:

$$\ln\left[\frac{p_i}{1 - p_i}\right] = b_0 + b_{tot}, \tag{8}$$

where P_i is equal to the probability of correctly responding to item i, $1 - p_i$ is equal to the probability of incorrectly responding to item i, b_0 is equal to the intercept, and b_{tot} is equal to the regression coefficient for total score. This is the base model in which to judge the presence of uniform and non-uniform DIF. Next, group membership is entered into the analysis:

$$\ln\left[\frac{p_i}{1-p_i}\right] = b_0 + b_{tot} + b_{group},\tag{9}$$

where b_{group} is equal to the regression coefficient for group membership. Lastly, an interaction term between total score and group membership is entered into the regression equation:

$$\ln\left[\frac{p_i}{1-p_i}\right] = b_0 + b_{tot} + b_{group} + b_{tot*group},\tag{10}$$

where $b_{tot*group}$ is equal to the regression coefficient for the interaction between total score and group membership.

To evaluate the statistical significance of DIF, one can conduct chi-square tests for both uniform and non-uniform DIF. This can be accomplished for uniform DIF by taking the chi-squared value for Equation (9) and subtracting it by the chi-squared value for Equation (8). The resultant value is compared to the chi-square probability with 1 degree of freedom. The statistical significance of non-uniform DIF can be evaluated in a similar fashion. More specifically, the chi-square value of Equation (10) is subtracted by the chi-square value of Equation (8). The resultant value is then compared to the chi-square probability with 1 degree of freedom.

In addition to statistical significance, measures of DIF magnitude (effect sizes) can also be evaluated. DeMars (2011) detailed three broad effect size classes in which logistic regression DIF results can be reported, which include log of the odds ratio, differences in the probability-correct (p metric), and proportion of variance accounted for (R^2). The effect size most often used is the proportion of variance accounted for. Although there are numerous R^2 measures (see Zumbo, 1999), Jodoin and Gierl (2001) developed a set of popular effect size guidelines based on Nagelkerke's weighted-least-squares R^2. Before applying the effect size guidelines, one must calculate the difference in R^2 between Equations (8) and (9) for uniform DIF, and the R^2 difference between Equations (8) and (10) for non-uniform DIF. Upon obtaining the incremental R^2, it can be applied to Jodoin and Gierl's recommendations, which classify negligible DIF by an incremental $R^2 < .035$, moderate DIF by an incremental $.035 < R^2 > .070$, and large DIF by an incremental $R^2 > .070$. Although these guidelines were developed for uniform DIF, they are also applied to non-uniform DIF (Gómez-Benito, Hidalgo, & Padilla, 2009).

One of the major advantages of utilizing the logistic regression DIF procedure lies in its ability to extend to ordinal scored items (Miller & Spray, 1993). An additional advantage of this method is its ability to evaluate both uniform and non-uniform DIF. In contrast, other observed score methods, such as MH, have difficulty in detecting non-uniform DIF for tests that are of moderate difficulty, which is common among most educational achievement tests (Rogers & Swaminathan, 1993). Furthermore, the logistic regression method can use a continuous matching variable, whereas the standardization index and Mantel-Haenszel methods typically require the division of a continuous score scale into discrete categories. With respect to sample size requirements, Zumbo (1999) suggested that for binary-scored items, 200 examinees per group were adequate. Lastly, this method does not require specialized DIF software and can be calculated in readily available statistical software packages such as SAS and SPSS. For detailed examples of how to conduct LR DIF analyses within SPSS, the reader is referred to Zumbo (1999) and Sireci (2011).

The one disadvantage noted for logistic regression DIF detection is that when the proficiency distributions for examinees in the reference and focal group do not overlap (i.e., there are large differences between the total test scores for the groups), and the sample size for one or both of the groups is small, the method can erroneously flag items for DIF (Narayanan & Swaminathan, 1996). This may occur because the logistic regression equation is fitting an equation where there are very little data for one or both groups. Other methods may also be problematic in this situation. We discuss this issue in a subsequent section.

Methods based on item response theory

Item response theory (IRT) describes a family of statistical models that describe the probability that an examinee with a specific level of proficiency will provide a specific response to an item. For example, the one-parameter logistic IRT model, which is designed for items that are scored correct/incorrect, can be specified as,

$$P_i(\theta) = \frac{e^{D(\theta - b_i)}}{1 + e^{D(\theta - b_i)}} \tag{11}$$

where P_i is probability of correct answer on item I, θ (theta) is examinee proficiency, b_i is item difficulty parameter, D is a scaling factor equal to 1.7, and e is base of the natural logarithm. Other IRT models have additional parameters; for example, the two-parameter logistic model adds a discrimination parameter, and the three-parameter model adds a lower asymptote to represent the probability that examinees with low proficiency will answer the item correctly. There are also models to handle multiple-category (polytomous) items. A review of all IRT models is beyond the scope of this article, and so readers are referred to Hambleton (1989) or Hambleton, Swaminathan, and Rogers (1991). What is relevant to DIF detection is that several DIF detection methods are based on IRT (e.g., Lord, 1980; Raju, 1988; Thissen, Steinberg, & Wainer, 1998, 1993). Here, we discuss two popular methods – Lord's chi-square and the IRT-based likelihood ratio test.

Lord's chi square

Lord's (1980) χ^2 statistic tests the hypothesis that the IRT model parameter values are identical across reference (R) and Focal (F) groups. For the aforementioned one-parameter logistic IRT model, Lord's χ^2 is:

$$\chi^2 = \frac{(b_{iR} - b_{iF})^2}{Var(b_{iR}) + Var(b_{iF})}, \tag{12}$$

where b_{iR} and b_{iF} are the difficulty parameter estimates for item i for the reference and focal groups, respectively. Although Equation (12) is specific to the one-parameter IRT model, the parameters in more complex models can be tested for statistically significant differences in similar fashion. The degrees of freedom are equal to the number of item parameters being compared (e.g., $df = 1$ for the one-parameter model).

The advantage of Lord's χ^2 is that it represents a statistical test that has been shown in most cases to control for Type I error (Kim, Cohen, & Kim, 1994; McLaughlin & Drasgow,

1987). When testing programmes are using IRT to calibrate items, it may be a particularly straightforward procedure. However, like all IRT approaches, moderate sample sizes are needed for stable item parameter estimation (e.g., at least 200 examinees per parameter per group), specialized IRT calibration software is needed, and the fit of the IRT model to the data must be appropriate.

IRT likelihood ratio

Some methods of fitting IRT models to assessment data compute a likelihood of obtaining the data, given the model. The likelihood associated with an IRT model fit to a data set can be used to evaluate DIF, by computing the parameters in two different ways – first, constraining the parameters to be equal across reference and focal groups and, second, by estimating separate parameters for each group. The difference in the likelihoods for each model is used to evaluate the invariance of the item parameters over groups.

The likelihood ratio (LR) test for DIF for a specific item proceeds as follows. First, item parameters are constrained equal across reference and focal groups for item i to represent the case of no DIF; that is, the same parameters can be used to characterize the item in both groups. This "no DIF" model is referred to as the compact model (C). Next, separate item parameters are used to calibrate item i across groups; that is, IRT parameters are fit to the data separately for each group, which allows the item parameters to differ to best fit the data for each group. This model is referred to as the augmented model (A). The fit of each model is evaluated using the likelihood ratio (LR) test,

$$G^2(df) = -2\ln\left[\frac{L(A)}{L(C)}\right], \tag{13}$$

where df is equal to the difference in the number of parameters between the augmented and compact models, $L(A)$ is equal to the likelihood function of the augmented model, and $L(C)$ is equal to the likelihood function of the compact model. The value of $G^2(df)$ is distributed as $x^2(df)$. Therefore, if the $G^2(df)$ value obtained exceeds the critical $x^2(df)$ value, then the compact model is rejected, suggesting that there are significant differences in item parameters across groups, and hence, DIF is present. This process can be conducted numerous times for item i depending on the number of augmented models specified by the researcher.

One of the advantages of the likelihood ratio procedure is that it easily extends to various types of items such as polytomous items found in educational tests and psychological surveys. It is also an extremely powerful method for evaluating DIF, and can even be applied to evaluate differential functioning of a larger set of items (i.e., "testlet" DIF, Wainer, Sireci, & Thissen, 1991). Like the logistic regression approach, it can also evaluate both uniform and non-uniform DIF, and like the logistic regression and standardization approaches, its results can be portrayed graphically.

The disadvantages of the IRT likelihood ratio approach are similar to Lord's χ^2 in that the IRT models must fit the data and adequate sample sizes are needed. In addition, specialized IRT software is needed to calibrate the items and calculate the likelihoods (e.g., MULTILOG; Thissen, 2003). The likelihood ratio procedure declined in popularity a few years ago due to the fact that multiple IRT models needed to be fit to isolate the items that exhibited DIF. However, a new programme designed to calibrate items and evaluate DIF using this procedure was recently made available (IRTLRDIF, Thissen, 2006), which makes DIF identification using the IRT likelihood ratio test much less laborious.[1]

Although IRT-based DIF detection procedures are attractive due to their flexibility and statistical power, there are no well-accepted effect size criteria for evaluating the magnitude of DIF using these approaches. Given the importance of effect sizes for distinguishing between substantive and negligible DIF, this is a serious limitation of the IRT approaches.

Summary of DIF detection methods

The five DIF detection methods we described are all popular but possess different advantages and disadvantages. Depending on sample sizes available, item format, statistical expertise, availability of software, and type of DIF, some methods are preferable to others. In Table 2, we provide a brief summary of the advantages and disadvantages of each method. The IRT-based methods are powerful and, like the logistic regression and standardization methods, can evaluate both uniform and non-uniform DIF, and display the results graphically. However, they require stronger model assumptions, larger sample sizes, more psychometric expertise, and specialized statistical software. The IRT-based methods are also limited in that there are no widely accepted effect size guidelines. They are likely to be best in large-scale assessment situations where sample sizes for all groups are large enough for stable item parameter calibration and the data are sufficiently unidimensional. In other cases, one of the other methods may be preferable, particularly if the data are dichotomous. If not, logistic regression may be best, assuming sufficient overlap among the reference and focal groups.

Decisions to be made in conducting DIF analyses

Up to this point, we stressed the importance of conducting DIF analyses and described five popular DIF detection methods. In this section, we describe the types of decisions that need

Table 2. Summary of advantages and disadvantages of selected DIF methods.

Method	Advantages	Disadvantages
Standardization Index	Easy to interpret, can weight score distributions, can handle relatively small samples, effect size guidelines	Discrete matching, no test for statistical significance
Mantel-Haenszel	Statistical test with good power, Type I error control, widely researched, effect size guidelines	Discrete matching, not good for detecting non-uniform DIF
Logistic Regression	Statistical test with good power, Type I error control, can use continuous matching variable, can detect non-uniform DIF, can handle polytomous data, can use multivariate matching, available in most statistical software packages, effect size guidelines	Problems when group proficiency distributions have little overlap
Lord's chi square	Statistical test with good power, Type I error control	Requires relatively larger sample sizes and assessment of model fit, no widely accepted effect size criteria
IRT-based likelihood ratio	Good statistical power, continuous matching variable, can detect non-uniform DIF, can handle polytomous data	Requires relatively larger sample sizes and assessment of model fit, no widely accepted effect size guidelines

to be made when doing DIF research. The first decision is choice of statistical method to use. Most of the subsequent decisions apply to all methods. Some focus on research design, while others focus on interpretation.

Choice of DIF method

Our preceding discussion of the strengths and limitations of each DIF method provided the essential background for selecting a DIF method for a particular situation. The nature of the data to be analysed will often determine the most appropriate methods. Sample size and data type are the two most important factors. With large sample sizes and dichotomous data, any of the five methods are good candidates. If the data are unidimensional and effect size criteria are not of interest, and the researcher has expertise in IRT, then IRT-based methods may be preferred. However, if there are many items, effect size criteria will be needed to distinguish between substantive DIF and statistically significant, but negligible DIF, and so one of the other methods may be preferred. Another issue is interpretation of results for communication with various audiences. If the audience is comprised of test developers and psychometricians, the results from any of the methods will be readily interpretable. If not, graphical display may be preferred, which would rule out the MH method. The advantages and disadvantages of each method that are summarized in Table 2 should be helpful in determining which method is best for a particular situation. However, there is no reason to limit the analysis to a single method. Where possible, researchers can use more than one DIF method and compare the results. By focusing on items flagged using more than one method, interpretation of DIF can be enhanced (Hambleton, 2006).

How to define groups to be studied

One decision to be made in using DIF to promote validity is which groups of examinees should be studied. In some cases, the examinee population may be homogeneous, and so only DIF across men and women may be of interest. Similarly, in some cases demographic information available for examinees may be limited to sex or ethnicity and so will dictate the groups to be studied. In other cases, however, judgement will be needed to combine examinees into groups for DIF analysis. For example, in many cases we are interested in evaluating whether items contain construct-irrelevant linguistic complexity that may be unfair to linguistic minorities. If we group examinees by native language (e.g., Spanish), we may be combining individuals who are culturally very different from one another (e.g., Spanish speakers from Spain, Puerto Rico, Mexico, etc.), which will obscure DIF effects. A similar situation arises when researchers use DIF to evaluate test accommodations for individuals with disabilities. Some disability categories have very small sample sizes (e.g., Braille, sign language interpreter) and may be combined together. Thus, researchers should consider the potential heterogeneity *within* potential focal groups before finalizing the groups to be studied (Buzick & Stone, 2011).

Matching criteria

In the introduction to this article, we stressed the importance of a conditioning (matching) variable to separate DIF from impact. The most common choice of matching variable is total test score because it is a convenient measure of the intended construct. One problem with using total score as a matching variable is that if the test is biased overall, it will be a biased matching criterion (Sireci, 1997). Although this situation may be rare, researchers should consider its possibility. If other variables relevant to the construct are available, they should be considered for use as the matching criterion, or as an additional criterion (i.e., multivariate matching). The logistic regression method may be the method of choice when more than one variable is used to match examinees, since it easily incorporates multivariate matching. When tests are composed of subscales, it may be preferable to use subscores, rather than total scores, in matching examinees, particularly if the subscores reflect multidimensionality. When different matching variables are available, researchers may want to run separate DIF analyses for each variable to acquire a more comprehensive analysis of potential DIF.

Purification of the matching variable

A related issue to choice of matching variable is whether the variable should be "purified" as the DIF analysis proceeds. Purifying the matching variable refers to the situation where total score is used to match examinees, and one or more items are flagged for DIF. When this occurs, some researchers have suggested removing the DIF items, recomputing the total score (to "purify" it), and then rerun the DIF analyses. Navas-Ara and Gomez-Benito (2002) found that purification improved IRT-based DIF analyses. French and Maller (2007) found that purification was not particularly helpful when using the logistic regression method, but Hidalgo and Gomez (2003) found that purification was helpful in detecting uniform DIF when using logistic regression. It appears purification may help improve DIF detection in some, but not all situations (Colvin, 2011). Thus, researchers may want to conduct DIF analyses both with and without purification to see which results are most interpretable.

Sampling and replication

Two concerns in conducting DIF analyses are Type I and Type II errors, which refer respectively to erroneously flagging items for DIF when they are not problematic, or not detecting items that do function differentially across groups. One way to mitigate these problems is to sample examinees and replicate the analyses. If the same results occur over replications, it is less likely they represent Type I or II errors. In some cases, the sample sizes for the reference group are much larger than for the focal group. When this occurs, multiple random samples can be taken from the reference group, and the analyses can be replicated using the same group of focal group examinees. In other cases, bootstrapping procedures may be helpful for gauging sampling variability and its effects on DIF detection.

Matching proficiency distributions

As mentioned earlier, DIF analyses are conditional, and so they compare individuals in different groups who are matched on the construct measured by the test. In some situations where there is little overlap among the distributions on the matching variable, it may be helpful to draw *matched* random samples from the reference group to focus the analysis on examinees who are more comparable to one another. Some research has found that when the total test score distributions exhibit little overlap, drawing stratified random samples from the reference group to match the score distribution of examinees in the focal group will reduce Type I errors and facilitate DIF interpretation (Sireci & Wells, 2010).

Effect size criteria

In many situations, investigating DIF will involve hundreds of analyses. Consider, for example, a test with 40 items and the desire to investigate DIF across men/women and four different ethnic groups. The endeavour would involve 200 comparisons (5 groups x 40 items). This number of comparisons will certainly flag many items for statistically significant DIF. To identify which items have substantive DIF and do not simply reflect Type I errors, effect size criteria are needed. For this reason, we were careful to include a discussion of effect size when describing each method. We believe the use of effect sizes will greatly improve interpretation of DIF results. That said, various effect size classes are differentially impacted by factors, such as item difficulty, item discrimination, and item lower asymptotes. Therefore, when choosing an effect size measure one must be cognizant of such factors (DeMars, 2011). Where possible, we recommend using more than one DIF detection method and focusing on items flagged for moderate or large DIF by both methods.

Level of analysis

In this article, we primarily discussed DIF analyses as analyses at the item level, which is the most typical situation. Before leaving our list of decisions, however, it is important to note that to use DIF analyses to promote validity two other issues should be considered – DIF cancelation and DIF amplification (Nandakumar, 1993; Wainer et al., 1991). DIF cancelation refers to the situation where items on an assessment may exhibit DIF, but the direction of the DIF (i.e., which group the item "favours") is balanced across groups such that the aggregate effect is essentially zero at the total test score level. In such cases, it may be acceptable to leave items flagged for DIF on the assessment, except when a clear interpretation of bias is present (Wainer et al., 1991). DIF aggregation refers to the situation where there may be no DIF observable at the item level, but small amounts of DIF aggregate across items to cause invariance at an item-set level. Wainer et al. (1991) called this testlet DIF, and illustrated how it could be manifested when items are grouped into sets based on a common stimulus such as a reading passage. Our recommendation is for researchers to consider aggregate effects of item-level DIF results and eliminate items when there seems to be an imbalance of direction across items flagged for DIF, and to consider eliminating or revising items when there is a large number of items flagged for small or negligible DIF all in the same direction.

Summary and recommendations

In this article, we discussed the importance of DIF analyses for promoting test score validity, described some of the most popular DIF detection procedures, and discussed some of the critical factors researchers must consider in conducting DIF analyses. Based on our review, we offer the following recommendations to those who wish to conduct DIF analyses in pursuit of more valid test score interpretations. Some, but not all of these recommendations have been previously suggested in the DIF literature (e.g., Hambleton, 2006).

(1) Select a DIF detection method that is best suited to the nature of the data to be analysed. Data features that will affect selection of a method include the number of score categories in an item, sample size, and dimensionality of the data.
(2) Where possible, use more than one DIF method to confirm items flagged for DIF.

(3) Use an effect size measure to distinguish substantive DIF from statistically significant DIF. Interpretation may be facilitated by focusing on items with non-negligible effect sizes identified by more than one method.

(4) Use graphical displays to better interpret DIF and communicate its effects.

(5) When DIF items are found, consider removing these items from the matching criterion (i.e., purifying) and repeating the analyses. Analysis of items flagged using the original and purified matching criterion may prove helpful.

(6) Use sensible sampling strategies to replicate DIF results. Items that are flagged for DIF across replications are likely to reflect true DIF rather than Type I errors.

(7) Consider drawing one or more matched random samples from the reference group when the proficiency distributions from the reference and focal groups do not sufficiently overlap (e.g., centre of distributions are more than one standard deviation apart).

(8) In interpreting DIF results, consider DIF direction, amplification, and cancelation; and their likely effects on interpretations at the total test score level.

We hope our review of methods and these recommendations are helpful to DIF researchers. We believe conducting conscientious analyses of DIF are important steps in promoting the validity of interpretations from educational and psychological assessments. Clearly, the statistical aspects of DIF research are helpful as a quality control procedure for facilitating validity, but, as Clauser and Mazor (1998) pointed out, "As with other aspects of test validation, DIF analysis is a process of collecting evidence. Weighting and interpreting that evidence will require careful judgment" (p. 40). Thus, our discussion and recommendations are designed as guidelines to better inform DIF researchers and test developers who will ultimately make the final judgments about how DIF results can be used to improve their assessments.

Note

1. IRTLRDIF for windows can be downloaded at http://www.unc.edu/ ~ dthissen/dl/irtlrdif201.zip, and for MAC at http://www.unc.edu/ ~ dthissen/dl/IRTLRDIF201.sit

References

American Educational Research Association, American Psychological Association, & National Council on Measurement in Education. (1999). *Standards for educational and psychological testing*. Washington, DC: American Educational Research Association.

Buzick, H., & Stone, E. (2011). *Recommendations for conducting differential item functioning (DIF) analyses for students with disabilities based on previous DIF studies*. Princeton, NJ: Educational Testing Service.

Camilli, G. (2006). Test fairness. In R. Brennan (Ed.), *Educational Measurement* (4th ed., pp. 221–256). Westport, CT: Praeger.

Camilli, G., & Penfield, D. A. (1997). Variance estimation for differential test functioning based on the Mantel-Haenszel log-odds ratio. *Journal of Educational Measurement, 34*, 123–139.

Camilli, G., & Shepard, L. A. (1994). *Methods for identifying biased test items*. Thousand Oaks, CA: Sage.

Clauser, B. E., & Mazor, K. M. (1998). Using statistical procedures to identify differential item functioning test items. *Educational Measurement: Issues and Practice, 17*, 31–44.

Clauser, B. E., Nungester, R. J., & Swaminathan, H. (1996). Improving the matching for DIF analysis by conditioning on both test score and an educational background variable. *Journal of Educational Measurement, 33*, 453–463.

Colvin, K. (2011). *A review of recent findings on DIF analysis techniques* (Center for Educational Assessment Research Report No. 797). Amherst, MA: Center for Educational Assessment, University of Massachusetts Amherst.

DeMars, C. E. (2011). An analytic comparison of effect sizes for differential item functioning. *Applied Measurement in Education, 24,* 189–209.

Dorans, N. J., & Kulick, E. (1986). Demonstrating the utility of the standardization approach to assessing the unexpected differential item functioning on the Scholastic Aptitude Test. *Journal of Educational Measurement, 23,* 355–368.

Emenogu, B. C., Falenchuk, O., & Childs, R. A. (2010). The effect of missing data treatment on Mantel-Haenszel DIF detection. *The Alberta Journal of Educational Research, 56,* 459–469.

Fidalgo, A. M., Mellenbergh, G. J., & Muñiz, J. (1998). Comparación del procedimiento Mantel Haenszel frente a los modelos loglineales en la detección del funcionamiento diferencial de los ítems [Comparison of the Mantel-Haenszel procedure versus the log linear models for detecting differential item functioning]. *Psicothema, 10,* 219–228.

French, B., & Maller, S. (2007). Iterative purification and effect size use with logistic regression for differential item functioning detection. *Educational and Psychological Measurement, 67,* 373–393.

Gómez-Benito, J., Hidalgo, M. D., & Padilla, J. L. (2009). Efficacy of effect size measures in logistic regression: An application for detecting DIF. *Methodology, 5,* 18–25.

Hambleton, R. K. (1989). Principles and selected applications of item response theory. In R. Linn (Ed.), *Educational measurement* (3rd ed., pp. 147–200). New York, NY: Macmillan.

Hambleton, R. K. (2006). Good practices for identifying differential item functioning. *Medical Care, 44,* 182–188.

Hambleton, R. K., Swaminathan, H., & Rogers, H. J. (1991). *Fundamentals of item response theory.* Newbury Park, CA: Sage.

Hidalgo, M. D., & Gomez, J. (2003). Test purification and the evaluation of differential item functioning with multinomial logistic regression. *European Journal of Psychological Assessment, 19,* 1–11.

Holland, P. W., & Thayer, D. T. (1988). Differential item performance and the Mantel-Haenszel procedure. In H. Wainer & H. Braun (Eds.), *Test validity* (pp. 129–145). Hillsdale, NJ: Lawrence Erlbaum Associates.

Jodoin, M. G., & Gierl, M. J. (2001). Evaluating power and Type I error rates using an effect size with the logistic regression procedure for DIF. *Applied Measurement in Education, 14,* 329–349.

Kim, S.-H., Cohen, A. S., & Kim, H.-O. (1994). An investigation of Lord's procedure for the detection of differential item functioning. *Applied Psychological Measurement, 18,* 217–228.

Lord, F. M. (1980). *Applications of item response theory to practical testing problems.* Hillsdale, NJ: Lawrence Erlbaum Associates.

Mazor, K. M., Clauser, B. E., & Hambleton, R. K. (1992). The effect of sample size on the functioning of the Mantel-Haenszel statistic. *Educational and Psychological Measurement, 52,* 443–452.

McLaughlin, M. E., & Drasgow, F. (1987). Lord's chi-square test of item bias with estimated and with known person parameters. *Applied Psychological Measurement, 11,* 161–173.

Miller, T. R., & Spray, J. A. (1993). Logistic discriminant function analysis for DIF identification of polytomously scored items. *Journal of Educational Measurement, 30,* 107–122.

Muñiz, J., Hambleton, R. K., & Xing, D. (2001). Small sample studies to detect flaws in item translations. *International Journal of Testing, 1,* 115–135.

Nandakumar, R. (1993). Simultaneous DIF amplification and cancellation: Shealy-Stout's Test for DIF. *Journal of Educational Measurement, 30,* 293–311.

Narayanan, P., & Swaminathan, H. (1996). Identification of items that show nonuniform DIF. *Applied Psychological Measurement, 20,* 257–274.

Navas-Ara, M. J., & Gomez-Benito, J. (2002). Effects of ability scale purification on the identification of dif. *European Journal of Psychological Assessment, 18,* 9–15.

Parshall, C. G., & Miller, T. R. (1995). Exact versus asymptotic Mantel-Haenszel DIF statistics: A comparison of performance under small-sample conditions. *Journal of Educational Measurement, 32,* 302–316.

Raju, N. S. (1988). The area between two item characteristic curves. *Psychometrika, 53,* 495–502.

Ramsey, P. A. (1993). Sensitivity review: The ETS experience as a case study. In P. W. Holland & H. Wainer (Eds.), *Differential item functioning* (pp. 367–388). Hillsdale, NJ: Erlbaum.

Robin, F. (2001). *STDIF: Standardization-DIF analysis program*. Amherst, MA: University of Massachusetts, School of Education.

Rogers, H. J., & Swaminathan, H. (1993). A comparison of the logistic regression and Mantel-Haenszel procedures for detecting differential item functioning. *Applied Psychological Measurement, 17*, 105–116.

Sireci, S. G. (1997). Problems and issues in linking tests across languages. *Educational Measurement: Issues and Practice, 16*, 12–19.

Sireci, S. G. (2011). Evaluating test and survey items for bias across languages and cultures. In D. Matsumoto & F. van de Vijver (Eds.), *Cross-cultural research methods in psychology* (pp. 216–243). New York, NY: Cambridge University Press.

Sireci, S. G., & Mullane, L. A. (1994). Evaluating test fairness in licensure testing: The sensitivity review process. *CLEAR Exam Review, 5*(2), 22–28.

Sireci, S. G., Patsula, L., & Hambleton, R. K. (2005). Statistical methods for identifying flaws in the test adaptation process. In R. Hambleton, P. Merenda, & C. Spielberger (Eds.), *Adapting educational and psychological tests for cross-cultural assessment* (pp. 93–115). Mahwah, NJ: Lawrence Erlbaum Associates.

Sireci, S. G., & Wells. C. S. (2010). Evaluating the comparability of English and Spanish video accommodations for English language learners. In P. Winter (Ed.), *Evaluating the comparability of scores from achievement test variations* (pp. 33–68). Washington, DC: Council of Chief State School Officers.

Spray, J. A. (1989). *Performance of three conditional DIF statistics in detecting differential item functioning on simulated tests* (Research Report No. 89-7). Iowa City, IA: American College Testing.

Stokes, M. E., Davis, C. S., & Koch G. G. (2000). *Categorical data analysis using the SAS system*. Cary, NC: SAS Institute and Wiley.

Swaminathan, H., & Rogers, H. J. (1990). Detecting differential item functioning using logistic regression procedures. *Journal of Educational Measurement, 27*, 361–370.

Thissen, D. (2003). MULTILOG 7: Multiple categorical item analysis and test scoring using item response theory [computer program]. Chicago, IL: Scientific Software.

Thissen, D. (2006). IRTLRDIF [computer program]. Retrieved from http://www.unc.edu/~dthissen/dl/irtlrdif201.zip

Thissen, D, Steinberg, L., & Wainer, H. (1988). Use of item response theory in the study of group differences in trace lines. In H. Wainer & H. I. Braun (Eds.), *Test validity* (pp. 147–169). Hillsdale, NJ: Lawrence Erlbaum.

Thissen, D., Steinberg, L., & Wainer, H. (1993). Detection of differential item functioning using the parameters of item response models. In P. Holland & H. Wainer (Eds.), *Differential item functioning* (pp. 67–113). Hillsdale, NJ: Lawrence Erlbaum Associates.

Wainer, H., Sireci, S. G., & Thissen, D. (1991). Differential testlet functioning: Definitions and detection. *Journal of Educational Measurement, 28*, 197–219.

Walker, C. M. (2011). What's the DIF? Why differential item functioning analyses are an important part of instrument development and validation. *Journal of Psychoeducational Assessment, 29*, 364–376.

Wood, R. (1988). Item analysis. In J. P. Keeves (Ed.), *Educational research, methodology, and measurement: An international handbook* (pp. 376–384). New York, NY: Pergamon Press.

Zieky, M. (1993). Practical questions in the use of DIF statistics in test development. In P. W. Holland & H. Wainer (Eds.), *Differential item functioning* (pp. 337–347). Hillsdale, NJ: Erlbaum.

Zumbo, B. D. (1999). *A handbook on the theory and methods of differential item functioning (DIF): Logistic regression modeling as a unitary framework for binary and Likert-type (ordinal) item scores*. Ottawa, Canada: Directorate of Human Resources Research and Evaluation, Department of National Defense.

Zwick, R., Donoghue, J. R., & Grima, A. (1993). Assessment of differential item functioning for performance tasks. *Journal of Educational Measurement, 30*, 233–251.

Zwick, R., Thayer, D. T., & Mazzeo, J. (1997). Descriptive and inferential procedures for assessing differential item functioning in polytomous items. *Applied Measurement in Education, 10*, 321–334.

Identifying differential item functioning in multi-stage computer adaptive testing

Mark J. Gierl, Hollis Lai and Johnson Li

Centre for Research in Applied Measurement and Evaluation, University of Alberta, Edmonton, Alberta, Canada

The purpose of this study is to evaluate the performance of CATSIB (Computer Adaptive Testing-Simultaneous Item Bias Test) for detecting differential item functioning (DIF) when items in the matching and studied subtest are administered adaptively in the context of a realistic multi-stage adaptive test (MST). MST was simulated using a 4-item module in a 7-panel administration. Three independent variables, expected to affect DIF detection rates, were manipulated: item difficulty, sample size, and balanced/unbalanced design. CATSIB met the acceptable criteria, meaning that the Type I error and power rates met 5% and 80%, respectively, for the large reference/moderate focal sample and the large reference/large focal sample conditions. These results indicate that CATSIB can be used to consistently and accurately detect DIF on an MST, but only with moderate to large samples.

Introduction

Assessment visionary, Dr. Randy Bennett (2001) claimed, more than a decade ago, that no topic would become more central to innovation and future practice in large-scale assessment than computers and the internet. His prediction has proven to be accurate. Large-scale assessment and computer technology have evolved at a staggering pace since 2001. As a result, many large-scale assessments, which were once administered in a paper-and-pencil format, are now administered by computer using the internet. Internet-based computerized assessment offers many advantages to examinees compared with more traditional paper-based assessments. For instance, computers support the development of innovative item types and alternative item formats (Sireci & Zenisky, 2006); items on computer-based tests can be scored immediately thereby providing examinees with immediate feedback (Dragsow & Mattern, 2006); computers permit on-demand testing for examinees (van der Linden & Glas, 2010). But the most important benefit of computer-based assessment is that it allows examiners to evaluate more complex performances by integrating test items and digital media to increase the types of knowledge, skills, and competencies that can be measured (Bartram, 2006; Breithaupt, Mills, & Melican, 2006; Zenisky & Sireci, 2002).

The advent of computer-based testing has also raised new challenges, particularly in the area of test fairness. Fairness is a broad and encompassing topic of importance and consequence in educational testing. In the *Standards for Educational and Psychological Testing* (American Educational Research Association [AERA], American Psychological Association [APA], & National Council on Measurement in Education [NCME], 1999), four characterizations of test fairness are presented. First, fair tests must be free from bias. Bias occurs when tests yield scores or promote score interpretations that result in different meanings for members of different groups. Second, test fairness requires that examinees receive just and equal treatment in the testing process. To achieve this outcome, both the test and the testing context must be considered when scores are interpreted for examinees. Third, test fairness requires equity in the outcomes of testing. Examinees must be given the chance to demonstrate their proficiency on the construct the test is designed to measure. Fourth, test fairness implies that examinees have had the opportunity to learn the content covered on the exam.

Differential item functioning (DIF) analyses can yield information about bias, which is the first characterization of fairness cited in the *Standards* (AERA, APA, & NCME, 1999). The development and application of DIF detection methods reflect a response to the legal and ethical need to assess examinees without bias. Bias occurs when tests produce scores or yield score interpretations that result in different meanings for different groups of examinees. To conduct DIF analyses, examinees are first divided into two groups, a *reference* and a *focal* group. DIF analysis then involves administering a test, matching members of the reference and focal group on a measure of ability derived from that test, and using statistical procedures to identify items that function differentially between the two groups. An item exhibits DIF when examinees from the reference and focal groups differ in the probability of answering that item correctly, after controlling for the measure of ability derived from the test. The bias occurs when the interpretation of this probability can be accounted for by construct-irrelevant variance that differentially affects reference and focal group performance.

DIF and computer adaptive testing

It is important to conduct DIF analyses with computer adaptive tests (CAT) to ensure that examinees are tested without bias. This need is amplified for internet-based CAT because these tests, increasingly, are being administered to large numbers of examinees around the world. Because testing has become a global enterprise, heterogeneous samples of examinees with different languages, cultures, educational backgrounds, learning opportunities, knowledge, skills, and access to computers and technology are writing the same exams that are expected to yield the same score interpretations. For example, Phillippe Grosskost, Managing Director of ETS Global for Europe, the Middle East, and Africa, claimed that "Scores on the TOEIC and TOEFL tests mean exactly the same thing regardless of whether the test was taken in Indonesia, Argentina, Hungary, or Egypt" (Educational Testing Service, 2007, p. 4). This strong assertion highlights the importance of testing without bias.

The need for DIF-free item administration also stems from the adaptive nature of CAT. As Zwick (2000, 2010) noted, examinees write fewer items in an adaptive testing context, meaning that each item contributes more to the final ability estimate. The presence of item bias, therefore, could exert a stronger affect on the examinees' estimates of ability. Bias could also affect the order of item administration, given that the selection of items on an adaptive test is determined by the examinees' response to the previous item.

But it is also particularly challenging to conduct DIF analyses with CAT. CAT requires large numbers of items because banks are needed to permit continuous testing while, at the same time, minimizing item exposure. As a result, these large item banks must first be developed and then continually replenished to minimize item exposure and maintain test security while allowing for continuous test administration. At the same time, policies, procedures, and reviews must be implemented to ensure each item meets the basic standards associated with fairness and equity. Sensitivity reviews – which entails having panels of content specialists review each item – are conducted to ensure items used for CAT meet these basic standards (e.g., Educational Testing Service, 2009; Zieky, 2006). Sensitivity reviews are also informed by the outcomes from DIF analyses because panelists can focus their interpretations on those items that contain large DIF value and, hence, produce large group differences. Unfortunately, the number of examinees who write any one item on an adaptive test may be small, particularly when the item bank is large, relative to the items on a paper-based exam. As a result, DIF methods designed to help monitor fairness must function in diverse testing environments and, often, when the total number of items in the bank is large but the number of examinees who respond to any one of those items is relatively small.

Given that DIF detection is both an important and challenging undertaking with CAT, it comes as *some surprise* that little research has been conducted on this topic in the last decade. In 2000, Zwick published a seminal chapter on DIF in CAT as part of the book *Computer Adaptive Testing: Theory and Practice* (van der Linden & Glas, 2000). She reviewed the three DIF detection methods that, at the time, were considered the main CAT DIF procedures – the Zwick, Thayer, and Wingersky CAT DIF method, the CAT version of the empirical Bayes Mantel-Haenszel DIF method of Zwick, Thayer, and Lewis, and CAT for SIBTEST (Simultaneous Item Bias Test) by Nandakumar and Roussos (CATSIB). Zwick (2000) provided a review of each method in its original, non-adaptive version. Then, she described each method in its modified, adaptive version. Finally, she presented some empirical results from simulation studies to support each CAT DIF method.

A decade later, in 2010, *Computer Adaptive Testing: Theory and Practice* (van der Linden & Glas, 2000) was revised and updated, and published as *Elements of Adaptive Testing* (van der Linden & Glas, 2010). The new volume featured revised chapters from many of the original authors as well as some new chapters. Zwick's chapter on DIF in CAT was included in the 2010 volume. The most striking feature of Zwick's revised chapter was how *little* the area of DIF in CAT had changed over the last 10 years. In the decade since the publication of her first chapter, no new DIF methods for CAT were introduced in Zwick's review. Moreover, only 10 new references were included in her updated manuscript (out of a total of 57 references in the 2010 chapter), of which 5 were published prior to the publication of Zwick's first chapter in 2000, 5 were published after 2000, and only 2 of the 5 references published after 2000 were found in referred journals (the other 3 citations appeared in technical reports). In short, relatively little research has been conducted on DIF in CAT since 2000 despite the explosion of research on and application of computer-based and computer adaptive testing over the same time period.

Using CATSIB to identify DIF IN CAT

In the current study, we begin to expand the research on DIF in CAT by evaluating the performance of CATSIB in a multi-stage adaptive testing environment. We begin with a short overview of this DIF detection statistic, and then we describe the two reasons for selecting this DIF method. CATSIB (Nandakumar & Roussos, 2004), a modification of SIBTEST (Shealy & Stout, 1993) intended for CAT, is a statistical procedure used to first match reference and focal group examinees on a regression-corrected IRT-based ability estimate, and then compare the examinees on a weighted mean difference to determine the presence of DIF. CATSIB is used to test the statistical hypotheses $H_0 : \hat{\beta}_{UNI} = 0$ versus

$\hat{\beta}_{UNI}$ where $\hat{\beta}_{UNI}$ is the parameter specifying the amount of DIF that occurs for an item when examinees in the reference and focal group are compared. More specifically, $\hat{\beta}_{UNI}$ serves as a measure of the expected probabilistic difference of a correct response between examinees in the reference and focal group. That is, $\hat{\beta}_{UNI} = ES_R(\theta) - ES_F(\theta)$, where $ES_R(\theta)$ and $ES_F(\theta)$ are the expected scores in the reference and focal groups, respectively, conditional on the matching subtest. But because $ES_R(\theta)$ and $ES_F(\theta)$ contain bias due to measurement error, a regression correction procedure is used to adjust these expected item scores so they yield more reliable estimates. The adjusted expected scores are denoted as $ES_R(\theta^*)$ and $ES_F(\theta^*)$ for the reference and focal groups, respectively. The adjusted scores more accurately reflect examinees of equal ability levels across groups and, thus, are more meaningful for comparing group differences on the studied items. CATSIB then uses the weighted average difference of these adjusted scores (weighted by the proportion of examinees obtaining matching subtest score θ^*) to estimate the DIF index $\hat{\beta}_{UNI}$, where $\hat{\beta}_{UNI} = \Sigma_{\theta*=\theta_{Min}*}^{\theta_{Max}*} \left[(ES_R(\theta^*) - ES_F(\theta^*)) \frac{N_R(\theta^*) + N_F(\theta^*)}{N} \right]$. In this formula, θ^* is the examinees' regression-corrected ability estimate on the matching subtest, $N_R(\theta^*)$ and $N_F(\theta^*)$ are the number of examinees obtaining matching subtest score θ^* from the reference and focal groups, respectively, and N is the total number of examinees. The $\hat{\beta}_{UNI}$ index is distributed as approximately normal assuming a null hypothesis of no DIF.

CATSIB was selected as the DIF detection method in the current study for two reasons. First, CATSIB, which is one of Zwick's (2000, 2010) three main CAT DIF methods, has received limited empirical evaluation in a small number of CAT environments. To date, CATSIB has only been evaluated in an item pretesting context in two studies. Nandakumar and Roussos (2004) first studied the performance of CATSIB on pre-test DIF items administered in a non-adaptive manner. In other words, adaptation affected the non-DIF items used to match examinees, but not the pre-test DIF items themselves. Hence, they evaluated the performance of CATSIB for DIF detection in a testing environment where the matching subtest (i.e., the subtest containing the non-DIF items) was created adaptively and assumed to be free from DIF, whereas the studied subtest (i.e., the subtest containing the DIF items) was not created adaptively and assumed to contain DIF. This design can be used when items on the matching subtest are either known or assumed to be free from DIF. The addition of new, presumably non-counting items (i.e., items not used for the final CAT ability estimate), are then evaluated for DIF. In this context, CATSIB performed well across a variety of study conditions in the Nandakumar and Roussos study.

Lei, Chen, and Yu (2006) also studied CATSIB using a pre-test design by comparing the Type I error and power rates of CATSIB, logistic regression, and the IRT likelihood-ratio test for identifying unidirectional and non-unidirectional DIF in a CAT environment. As with Nandakumar and Roussos (2004), Lei et al. (2006) evaluated the performance of CATSIB in a testing environment where the matching subtest was created adaptively and assumed to be free from DIF and a studied subtest that was not created adaptively. Again, CATSIB performed well across those conditions that were similar to Nandakumar and Roussos for detecting unidirectional (i.e, uniform) DIF, but CATSIB was less effective when attempting to identify non-unidirectional (i.e., non-uniform) DIF. Lei et al. also found that CATSIB was more accurate for detecting unidirectional DIF when the samples sizes were balanced (i.e., 500 examinees in the reference and focal groups) compared to conditions where the sample sizes were unbalanced. Taken together, these two studies provide important information on key variables that affect CATSIB DIF detection in a pretesting context using adaptively administered non-DIF items and non-adaptively administered DIF items. Unfortunately, their results may not generalize to the performance of CATSIB DIF detection in a purely adaptive context, meaning when items in both the matching and studied subtests are administered adaptively. Therefore, additional research is required to evaluate the performance of CATSIB in more diverse CAT environments, particularly when both DIF and non-DIF items are administered adaptively.

The second reason CATSIB was selected is that it is a psychometric method embedded in the multidimensional differential item functioning analysis paradigm proposed by Roussos and Stout (1996) that unifies substantive and statistical DIF analyses by linking both to the Shealy-Stout multidimensional model for DIF (Shealy & Stout, 1993). This paradigm is unique in the DIF research area because it is designed to help researchers and practitioners understand *why* DIF occurs. Typically, DIF statistical analyses are followed by sensitivity reviews to identify the sources and probable causes of DIF. Reviewers are asked to study DIF items and describe why these items are more difficult for one group of examinees compared to another (see, e.g., Camilli & Shepard, 1994, p. xiii). But researchers found that reviewers were generally poor at predicting which items would function differently across groups (e.g., Englehard, Hansche, & Rutledge, 1990; Plake, 1980). Practitioners also claimed it is difficult to interpret DIF using the judgemental approach (e.g., Camilli & Shepard, 1994; O'Neill & McPeek, 1993; Roussos & Stout, 1996; AERA, APA, & NCME, 1999). To overcome this problem, Roussos and Stout proposed a confirmatory two-stage approach. The first stage is a substantive analysis where DIF hypotheses are generated. The second stage is a statistical analysis of the DIF hypotheses. By combining substantive and statistical analyses in a confirmatory framework, researchers can identify and study the sources and probable causes of DIF (e.g., Gierl, 2005; Gierl, Bisanz, Bisanz, & Boughton, 2003; Gierl, Bisanz, Bisanz, Boughton, & Khaliq, 2001; Gierl & Khaliq, 2001). But before researchers and practitioners can address the question of why DIF occurs, they must first identify items that produce these group differences using statistical methods such as CATSIB. To date, however, no research has been conducted with CATSIB to evaluate its performance for identifying DIF when items from both the matching and studied subtests are administered adaptively.

Purpose of study

The purpose of our study is to evaluate the performance of CATSIB for detecting DIF when both the matching and studied subtest items are administered adaptively in the context of a realistic multi-stage adaptive testing environment. Our research contributes to the study of DIF in CAT in two ways. We will evaluate CATSIB when items on the studied and matching subtests are administered adaptively. Nandakumar and Roussos (2004) and Lei et al. (2006) only evaluated CATSIB when items on the matching subtest were administered adaptively. But in situations where pretesting does not occur, DIF analyses should still be conducted to evaluate item quality. Our study provides a method and highlights the expected results for these types of situations. We will also evaluate CATSIB in the realistic and, increasingly, popular CAT context of multi-stage adaptive testing (MST). MST involves adaptive selection on sets of items, rather than a single item as with CAT, for sequential administration. It is a form of adaptive testing that has been evaluated, scrutinized, and empirically supported (see, e.g., the studies presented in Mead, 2006). As a result, MST is growing in popularity and, currently, is implemented, to cite but a few examples, in well-known testing programmes such as the American Institute of Certified Public Account's Uniform CPA examination, which is used to license public accountants in the United States, and the Medical Council of Canada's Qualifying Exam Part I, which is used to admit medical students into supervised clinical practice in Canada. Just as DIF on CAT can adversely affect the adaptive item administration procedures, the consequences of DIF on MST could exert a negative affect on the examinees' estimate of ability because bias could affect the order of administration for the sets of items on an MST. To date, however, there has been little research on DIF in MST (Richard Luecht, personal communication, December 13, 2010; see Zwick & Thayer, 2002, for an early evaluation of DIF in MST using the Mantel-Haenszel method).

Methods

We evaluated the performance of CATSIB for detecting DIF when both the matching and studied subtest items were administered adaptively in the context of a simulated MST. We begin by describing the MST testing context, the data generation process, and the independent variables (module difficulty level; sample size; balanced/unbalanced design). Then, we present the dependent variables (Type I error; power) used in our study to evaluate the performance of CATSIB.

Testing context, data generation process, and independent variables

Many different variations of MST are permissible (Zenisky, Hambleton, & Luecht, 2010). However, some key concepts do exist across these variations. A block or set of items is referred to as a *module* (Luecht & Nungester, 1998). Each module contains a set of items that adhere to specific content requirements while also meeting strict statistical specifications. These modules then become part of a computer-adaptive process, in which modules with different difficulty levels are administered to examinees. Although each examinee completes all of the items administered within a module, any two examinees need not receive the same module or sequence of modules because the module and its administration order is based on each examinees' ability estimate. The modules are administered in stages called *panels* to facilitate the adaptive process. In each panel, the module is created to meet a specific level of difficulty, where the difficulty level is matched to the examinee's provisional ability level as estimated from their performance on the modules administered during the previous panel. Within any one panel, the modules typically have two or more difficulty levels and, hence, permit adaptive sequencing for test administration. After the examinee completes the items for one module, the ability estimate is updated and, based on the estimate, the module in the next panel that provides the most measurement information is presented to the examinee.

For the current study, a MST environment was developed using the R programming language (R Development Core Team, 2005). Our simulated MST used a four-item module in a seven-panel administration, where the first panel contained a single module that was common to all examinees, while the second through seventh panels each contained three modules with items at three different difficulty levels (see Figure 1). Using this structure, each examinee completed seven modules and wrote a total of 28 items. Each module contained items at three levels of difficulty – easy, medium, and hard. Because item difficulty could affect CATSIB DIF detection, particularly when variation among the levels differs, it served as the first independent variable in this study. The parameter estimates for the generated items at each of the three levels are provided in Table 1. The items were generated using a two-parameter logistic item response theory (2PL IRT) model. The a-parameter was generated with a mean of 0.80 ($SD = 0.20$) across the three difficulty

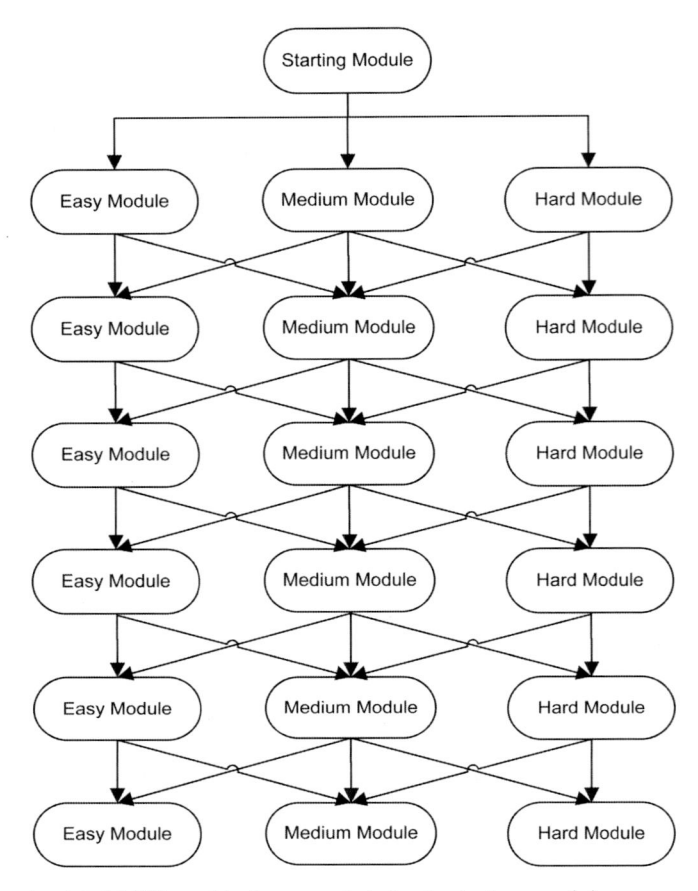

Figure 1   The simulated MST used in the current study: A nineteen-module, seven-panel MST with four-items per module.

Table 1.   The generated item difficulty parameters for the easy, medium, and hard MST modules.

Difficulty Level	a-parameter		b-parameter		Number of Items	
	Mean	*SD*	Mean	*SD*	Non-DIF	DIF
Easy	0.80	0.20	−1.25	0.50	90	10
Medium	0.80	0.20	−0.25	0.25	90	10
Hard	0.80	0.20	0.25	0.25	90	10

levels indicating that, overall, the quality of the items was high, but that the bank also contained items with a range of discrimination power as one might expect in an operational computer-based testing situation. The b-parameter was variable across three levels of difficulty: The easy level had a mean of −1.25 (SD = 0.50); the medium level had a mean of −0.25 (SD = 0.25); the hard level had a mean of 0.25 (SD = 0.25). These parameters are based on the difficulty levels from an operational MST item bank used by the Medical Council of Canada. Hence, our goal was to model an operational testing situation. We simulated more variation among the items in the easy level because, in our experience, easy items are more readily created and hence more common in an item bank. Moreover, the operational MST item bank from the Medical Council of Canada contained more variation among the easier items relative to medium and hard items. Item difficulty should be manipulated at different levels in future studies to further evaluate the effect of item difficulty on the DIF detection rates.

Examinees were routed in the simulated MST using a simple strategy determined by their number correct score. Examinees who answered all four items correctly moved to a harder module; examinees who scored 0 or 1 moved to an easier module; examinees who scored 2 or 3 moved to a module with the same difficulty level. The bank size for our MST simulation was fixed, as it contained 100 items at each difficulty level, with 90 non-DIF and 10 DIF items per level (the procedure used to generate these DIF items is described in the last paragraph of the Methods section). The items were randomly selected at each difficulty level during the adaptive test administration. Examinees' ability estimates in the MST simulation were generated from a bimodal distribution to ensure equal participation (i.e., exposure) rates across the three difficulty levels. In other words, the same distribution was used to generate examinees in the reference and focal groups meaning that there was no systematic difference in ability between these two groups (this condition is often referred to as *no impact* in the DIF literature; see, e.g., Lei et al., 2006, p. 248). By combining the examinee generation process using the bimodal distribution with the number-correct routing strategy, an expected use rate could be anticipated for each item (for a small-scale simulation study evaluating the effect of impact on CATSIB DIF detection, see Chu, Lai, & Wang, 2012).

For the condition with 3,000 examinees (1,500 examinees in both the reference and focal groups), the adaptive process combined with our fixed-length item bank yields approximately 100–175 examinees per group who responded to each item. That is, 3,000 examinees were administered 28 items adaptively using a bank of 300 items. With the bank containing 100 items per difficulty level, this resulted in an exposure rate ranging from 6.67% to 11.67% per item. With examinees from the reference and focal groups each having an equal chance of receiving an item from the bank, this resulted in 100–175 examinees per group who responded to each item (i.e., 6.67% x 3,000 / 2 = 100; 11.67% x 3,000 / 2 = 175). For the condition with 6,000 examinees (3,000 examinees in both the reference and focal groups), the adaptive process combined with our fixed-length item bank yields approximately 200–300 examinees per group who responded to each item. For the condition with 9,000 examinees (4,500 examinees in both the reference and focal groups), the adaptive process combined with our fixed-length item bank yields approximately 300–450 examinees per group who responded to each item.

Sample size, then, serves as the second independent variables in our study – it may also be one of the most important variables to consider when computing DIF in CAT because sample sizes are typically very small, especially compared to paper-based tests where every item is administered to all examinees. In CAT, the number of examinees who write any one item is limited because item exposure rates are often kept to a minimum to ensure test security. As a result, DIF methods designed to help monitor bias must function in testing environments where the total number of items in the bank may be large but the number of examinees who respond to any one of those items is relatively small. For instance, if 1,000 examinees write an MST, but the item exposure rate is 10%, then each item would only be administered to 100 examinees. The problem is compounded when these 100 examinees are further divided into the reference and focal groups, and then separated by ability prior to computing the DIF statistic. Three different sample sizes were evaluated in the current study – small (i.e., 100–175 examinees per group per item), moderate (i.e., 200–300), and large (i.e., 300–450). We also evaluated the consequences of balanced (i.e., same sample size range in the reference and focal groups) and unbalanced (i.e., different sample size range in the reference and focal groups) sample sizes on DIF detection, which serves as our third independent variable, as this was an important factor that affected CATSIB performance in the Lei et al. (2006) study.

For DIF studies using paper-based test administration (i.e., studies with no adaptation, where every examinees writes every item), the magnitude of DIF is controlled during the simulation of sample responses, meaning the examinee responses vectors can be modified to fit the expected magnitude of DIF. This approach helps ensure that an expected level of DIF is generated for any given item in the study. For DIF studies using CAT administration, the DIF items cannot be generated in this manner because the examinee item responses are dynamic thereby affecting the expected level of DIF. That is, the simulated examinee item responses produced with an adaptive testing process affect the magnitude of DIF. To address this problem, the DIF items were generated according to a normal distribution, with the mean of $\hat{\beta}_{UNI} = 0.11$ and standard deviation $\hat{\beta}_{UNI} = 0.04$. This DIF magnitude is considered large (Nandakumar & Roussos, 2004), indicating that matched reference and focal group examinees differ, on average, by 1/9 of a score point. Only items that produced large DIF were simulated and, hence, evaluated in our study.

Dependent variables

Two types of dependent variables were used to evaluate the performance of CATSIB: Type I error and power. Type I error refers to the probability that CATSIB will incorrectly identifying an item as displaying DIF when, in fact, it does not. We can call this concept a "false alarm", meaning a non-DIF item is falsely signalled as a DIF item. Type I error was calculated across 100 simulated analyses for the 270 non-DIF items (i.e., of the 300 items in the bank, only 10 DIF items were simulated at each of the three difficulty levels). Ideally, when an item is specified as a non-DIF item, the probability of detecting this item mistakenly as a DIF item (i.e., Type 1 error) should be close to 0%. In practice, however, we never use a test that maintains a Type I error rate of 0% because this outcome would adversely affect power, given that Type I error and power depend on one another (see Figure 2). Hence, we use the nominal level of 0.05 or 5% to assess the Type I error performance of the non-DIF items in our study. This 5% level corresponds to a $\hat{\beta}_{UNI}$ value of 0.08.

Power refers to the probability of correctly detecting a DIF item. We call this concept a "correct decision" because we are identifying DIF items correctly. Power was calculated across 100 simulated analyses for the 30 DIF items. Ideally, the probability of detecting a DIF item correctly should be 100%. Unfortunately, high power rates can also lead to unreasonably high Type I error rates (i.e., all items are identified as DIF items regardless of their true designation as DIF or non-DIF). For this study, a $\hat{\beta}_{UNI}$ value of 0.08 is used as the criterion for identifying a DIF item, meaning that items with $\hat{\beta}_{UNI} = 0.08$ or greater are considered DIF items. That is, by generating a normal distribution of DIF items where the $\hat{\beta}_{UNI}$ has a mean of 0.11 and a standard deviation of 0.04, the criterion of 0.08 is used to identify DIF items because this value is two standard deviations above the null distribution of no DIF (see Figure 2) and would represent a large difference between the performance of the reference and focal group examinees. A nominal level of 0.80 or 80% is used to assess the power of CATSIB to correctly detect DIF items in our study. This 80% level corresponds to a $\hat{\beta}_{UNI}$ value of 0.11.

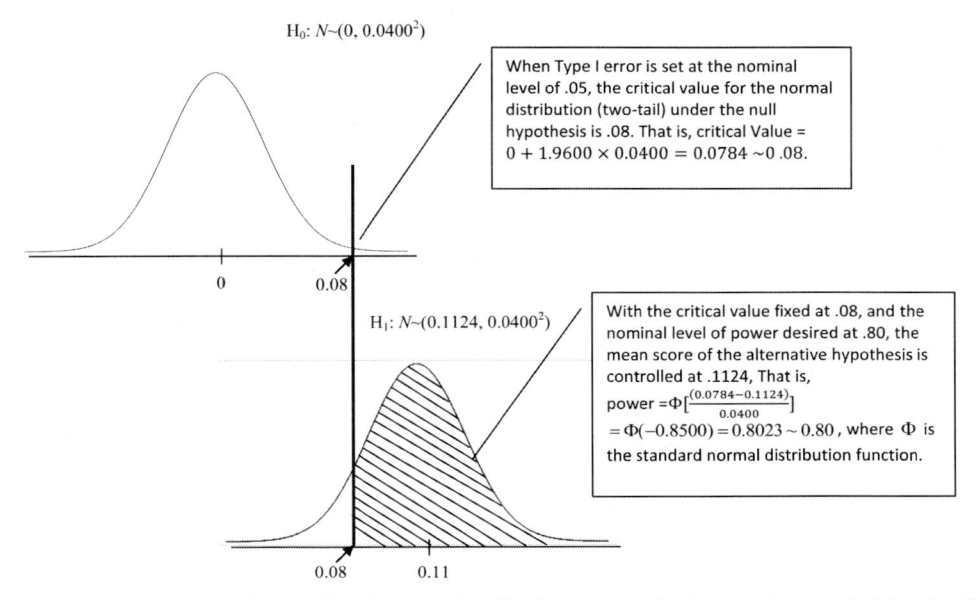

Figure 2   A summary of the null and alternative distributions required to set the nominal levels of Type I error and power in our study. The region in the null distribution represents the nominal level of Type I error (i.e., 5%), whereas the region in the alternative distribution indicates the nominal level of power (i.e., 80%).

Results

We present the results in two sections. First, we present the results for the balanced sample size conditions. The Type I error and power rates as a function of the item difficult level in each module are described. Second, we present the results for the unbalanced sample size conditions.

Balanced sample size

With a small (100–175) number of examinees per group, the Type I error differed across the three difficulty levels (see Table 2). The rate for the easy items was 0.17; the rate for the medium items was 0.22; the rate for the hard items was 0.21. Across all three difficulty

Table 2.   The Type I error and power rates for the balanced sample size conditions.

Focal/Reference Group Size	Difficulty Level	Type 1 Error	Power
Small (100–175)/Small (100–175)	Easy	0.17	0.74
	Medium	0.22	0.72
	Hard	0.21	0.74
	Total	0.20	0.73
Moderate (200–300)/Moderate (200–300)	Easy	0.05	0.80
	Medium	0.08	0.80
	Hard	0.07	0.78
	Total	0.07	0.79
Large (300–475)/Large (300–475)	Easy	0.02	0.85
	Medium	0.03	0.84
	Hard	0.03	0.84
	Total	0.02	0.84

levels, the overall Type I error rate was 0.20. The power rates also differed across the three difficulty levels. Power for the easy items was 0.74; power for the medium items was 0.72; power for the hard items was 0.74. The overall power rate was 0.73. These results reveal that when sample sizes are small, both the Type I error and power rates fail to meet our acceptable level of performance of 0.05 and 0.80, respectively.

With a moderate (200–300) number of examinees per group, the Type I error and power rates also differed across the three difficulty levels and improved, relative to the results in the small sample condition. The Type I error for the easy items was 0.05; the rate for the medium items was 0.08; the rate for the hard items was 0.07. The overall Type I error rate was 0.07. Power for the easy items was 0.80; power for the medium items was 0.80; power for the hard items was 0.78. The overall power rate was 0.79. These results, although better than the previous condition, again failed to meet our acceptable level of performance of 0.05, and 0.80, respectively, except for the easy items. Power did, however, either meet or approach our criterion of 0.80 for the medium and overall difficulty levels.

With a large (300–475) number of examinees per group, the Type I error and power rates produced the most acceptable results in our simulation study and met both our criteria. The Type I error for the easy items was 0.02; the rate for the medium items was 0.03; the rate for the hard items was 0.03. The overall Type I error rate was 0.02. Power for the easy items was 0.85; power for the medium items was 0.84; power for the hard items was 0.84. The overall power rate was 0.84.

Unbalanced sample size

With a small focal sample (100–175 examinees per group) and a moderate reference sample (200–300 examinees per group), the Type I error rates, again, differed across the three difficulty levels (see Table 3). The rate for the easy items was 0.10; the rate for the medium items was 0.15; the rate for the hard items was 0.14. The overall Type I error rate was 0.13. The power rates also differed across the three difficulty levels. Power for the easy items was 0.76; power for the medium items was 0.82; power for the hard items was 0.80. The overall power rate was 0.79. These results reveal that with a small focal and moderate reference sample, the Type I error rates fail to meet the acceptable criterion of 0.05, but the power rate was acceptable for the medium and hard difficulty levels and approached the criterion of 80% for the overall rate.

Table 3. The Type I error and power rates for the unbalanced sample size conditions.

Focal/Reference Group Size	Difficulty Level	Type 1 Error	Power
Small (100–175)/Moderate (200–300)	Easy	0.11	0.76
	Medium	0.15	0.82
	Hard	0.14	0.80
	Total	0.13	0.79
Small (100–175)/Large (300–475)	Easy	0.09	0.79
	Medium	0.13	0.75
	Hard	0.13	0.77
	Total	0.11	0.77
Moderate (200–300)/Large (300–475)	Easy	0.03	0.85
	Medium	0.05	0.80
	Hard	0.05	0.82
	Total	0.04	0.82

With a small focal sample (100–175 examinees per group) and a large reference sample (300–475 examinees per group), the Type I error rates remained below the acceptable standard of performance, whereas the power rate approached the criterion, but only for the easy difficulty level. The Type I error for the easy items was 0.08; the rate for the medium items was 0.13; the rate for the hard items was 0.13. The overall Type I error rate was 0.11. Power for the easy items was 0.79; power for the medium items was 0.75; power for the hard items was 0.77. The overall power rate was 0.77.

With a moderate focal sample (200–300 examinees per group) and a large reference sample (300–475 examinees per group), the Type I error rates and power rates met the acceptable criterion of 0.05 and 0.80 for all difficulty levels. The Type I error for the easy items was 0.03; the rate for the medium items was 0.05; the rate for the hard items was 0.05. The overall Type I error rate was 0.04. Power for the easy items was 0.85; power for the medium items was 0.80; power for the hard items was 0.82. The overall power rate was 0.82.

A summary of the overall results (i.e., results across the three difficulty levels), relative to our acceptable Type I error and power criteria, is presented in Table 4. The Type I error criterion of 0.05 was met for two of the six sample size conditions – large reference/moderate focal and large reference/large focal. The power criterion of 0.80 was also met in two of the MST sample size conditions – large reference/moderate focal and large reference/ large focal. The results from the moderate reference/moderate focal approached the criterion, with an overall power result of 0.79.

Summary, conclusions, and directions for future research

The purpose of this study was to evaluate the performance of CATSIB for detecting DIF when items in both the matching and studied subtest were administered adaptively in the context of a realistic multi-stage adaptive test. Our research contributes to the study of DIF in CAT in two ways. First, we evaluated CATSIB when items on the studied and matching subtests were administered adaptively. Nandakumar and Roussos (2004) and Lei et al. (2006) only evaluated CATSIB when items on the matching subtest were administered adaptively. Second, we evaluated CATSIB in the realistic and, increasingly, popular CAT context of multi-stage adaptive testing (MST). To date, there has been little research on DIF in MST. We simulated MST using a four-item module in a seven-panel administration, where the first panel contained a single four-item module that was common to all examinees. The second to seventh panels each contained three modules with four items per module at three different difficulty levels.

Table 4. Summary of sample size results relative to the Type I error and power criteria of 5% and 80%, respectively.

| | Focal Group | | | | | |
| | Small (100–175) | | Moderate (200–300) | | Large (300–475) | |
Reference Group	Type 1 Error	Power	Type I Error	Power	Type 1 Error	Power
Small (100–175)	NO	NO	–	–	–	–
Moderate (200–300)	NO	NO	NO	NO	–	–
Large (300–475)	NO	NO	YES	YES	YES	YES

CATSIB met the acceptable criteria, meaning that the Type I error and power rates met 5% and 80%, respectively, for the large reference/moderate focal sample and the large reference/large focal sample conditions. The criteria were also met in only one other study condition – easy difficulty level with a moderate number of reference and focal group examinees. For the conditions evaluated in this study, our results indicated that CATSIB can be used to consistently and accurately detect DIF on an MST, but only with moderate to large samples. In other words, CATSIB will identify DIF items with adequate Type I error protection and power across a range of module difficulty levels when a minimum sample size of 475 examinees (i.e., 175 focal group + 300 reference group) is used. CATSIB performs even better, meaning lower Type I errors and higher power, with 600 examinees (i.e., 300 examinees in the focal and reference groups).

Synthesis of existing research on sample size and DIF detection with CATSIB

Sample size is one of the most important variables to consider when computing DIF in CAT because sample sizes are typically small, given the number of examinees who write any one item is limited because item exposure rates must be minimized to ensure test security. Although there is little research on the effects of small sample size DIF detection with CATSIB, the studies by Nandakumar and Roussos (2004) and Lei et al. (2006) provide an important point of reference for the current study. Recall that Nandakumar and Roussos and Lei et al. both used a pre-test design where single items in the matching subtest were administered adaptively but items on the studied subtest were not. The current study, by comparison, assessed modules of items in the matching and studied subtest where the items in both subtests were administered adaptively. To evaluate Type I error, Nandakumar and Roussos used six non-DIF items with b-parameters ranging from –2 to 2, a-parameters ranging from 0.5 to 1.7, and c-parameters ranging from 0.12 to 0.22. Using a two-tailed test with no ability differences between groups (i.e., no impact), the average Type I error across the six items was 0.05 with 250 reference/250 focal group examinees, 0.05 with 500 reference/250 focal group examinees, and 0.06 with 500 reference/500 focal group examinees. Lei et al. used 16 non-DIF items with b-parameters ranging from –1.95 to 1.95, a-parameters ranging from 0.74 to 1.5, and c-parameters fixed at 0.15. Using a two-tailed test with no ability differences between groups, the average Type I error across the 16 items was 0.06 with 500 reference/500 focal group examinees. In the current study, b-parameters in four-item modules at three difficulty levels ranged from –1.25 to 0.25, a-parameters were generated with a mean of 0.80 and a standard deviation of 0.20, and c-parameters were fixed at 0. Using a two-tailed test with no ability differences between groups, the average Type I error across the module difficulty levels was 0.07 with 200–300 reference/200–300 focal group examinees, 0.04 with 300–475 reference/200–300 focal group examinees, and 0.02 with 300–475 reference/300–475 focal group examinees. In short, the CATSIB Type I error rates are quite consistent across the three studies (i.e., Type I error rates ranged from 0.02 to 0.07).

The outcomes across the three studies are also comparable, generally speaking, for the power rates. To evaluate power, Nandakumar and Roussos (2004) assessed medium and large DIF items. We focus only on the results for the six large (i.e., $\hat{\beta}_{UNI} = 0.10$) DIF items so comparisons can be made with the current study. The average power across these six DIF items was 0.73 with 250 reference/250 focal group examinees, 0.84 with 500 reference/250 focal group examinees, and 0.94 with 500 reference/500 focal group examinees. Lei et al. (2006) also evaluated large DIF in one set of their study conditions. Using eight large DIF items, meaning the area between the unidirectional item characteristic curves for the reference and focal groups was set to 0.60, the average power was 1.00 with 500 reference/500 focal group examinees. In the current study, the average power for the 30 large DIF items across 100 replications in the modules was 0.79 with 200–300 reference/ 200–300 focal group examinees, 0.82 with 300–475 reference/200–300 focal group examinees, and 0.84 with 300–475 reference/300–475 focal group examinees. In sum, CATSIB can effectively identify large DIF items across a variety of sample size conditions. Power rates, across the three studies, ranged from a low of 0.73 for samples with 500 examinees in total to 1.00 for samples with 1000 examinees in total. The consistent Type I error and power results between Nandakumar and Roussos and Lei et al. with the current study also provide corroborating evidence to support our recommendation that samples as small as 475 examinees in total (i.e., 175 focal group + 300 reference group) can be used to identify large DIF items in CAT with CATSIB, but that 600 examinees in total (i.e., 300 examinees in the focal and reference groups) is preferred.

Two directions for future research

We conclude by describing two areas where future research could be conducted. First, future research should focus directly on the CATSIB statistic itself. Research could be conducted to evaluate the potential to improve the accuracy of the examinees' regression-corrected ability estimate ($\theta*$) by using the standard error of measurement (*SEM*) conditional on each examinee rather than the overall *SEM*. In the current study, the $\theta*$s were estimated based on the regression correction formula for Shealy and Stout's (1993) SIBTEST, in which the overall *SEM* is assumed to be identical across the examinees in focal and reference groups. The overall *SEM* was also used by Nandakumar and Roussos (2004) in their initial description and evaluation of CATSIB. The use of an overall *SEM*, however, may lead to a potential limitation – examinees in the same group (either focal or reference) are assumed to share the same error variance, even when they possess different ability levels. For instance, when an examinee with a high ability level answers a difficult item, it tends to yield a small *SEM* for that examinee. Conversely, when an examinee with low ability level attempts the same item, it yields a large *SEM* for that examinee. In this example, the ability estimates ($\theta*$s) may be biased because the current version of CATSIB applies the overall *SEM* to both examinees. To correct for this bias, Raju, Price, Oshima, and Nering (2007) proposed a procedure which can estimate the *SEM* for each examinee, conditional on their ability level. Additional research should be conducted to combine the CATSIB procedure described in this study with Raju et al.'s procedure to evaluate the performance of a *modified CATSIB* approach. A modified CATSIB procedure is expected to yield more accurate *SEM*s and $\theta*$s for each examinee, thereby leading to a decrease in Type I error and an increase in power which means improved statistical DIF detection in CAT.

Second, future research should focus on using CATSIB with the Roussos and Stout (1996) DIF analysis paradigm to understand why DIF occurs in CAT. DIF studies are undertaken for many reasons. One reason to conduct a DIF study may be to identify and remove items that elicit large group differences, even when the reasons for these differences are not apparent. Another reason to conduct a DIF study is to better understand the nature of these group differences. The DIF analysis paradigm is used to address the second reason. Roussos and Stout (1996) developed this framework to unify the substantive and statistical analyses because many researchers and practitioners reported that the outcomes from DIF statistical analyses alone were not interpretable. It serves as one of the first model-based approaches for identifying and interpreting the factors that elicit group differences. Because the independent variables that affect CATSIB's statistical performance are becoming more apparent, researchers and practitioners can also begin to use this psychometric procedure to start to evaluate the factors that could explain the presence of DIF. Zwick (2000, 2010) claimed, for instance, that computer-based test administration might elicit several new and important sources of DIF that are not present in paper-based testing, including differential computer familiarity, facility, and anxiety. These hypotheses can now be assessed, at least in some CAT conditions, by using CATSIB with the DIF analysis paradigm to study the factors that could explain why DIF occurs.

References

American Educational Research Association, American Psychological Association, & National Council on Measurement in Education. (1999). *Standards for educational and psychological testing* (2nd ed.). Washington, DC: American Educational Research Association.

Bartram, D. (2006). Testing on the internet: Issues, challenges, and opportunities in the field of occupational assessment. In D. Bartram & R. Hambleton (Eds.), *Computer-based testing and the internet* (pp. 13–37). Hoboken, NJ: Wiley.

Bennett, R. (2001). How the internet will help large-scale assessment reinvent itself. *Educational Policy Analysis Archives, 9*, 1–23.

Breithaupt, K. J., Mills, C. N., & Melican, G. J. (2006). Facing the opportunities of the future. In D. Bartram & R. Hambleton (Eds.), *Computer-based testing and the internet* (pp. 219–251). Hoboken, NJ: Wiley.

Camilli, G., & Shepard, L. (1994). *Methods for identifying biased test items*. Newbury Park, CA: Sage.

Chu, M.-W., Lai, H., & Wang, X. (2012, April). *Detecting directional DIF using CATSIB with impact present*. Poster presented at the annual meeting of the National Council on Measurement in Education, Vancouver, BC.

Drasgow, F., & Mattern, K. (2006). New tests and new items: Opportunities and issues. In D. Bartram & R. Hambleton (Eds.), *Computer-based testing and the internet* (pp. 59–76). Hoboken, NJ: Wiley.

Educational Testing Service. (2007). *Innovations: News on research, products, and solutions for learning and education, Summer 2007*. Princeton, NJ: Author.

Educational Testing Service. (2009). *ETS guidelines for fairness review of assessments*. Princeton, NJ: Author.

Englehard, G,. Hansche, L., & Rutledge, K. E. (1990). Accuracy of bias review judges in identifying differential item functioning on teacher certification tests. *Applied Measurement in Education, 3*, 347–360.

Gierl, M. J. (2005). Using a dimensionality-based DIF analysis paradigm to identify and interpret constructs that elicit group differences. *Educational Measurement: Issues and Practice, 24*(1), 3–14.

Gierl, M. J., Bisanz, J., Bisanz, G., & Boughton, K. (2003). Identifying content and cognitive skills that produce gender differences in mathematics: A demonstration of the DIF analysis framework. *Journal of Educational Measurement, 40*, 281–306.

Gierl, M. J., Bisanz, J., Bisanz, G., Boughton, K., & Khaliq, S. (2001). Illustrating the utility of differential bundle functioning analyses to identify and interpret group differences on achievement tests. *Educational Measurement: Issues and Practice, 20*(2), 26–36.

Gierl, M. J., & Khaliq, S. N. (2001). Identifying sources of differential item and bundle functioning on translated achievement tests. *Journal of Educational Measurement, 38*, 164–187.

Lei, P. W., Chen, S. Y., & Yu, L. (2006). Comparing methods of assessing differential item functioning in a computerized adaptive testing environment. *Journal of Educational Measurement, 43*, 245–264.

Luecht, R., & Nungester, R. (1998). Some practical examples of computer-adaptive sequential testing. *Journal of Educational Measurement, 35*, 229–249.

Mead, A. D. (Ed.). (2006). An introduction to multistage testing [Special issue]. *Applied Measurement in Education, 19*(3).

Nandakumar, R., & Roussos, L. (2004). Evaluation of the CATSIB DIF procedure in a pretest setting. *Journal of Educational and Behavioral Statistics, 29*, 177–199.

O'Neill, K. A., & McPeek, W. M. (1993). Item and test characteristics that are associated with differential item functioning. In P. W. Holland & H. Wainer (Eds.), *Differential item functioning* (pp. 255–276). Hillsdale, NJ: Lawrence Erlbaum.

Plake, B. S. (1980). A comparison of a statistical and subjective procedure to ascertain item validity: One step in the validation process. *Educational and Psychological Measurement, 40*, 397–404.

R Development Core Team. (2005). *R: A language and environment for statistical computing* (Reference index version 2.2.1). Vienna, Austria: R Foundation for Statistical Computing.

Raju, N. S., Price, L. R., Oshima, T. C., & Nering, M. L. (2007). Standardized conditional *SEM*: A case for conditional reliability. *Applied Psychological Measurement, 31*, 169–180.

Roussos, L., & Stout, W. (1996). A multidimensionality-based DIF analysis paradigm. *Applied Psychological Measurement, 20*, 355–371.

Shealy, R., & Stout, W. F. (1993). A model-based standardization approach that separates true bias/DIF from group differences and detects test bias/DIF as well as item bias/DIF. *Psychometrika, 58*, 159–194.

Sireci, S. G., & Zenisky, A. L. (2006). Innovative item formats in computer-based testing: In pursuit of improved construct representation. In S. M. Downing & T. M. Haladyna (Eds.), *Handbook of test development* (pp. 329–348). Mahwah, NJ: Erlbaum.

van der Linden, W. J., & Glas, C. A. W. (Eds.). (2000). *Computerized adaptive testing: Theory and practice*. Dordrecht, The Netherlands: Kluwer.

van der Linden, W., & Glas, C. A. W. (Eds.). (2010). *Elements of adaptive testing*. New York, NY: Springer.

Zenisky, A., Hambleton, R., & Luecht, R. (2010). Multistage testing: Issues, designs, and research. In W. J. van der Linden & C. A. W. Glas (Eds.), *Elements of adaptive testing* (pp. 355–372). New York, NY: Springer.

Zenisky, A. L., & Sireci, S. G. (2002). Technological innovations in large-scale assessment. *Applied Measurement in Education, 15*, 337–362.

Zieky, M. (2006). Fairness reviews in assessment. In S. M. Downing & T. M. Haladyna (Eds.), *Handbook of test development* (pp. 359–376). Hillsdale, NJ: Erlbaum.

Zwick, R. (2000). The assessment of differential item functioning in computer adaptive tests. In W. J. van der Linden & C. A. W. Glas (Eds.), *Computerized adaptive testing: Theory and practice* (pp. 221–244). Dordrecht, The Netherlands: Kluwer.

Zwick, R. (2010). The investigation of differential item functioning in adaptive tests. In W. J. van der Linden & C. A. W. Glas (Eds.), *Elements of adaptive testing* (pp. 331–352). New York, NY: Springer.

Zwick, R., & Thayer, D. T. (2002). Application of an empirical Bayes enhancement of Mantel-Haenszel differential item functioning analysis to a computerized adaptive test. *Applied Psychological Measurement, 26*, 57–76.

Assessing statistical aspects of test fairness with structural equation modelling

Rex B. Kline

Concordia University, Montréal, Québec, Canada

Test fairness and test bias are not synonymous concepts. Test bias refers to statistical evidence that the psychometrics or interpretation of test scores depend on group membership, such as gender or race, when such differences are not expected. A test that is grossly biased may be judged to be unfair, but test fairness concerns the broader, more subjective evaluation of assessment outcomes from perspectives of social justice. Thus, the determination of test fairness is not solely a matter of statistics, but statistical evidence is important when evaluating test fairness. This work introduces the use of the structural equation modelling technique of multiple-group confirmatory factor analysis (MGCFA) to evaluate hypotheses of measurement invariance, or whether a set of observed variables measures the same factors with the same precision over different populations. An example of testing for measurement invariance with MGCFA in an actual, downloadable data set is also demonstrated.

Introduction

The concept of test fairness includes two distinctly different aspects, one more subjective that concerns societal values and the other more objective that involves statistical evidence about test psychometric characteristics. Messick (1998) referred to these facets as, respectively, the *consequential aspect* versus the *evidential aspect* of test outcomes. The former refers to intended or unintended consequences of test use that can be evaluated from social perspectives about distributive justice. Such values are often the subject of intense, passionate debate in the public square about the perceived common good. These debates often involve the tension between concern for the treatment of disenfranchised groups, such as cultural minorities or women, and broader notions of fairness and equity that supposedly apply to all persons. Such debate is ongoing and without permanent resolution because societal values change over time. It is also not strictly within the realm of science for the same reason.

The evidential aspect of test fairness concerns *test bias*, which has a more empirically accessible definition and for which there is a set of more-or-less standard statistical techniques for evaluating the extent of bias. Test bias involves constant or systematic error due to group membership or some other nominal variable in the estimation of scores on psychological tests or on performance criteria (Reynolds, 1982). It occurs when the psychometric properties of scores or their interpretation depend on gender, ethnicity, or other characteristics, especially when such differences are not theoretically expected. Another way to describe test bias is to say that it happens when people from two different groups who have the same observed test score do not have the same status on the latent variable (trait, hypothetical construct) that the test is supposed to measure.

It is important to understand that use of a test in a particular population can be judged as unfair even when there is little statistical evidence for test bias. The basis for such a judgement rests on observed consequences of the testing process instead of solely on the statistical characteristics of individual tests. That is, if outcomes based on test scores are deemed to be unequal or discriminatory for certain groups, then use of that test may be considered unfair. This principle is illustrated by various rulings in the *Larry P. v. Riles* (1972) case by the Federal Ninth Circuit Court of Appeals in the state of California in the United States concerning the use of standardized intelligence (IQ) with African American school children. Based on (a) the observation that IQ scores classified higher proportions of minority children than White children as exhibiting an educational disability – especially the category *educable mentally retarded* (EMR) – and (b) the court's finding that EMR classes did little to help children learn essential scholastic skills, the use of IQ tests with African American children was banned in California except when the court gave permission. Some researchers at the time argued that there was little statistical evidence that IQ tests constructed according to proper psychometric standards were biased against African American children (e.g., Jensen, 1980), but see Harrington (1984) for a different view. The main point here is that although evidence for test bias may justify a determination of test unfairness, test bias is *not* required to conclude test unfairness. See the report of the Board on Testing and Assessment of the National Research Council in the United States for a succinct summary on the use of IQ tests with minority children in school settings (Morison, White, & Feuer, 1996).

There is also no direct correspondence between the finding of statistical significance in test bias studies when the "no bias" null hypothesis is rejected and the conclusion about whether the test is fair or unfair. Indeed, there is no necessary link between the two at all. One reason was mentioned: A test could be deemed to be unfair based on differential outcomes over groups in the absence of systematic test bias. Another is that statistical significance says little about effect size. Specifically, a result of trivial magnitude can be statistically significant in large samples, but effects of appreciable size may not be statistically significant in small samples. The realization that statistical significance does not directly measure effect size has motivated the development of various methods for estimating effect size apart from statistical significance (e.g., Ellis, 2010; Grissom & Kim, 2011). Likewise, statistical significance in the analyses described later in this article does *not* automatically lead to the decision that a test is unfair. This is because both context and evaluation of test outcomes must be considered along with the available statistical evidence.

There is a similar gap between statistical significance and evaluation of the results in treatment outcome studies. That is, whether any difference between treated and control cases is statistically significant has nothing to do with *clinical significance*. The latter concerns whether an intervention leads to any tangible benefit in the real world, such as when treated cases can no longer be distinguished from control cases not meeting the same criteria. The evaluation of clinical significance is a rationale exercise that requires strong knowledge of the illness or disorder under study, real-world implication of scores on outcome variables, and results from extant empirical studies (e.g., Blanton & Jaccard, 2006; Kazdin, 2006). This means that (a) treatment effects can be statistically significant yet judged to be clinically irrelevant if such effects are not of appreciable magnitude, and (b) clinically meaningful effects are not always statistically significant. The latter can occur in small pilot studies with low statistical power. The issues just discussed are also part of the realization over more and more disciplines that statistical significance per se has little to do with scientific relevance (e.g., Kline, 2013a; Lambdin, 2012; Ziliak & McCloskey, 2008).

Types of test bias

There are three basic kinds of test bias, content, predictive (criterion-related), and construct. Briefly, *content bias* is indicated when a test item or subscale is relatively more difficult for members of one group than for members of another after controlling for the overall levels of the groups on the construct of interest (Reynolds & Kaiser, 1990). This phenomenon is *differential item functioning* (DIF), and in this context it implies that different groups have different probabilities of getting an item correct. Content bias can occur due to group differences in exposure to the material or knowledge required to select or derive the right answer. Rational evaluation by content experts of the wording or representativeness of items during test construction may prevent some instances of content bias, but judges often fail to detect biased items. A related consideration is whether a set of items covers the full conceptual bandwidth of the construct as defined by theory (Gunnell, Wilson, Zumbo, Mack, & Crocker, 2012). Evidence for content bias is often estimated at the level of individual test items. Note that items that exhibit content bias may also exhibit construct bias, but this is not guaranteed. That is, items that are differentially difficult over groups do not necessarily have appreciably different factor loadings across the same groups.

Construct bias occurs when a test measures different hypothetical constructs (traits) for one group than another or reflects the same basic dimensions but with different degrees of accuracy (Reynolds, 1982). The basic issue is whether observed test scores have the same meaning or interpretation over different groups. In the method of factor analysis, the phenomenon of DIF is most consistent with the case where (a) the same basic factor solution – including both the number of factors (e.g., 3) and the correspondence between indicators (items) and factors – holds over different groups but where (b) some items relate to their corresponding factors in different ways. The latter is evidenced when values of the unstandardized pattern coefficients (factor loadings) for the same indicator vary appreciably across the groups. Note that the observation of statistically significant group differences in factor loadings for the same indicators does *not* establish that those loadings are substantively different. A more extreme form of construct bias occurs when the factor solution varies over groups, such as when a particular set of indicators measures two factors for men but three factors for women. This outcome suggests that the indicators measure different constructs altogether in one population versus another.

The complement of construct bias is *measurement invariance*, or the degree to which a test measures the same constructs across different groups. Measurement invariance is not an all-or-none property of a set of indicators. Specifically, if the same basic factor solution does not hold over different groups, then measurement invariance does not exist at all. Otherwise, there can be different levels of measurement invariance that depend on whether the indicators relate to their factors in the same way in each group (i.e., is there evidence for DIF?) among other considerations explained later. The idea of measurement invariance also applies to times, forms of tests, and modes of test administration (Gunnell et al., 2012). For example, *longitudinal invariance* concerns whether a test reflects the same constructs in the same group but tested at different occasions (e.g., Brown, 2006, pp. 252–266). It is also possible to assess whether what a test measures depends on its format, such as paper-and-pencil administration versus computer administration of the same items in the same group (e.g., Whitaker & McKinney, 2007).

Predictive bias is usually estimated at the level of test summary (total) scores, and it concerns the regression of scores from an external criterion on test summary scores. Predictive bias occurs when there is constant error in prediction as a function of group membership (Reynolds & Kaiser, 1990). There are two general kinds, *slope bias* and *intercept bias*. The former occurs when the slopes of regression lines for predicting the criterion from the test differ appreciably over groups, and the latter is apparent when the intercepts of those regression lines depend on group membership. A related concept is that of *selection bias*, which occurs when the sensitivity or specificity of a screening measure depend on group membership (Borsboom, Romeijn, & Wicherts, 2008). Sensitivity is the proportion of screening test scores from cases with a known disorder that are correct (valid positives), and specificity is the proportion of scores from a control group without the disorder that are correct (valid negatives). For example, Moons, Van Es, Deckers, Habbema, and Grobbee (1997) found that sensitivity and specificity values for the exercise (stress) test for coronary disease varied by gender and systolic blood pressure at baseline. It should be noted that the items on which a summary score is based should have similar difficulties and factor loadings; otherwise, content or construct bias may be confounded with predictive bias.

Standard statistical techniques for analysing test bias

Described next are some standard kinds of statistical techniques used to evaluate test bias. The technique of *moderated multiple regression* (MMR) is widely used to evaluate predictive bias for test summary scores (e.g., Aguinis, 2004). In this approach, predictive bias is estimated by entering into the equation special product terms that represent group × test interactions along with main effect terms that represent continuous test scores and categorical group membership, such as gender. Appreciable interaction effects in MMR indicate the presence of slope bias or intercept bias (or both); see Preacher, Curran, and Bauer (2006) for more information.

Item response theory (IRT) offers an extremely powerful set of statistical techniques for detecting DIF within a set of items presumed to measure a common underlying factor (i.e., unidimensionality within the item set is assumed). Through the analysis of *item characteristic curves*, the presence of DIF is indicated when item difficulty, discrimination, or lower asymptote (e.g., due to a guessing effect) parameter estimates differ appreciably across groups with the same underlying true ability; see Zumbo (2007), for more information. There are also IRT-based methods that estimate the degree of *differential test functioning* (DTF), or whether total scores based on cumulative responses over a set of items relate to the underlying (latent) dimension in the same over different populations. Oliveri, Olson, Ercikan, and Zumbo (2012) described the application of parametric and nonparametric forms of IRT and the technique of ordinal logistic regression to simultaneously estimate DIF and DTF over samples of English- versus French-speaking students who completed an objective measure of problem solving. They found that differential functioning at the item level was not generally detected by analysis at the test level. This is because the direction of DIF was such that some items favoured English-speaking students and others favoured French-speaking students, so the overall effect of bias at the item level cancelled out when item responses were summed to form total scores.

Exploratory factor analysis (EFA) is a major statistical technique for evaluating construct bias at the level of either individual items or summary scores. Standard EFA procedures generally work better with continuous summary scores than with categorical items, such as those with true-false (i.e., binary) formats or Likert-type response formats (e. g., 0 = *disagree*, 1 = *uncertain*, 2 = *agree*). But there are some special factor analytic methods for categorical indicators. They generally analyse polychoric (estimated) correlations among the items assuming that the underlying construct is continuous (see Wirth & Edwards, 2007). Some of these methods also estimate item *thresholds*, or points through the normally distributed latent response distribution that give rise to the selection of one response alternative versus another in items with Likert scales. In the analysis of measurement invariance, there are also various statistical indexes of the similarity or convergence of factor solutions for the same indicators over different groups that can be calculated in EFA (Reynolds & Kaiser, 1990); see also Nimon and Reio (2011). A drawback of EFA is that it analyses *unrestricted measurement models* where each and every indicator is allowed to load on (correlate with) each and every factor. That is, the method does not directly test the hypothesis that different subsets of indicators are each uniquely associated with the factors. This restriction does not apply to confirmatory factor analysis, which is considered next.

Structural equation modelling techniques for analysing test bias

The SEM family of techniques has also been extensively applied to the evaluation of test bias. Briefly, all SEM techniques analyse *covariance structures*, which are a priori statistical models that represent hypotheses about why observed variables vary and covary. These hypotheses may reflect presumed direct or indirect causal effects among observed or latent variables, and sometimes the term "causal modelling" has been used to describe this aspect of SEM. The original SEM technique of path analysis, which was developed in genetics research and dates to the 1920s, estimates direct and indirect effects among observed variables. Later developments in SEM integrated regression-type techniques with factor analytic methods in a framework where observed or latent variables can be specified as predictors or as outcomes in a model that can also represent presumed direct or indirect effects (Matsueda, 2012).

In contrast to standard multiple regression where it is assumed that all predictors have perfect score reliabilities, measurement error can be explicitly represented and estimated in SEM, which controls for it. This capability can give a more realistic tenor to the analysis. It is also possible in SEM to simultaneously analyse multiple outcomes (criteria), but just one criterion can be analysed at a time in standard multiple regression. For example, Lynam, Moffitt, and Stouthamer-Loeber (1993) analysed path models of scholastic achievement and delinquency in samples of White and African American adolescents from low-income neighbourhoods where both variables just mentioned were the outcome variables. They found that direct effects of scholastic achievement on delinquency were appreciably stronger among African American youth than among White teenagers, which is evidence for differential prediction of delinquency by race (i.e., predictive bias). This analysis by Lynam et al. is an example of *multiple-group path analysis* where the same path model is simultaneously analysed across samples from at least two different populations.

The SEM method of factor analysis is confirmatory factor analysis (CFA). An advantage over EFA is that CFA estimates *restricted measurement models* where the researcher must specify both the specific number of factors and the exact correspondence between indicators and factors, which permits of tests of stronger hypotheses about measurement compared with EFA. Brown (2006) and Kline (2013b) considered other differences between EFA and CFA. Just as in EFA, there are also methods in CFA for analysing indicators that are categorical items instead of continuous variables, or summary scores (e.g., Bovaird & Koziol, 2012).

The technique of *multiple-group confirmatory factor analysis* (MGCFA) is used in some research areas to evaluate measurement invariance within the bounds of this concept for factor analytic methods outlined earlier (e.g., Nimon & Reio, 2011). It is critical in any application of SEM, including MGCFA, that the model specified by the researcher is reasonably correct. Indeed, estimation of model parameters in SEM assumes that the model is correctly specified, a very strong assumption not always fully appreciated in practice (Kline, 2012). Serious specification error in the analysis can prevent the researcher from discovering the "true" model. In MGCFA, it can happen that specification error leads to the failure to discover either that a test really measures different factors over groups or that measurement is actually invariant at some level. Suppose that measurement is actually invariant over groups. Specification of a measurement model with either the wrong number of factors or the wrong correspondence between indicators and factors could lead to model-data correspondence so poor that the model is rejected. But if the fit of the model is poor in all samples, then the only viable conclusion is that there may be specification error so severe that none of the within-group covariances are adequately explained. The hypothesis that the test measures different factors over groups would be supported only if different measurement models are each found to have adequate fit within their respective groups. In any event, results in SEM, including MGCFA, depend heavily on the accuracy of the specifications on which the analysis is based.

Whether indicators measure the same factor in different ways over groups can be estimated in both MGCFA and with IRT-based techniques, so a brief comparison of the two techniques is warranted. Only CFA can estimate models where two or more latent variables are assumed to covary. Results in CFA not only directly estimate factor covariances but also control for these covariances in the calculation of parameters for items, such as factor loadings. In contrast, IRT analysis deals with a single latent variable at a time. More item parameters are estimated in IRT methods, which potentially yields more psychometric information. Both techniques require large samples, but even larger samples are generally needed for IRT analyses. It was mentioned earlier that IRT methods can estimate both DIF at the item level and DTF at the level of cumulative responses over items (e.g., Oliveri et al., 2012). I am aware of no similar capability in MGCFA. See Meade and Lautenschlager (2004) and Kim and Yoon (2011) for additional comparisons of MGCFA and IRT techniques.

Hierarchy of invariance hypotheses in confirmatory factor analysis

The basic logic of testing for measurement invariance when applying CFA over multiple samples is outlined next; see Brown (2006, Chapter 8), Cheung and Rensvold (2002), or Schmitt and Kuljanin (2008) for more information. The most basic form of measurement invariance is *configural (equal form) invariance*.[1] It is tested by specifying the same factor structure for the same set of indicators within each group. In this model, both the number of factors and the correspondence between indicators and factors are the same, but all model parameters are freely estimated within each group. If this model is rejected as inconsistent with the data, measurement invariance does not hold at any basic level. Otherwise, the hypothesis of configural invariance is retained, which says that the same factors are manifested in somewhat different ways in each group. These "different ways" refer to the unstandardized factor loadings, which were freely estimated in each group.

This means that if factor scores were calculated at this point, a different weighting scheme could be applied to the indicators in each group.

If the hypothesis of configural invariance is not rejected, stronger forms of measurement invariance can be considered. One is *full metric invariance*, which means that the unstandardized factor loadings of each indicator are equal across the groups. If this hypothesis is retained, the researcher could conclude that the constructs are manifested in the same way (they have the same meaning) in each group. This implies that if factor scores were calculated now, the same weighting scheme could be applied across all groups. A related conclusion is that there is no evidence for slope bias concerning the regression of each indicator on its corresponding factor across the groups. A less strict form is *partial metric invariance*, which means that some, but not all, of the unstandardized factor loadings for the same indicator(s) are equal across the groups. Indicators with appreciably different loadings across the groups exhibit DIF, and they relate to their respective factors in different ways over groups (i.e., the slopes vary). If no form of the partial metric invariance hypothesis is supported, then only configural invariance is consistent with the data.

Evaluating measurement invariance hypotheses beyond those described so far requires (a) the analysis of indicator means as well as covariances and (b) the specification of a measurement model with a *mean structure* in addition to its basic covariance structure. Measurement models with mean structures have additional parameters that include intercept terms for the regressions of the indicators on the factors and means of the factors. The intercepts estimate the score on each indicator when the true score on the corresponding factor is zero. Assuming at least partial metric invariance, the hypothesis of *full scalar invariance* is that intercepts for each indicator are equal over groups. If so, then different groups use the response scale of the corresponding indicator in the same way. This means that a person from one group and a person from a different group with the same level on the underlying factor should select the same response option on the indicator. It could also be said that there is no intercept bias over groups concerning the regressions of indicators on factors. But if none of the intercepts are invariant, there is evidence for a *differential additive response (bias) style* over groups.

The combination of full metric invariance and full scalar invariance says that both the units (factor loadings) and origins (intercepts) are invariant over groups. This combination is referred to as the hypothesis of *strong factorial invariance*. A weaker form of strong factorial invariance allows for partial metric invariance or partial scalar invariance (or both). This weaker form controls for unequal indicator loadings or intercepts across the groups in the estimation of factor means. But if *none* of the loadings or indicators are equal over groups (i.e., the weaker form of strong factorial invariance does not apply), then there are no grounds for interpreting factor mean contrasts.

An even stronger form of invariance is that of *strict factorial invariance*, which assumes full metric invariance, full scalar invariance, and equal measurement error variances and error covariances (if any) for each indicator across the groups. DeShon (2004) argued that error variance (and covariance) homogeneity is critical to claiming that a set of indicators measures the same factors with the same degree of precision. This is because unmodelled systematic effects on observed scores can be confounded with differences in factor loadings or intercepts over groups. This is another kind of potential specification error in MGCFA. It is also true that if strict factorial invariance holds, expected group differences in composite means and variances on the indicators are unbiased estimates of the corresponding differences in both factor means and variances (Gregorich, 2006). A weaker form of strict factorial invariance allows for partial metric, scalar, or error term invariance, and it is the minimum requirement for meaningful group comparisons on indicator means.

Assuming at least this weaker form of strict factorial invariance, it is also possible to directly test the hypothesis of *equal construct (factor) variances and covariances*, if either expectation is theoretically relevant.

The concept of partial measurement invariance is problematic because it requires only that a single parameter estimate is invariant over groups, such as the loading of the same indicator for partial metric invariance. Unfortunately, there are no clear guidelines for determining the degree of partial invariance (i.e., ≥ 1 invariant parameters) that would be acceptable in all situations for concluding that the indicators measure approximately the same things over groups. I suggest that at least the *majority* of indictor loadings, error variances, and error covariances (if any) should be invariant before coming to the conclusion just stated. Steenkamp and Baumgartner (1998) discussed the evaluation of partial measurement invariance in studies of cross-national consumer research.

Testing strategy

Described next is a strategy for testing increasingly stronger forms of hypotheses about measurement invariance. The particular sequence used in an actual study may vary somewhat from the order outlined here depending on the number and priority of invariance hypotheses, but the basic logic in perhaps most invariance analyses will roughly follow these steps; see Schmitt and Kuljanin (2008) for more information.

Testing for measurement invariance in CFA usually begins with the specification of a model that corresponds to configural invariance. If this model is not rejected, then increasingly more constrained models are specified and tested. The degree of metric variance is usually tested in the second step by imposing equality constraints on the unstandardized loading of each indicator across all groups. The relative fits to the data of this full metric invariance model at the second step and the configural invariance model from the first step can be tested with the chi-square difference statistic, χ_D^2, the difference between the model chi-square statistics from each of the two nested models (configural invariance vs. full metric invariance). The degrees of freedom for this test statistic, df_D, equals the difference in the model degrees of freedom for the two models. If the probability level of χ_D^2 is $p < .05$, the fit of the less constrained configural invariance model is statistically better than that of the more constrained full metric invariance model at the .05 level. If so, next the hypothesis of partial metric invariance would be tested where some, but not all, factor loadings are constrained to equality. If no variation of the partial metric invariance hypothesis is retained, invariance testing stops.

The model specified at the third step is usually that of full scalar invariance where the intercept of each indicator is constrained to equality across the groups. The relative fits of this full scalar invariance model at the third step with that of the model retained at the second step (metric invariance, full or partial) are again compared with the chi-square difference test. If the full scalar invariance model is rejected, then models of partial scalar invariance where some, but not all, intercepts are constrained to equality over the groups can be tested. Any scalar invariance model (full or partial) retained as consistent with the data at the third step would be compared with the metric invariance model from the second step. But if no form of partial scalar invariance is supported (i.e., all intercepts must be freely estimated within each group in order for the model to have acceptable fit), then invariance testing is halted.

Cheung and Rensvold (2002) remind us that the chi-square difference test is affected by sample size. In invariance testing, this means that χ_D^2 could be statistically significant even though the absolute differences in parameter estimates are of trivial magnitude. That is, the outcome of the chi-square difference test could indicate lack of measurement invariance when the imposition of cross-group equality constraints makes relatively little difference in fit. One way to detect this outcome is to compare the unstandardized solutions across the groups.[2] Another is to inspect changes in approximate fit indexes – which are intended as continuous measures of model-data correspondence (e.g., Kline, 2010, Chapter 8) – but there are few guidelines for doing so in invariance testing. An exception is for the Bentler comparative fit index (CFI), which Cheung and Rensvold (2002) found in computer simulation studies to be relatively unaffected by model characteristics such as the number of factors or number of indicators per factor. They suggested that change in CFI values less than or equal to .01 (i.e., ΔCFI $\leq$ .01) indicate that the stricter invariance hypothesis should *not* be rejected. If all group sizes exceed, say, 1,000 cases, the ΔCFI $\leq$ .01 rule may be useful.

It is common but *poor* practice in SEM to base the decision about whether to retain the model solely on values of model test statistics or approximate fit indexes while ignoring the residuals, or differences between observed (sample) covariances and those predicted by the model. If these residuals are excessively large, the model should be rejected even if values of its fit statistics look favourable (e.g., Hayduk, Cummings, Boadu, Pazderka-Robinson, & Boulianne, 2007; Kline, 2010, Chapter 8). One definition of an "excessively large" departure between model and data is when an absolute *correlation residual*, or the difference between a sample correlation and the value predicted by the model for the same pair of observed variables, exceeds .10. If several absolute correlation residuals exceed .10, especially in a smaller model, the model is clearly inadequate. There is no golden rule about how many high absolute correlation residuals is too many, but the more that exceed .10, the worse is the explanatory power of the model. Inspection of the residuals in SEM is a best practice that should be routine in all analyses. This is because it is *not* adequate to adjudge model fit based solely on values of summary fit statistics.

It can also be informative to inspect *standardized covariance residuals*, or statistical tests (in the form of normal deviates, z), of whether the corresponding *covariance residuals*, or differences between observed and predicted covariances, differ statistically from zero. In analyses of means in SEM, there are also *standardized mean residuals*, and they test whether differences between sample means and those predicted by the model differ statistically from zero. These tests are sensitive to sample size, so their outcomes can be statistically significant even when the corresponding covariance residual or mean residual differs trivially from zero when the group sizes are very large. The same limitation applies to *modification indexes*, which are interpreted as chi-square statistics where $df = 1$ that estimate the reduction in the overall model chi-square (i.e., χ^2_D) if the corresponding parameter constraint were released (e.g., the requirement that a pair of unstandardized factor loadings is equal across two groups). These statistics can be significant even though the corresponding constraint makes relatively little difference in overall model fit. Inspecting the absolute value of the corresponding parameter change when the constraint is released may help to detect this problem.

Empirical example

The data for this example are from Radloff (1977), who evaluated psychometric characteristics of items from the Center for Epidemiologic Studies Depression (CES–D) scale in White ($n_1 = 2004$) and African American samples ($n_2 = 248$). The five CES–D items analysed next, all have the same Likert-type response format (0–3) where higher scores indicate greater complaints about somatic correlates of depression, such as reduced appetite and increased restlessness. Reported in Table 1 are summary statistics (covariances, means)

Table 1.   Input data (covariances, means) for analysis of a one-factor model of somatic complaints analysed across ethic samples.

Indicators	1	2	3	4	5
		White (n_1 = 2004)			
1. Bothered	.49822				
2. Restless	.12634	.42714			
3. Get Going	.20046	.17796	.76513		
4. Appetite	.18179	.17049	.27322	.82264	
5. Effort	.16644	.16163	.31836	.24146	.63059
M	.32834	.24002	.48553	.61228	.43713
		African American (n_2 = 248)			
1. Bothered	.49587				
2. Restless	.16935	.57562			
3. Get Going	.19368	.17265	1.29030		
4. Appetite	.14082	.13106	.31683	.87469	
5. Effort	.18769	.12476	.34361	.34361	.66199
M	.35081	.34677	.80645	.58871	.45565

Note: These indicators correspond to, respectively, Items 1, 2, 7, 11, and 20 from the Center for Epidemiologic Studies Depression scale (Radloff, 1977). Internal consistency reliabilities (Cronbach's alpha) in the White and African American samples based on all five items are, respectively, .703 and .661.

for these five items in both groups. These summary data can also be freely downloaded over the Internet.[3]

The one-factor measurement model with a mean structure presented in Figure 1 was fitted to the data in Table 1 using Mplus (Muthén & Muthén, 1998–2010) and default maximum likelihood estimation, which treats the items as continuous variables. This is not ideal because Likert-scale items are not usually considered as continuous (e.g., Millsap & Yun-Tein, 2004). Gregorich (2006) analysed the same data using MGCFA and reported model test statistics corrected for non-normality, but his results are generally similar to those described next for this pedagogical example. Best practice in CFA is to analyse Likert-type items with methods intended for ordered-categorical (ordinal) variables that were mentioned earlier. A drawback of doing so for this pedagogical example is that raw data files are required for such methods, and raw data files are not publicly available for this problem. In contrast, assuming that the items are continuous variables and using standard maximum likelihood estimation permits the analysis of summary statistics (covariances and means) instead of raw data. Thus, readers can freely download all Mplus syntax (input), data, and output files for the analyses outlined next.[4] Readers with access to Mplus can not only reproduce these analyses but also test additional models not considered here. Because all input and output files are simply text (ASCII) files, readers without access to Mplus can nevertheless open these files using any basic text editor, such as Microsoft Windows Notepad.

Results of a recent computer simulation study by Koh and Zumbo (2008) offer some encouragement that the results described next may not be grossly inaccurate. They estimated effective rates of Type I error in MGCFA when Likert-type items are analysed using methods for continuous variables (i.e., standard maximum likelihood) over simulated samples that varied in group size (n = 200–800), degree of imbalance in group sizes (e.g., n_1 = n_2 = 200 vs. n_1 = 250, n_2 = 500), and proportions of items with a dichotomous format versus a 3-point response format (i.e., item response is mixed). The two simulated populations had equal parameters for the same measurement model, so the invariance hypothesis was true. Observed rates of Type I error where the invariance hypothesis was falsely rejected did not generally vary a great deal from nominal values, such as α = .05, in the

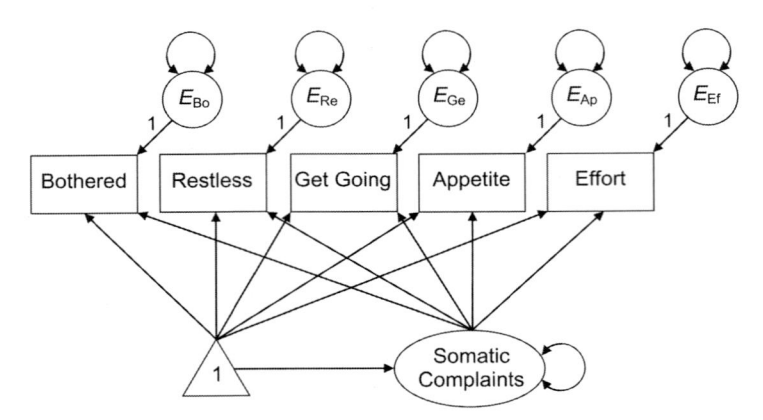

Figure 1. Single-factor model of somatic complaints with a mean structure analysed across ethnic samples.

chi-square difference test. These results suggest that the use of sub-optimal methods within the scope of the variables tested by Koh and Zumbo (2008) may not systematically lead researchers to reject true measurement invariance hypotheses.

Another limitation is that it is not possible in this secondary analysis to specify a priori hypotheses about *which particular* parameters may be invariant or not invariant over the White and African American samples, given the content of the items. This means that there is an unavoidable exploratory bent to the analyses described next as the model is modified to better fit the data. It is better practice in actual primary analyses to respecify models according to theoretical predictions or results of previous empirical studies; see Hoyle (2012) for more information about this issue.

The five indicators in Figure 1 are specified to measure a common somatic complaints factor, and estimates of the direct effects of the factor on the indicators are factor loadings. The symbol $\triangle$ in the figure represents a constant with direct effects on the indicators and factor, which altogether make up the mean structure of the model. Unstandardized estimates of direct effects of the constant on the indicators are intercepts for regressions of the latter on their common factor, but the coefficient for the direct effect of the constant on the factor estimates the factor mean. The curved lines with two arrowheads in Figure 1 represent the variances of the factor and indicator measurement errors, which are all model parameters that require statistical estimates. The factor loadings and intercepts are the other parameters of the measurement model with structured means.

There are three basic options to scale the factor and identify the model in Figure 1, which makes it possible for the computer to derive unique estimates of each parameter (Little, Slegers, & Card, 2006). It is important to note that all three methods outlined next generate the same value of the model chi square and all other fit statistics for the same model and data. In the *reference-group method*, one group is selected as the reference group, and the factor variance and mean are fixed to equal, respectively, 1.0 and 0 in this group. With the loadings and intercepts equated across all groups, factor means and variances are freely estimated in the other groups each scaled relative to the values in the reference group (i.e., 0 for the mean, 1.0 for the variance). A second option is the *marker-variable method* where the unstandardized loading of one indicator per factor is fixed to 1.0 and its intercept is fixed to 0. The remaining loadings and intercepts are freely estimated but equated across the groups. This method scales each factor in a metric related to that of the explained variances of the corresponding marker variable.

A drawback of both methods just described is that the selection of a reference group or marker variable may be arbitrary. Also, the reference-group method and the marker-variable method both require a homogeneity (invariance) assumption, but of a different type for each method. Because all factor variances are fixed to 1.0 in the reference group method, it must be assumed that the true factor variances of this group are the same as in all other groups for each and every corresponding factor. Because the loadings of marker variables are fixed to 1.0 in all groups in the marker-variable method, it must be assumed that the true factor loadings of the marker variables are also invariant across all groups. But if these assumptions are untenable, then the results may be inaccurate.

A third option to scale the factors for models where all indicators have exactly the same metric is the *effects-coding method* where (1) the *average* unstandardized loading for the indicators of each factor is fixed to 1.0 and (2) their *average* intercept is fixed to 0. This method scales each factor in a metric related to that of the average explained variance over all its indicators. Factor means, variances, and indicator loadings and intercepts are all freely estimated in each group, that is, no invariance assumptions about factor variances or indicator loadings are required. As mentioned, the use of the three methods to scale the factors just described does not affect the overall fit of the model; see Little et al. (2006) for more information. The effects-coding method is used in this example and is implemented in the Mplus syntax for the results described next. Because not all group sizes exceed 1,000 in this example, the ΔCFI $\leq$ .01 rule of Cheung and Rensvold (2002) is not applied to compare the models analysed next.

Summarized in Table 2 are values of the model chi-statistic for a total of five hierarchically related single-factor models with structured means fitted to the multiple group data in Table 1. Also reported in Table 2 are results of the chi-square difference test for comparisons between adjacent models and values of the Steiger-Lind root mean square error of approximation (RMSEA) with its 90% confidence interval for each model. Values of the RMSEA < .08 are generally preferred, but any single-number fit statistic says little about the residuals. For this reason, I inspected the residuals for each and every model described next. Model 1 represents the hypothesis of configural invariance. This model fails the chi-square test, χ^2_M (10) = 25.114, p = .005. Values of all absolute correlation residuals are close to zero in the White sample, but the residual correlation in the African American sample for the Bothered and Restless indicators is .119, which says that the model underpredicts the corresponding sample correlation by this amount. One interpretation is that this pair of indicators shares systematic variance not due to the common factor. Accordingly, Model 2 was specified to include an error covariance between the Bothered and Restless indicators in the African American sample only. This model marginally fails the chi-square test, χ^2_M (9) = 17.290, p = .044, but all absolute correlation residuals in both groups are < .10. Model 2 also has statistically better fit to the data compared with Model 1, χ^2_D (1) = 6.824, p = .009 (see Table 2), so this modified model of configural invariance is retained.

Note that the claim for configural invariance (Model 2) is possibly confounded with unmodelled systematic effects that underlie the error covariance between the Bothered and Restless items in the African American sample only. Here, I remind the reader of DeShon's (2004) argument that error covariance homogeneity is required in order to claim that the five indicators measure the sole factor with the same degree of precision, so there is some doubt for these data about the hypothesis of full metric invariance. On the positive side, all indicator error variances are generally similar across the two samples. With the caveat just mentioned in mind, we continue with testing additional invariance hypotheses.

Each factor loading is constrained to equality across the groups in Model 3, which tests the hypothesis of full metric invariance. This model passes the chi-square test,

Table 2. Values of fit statistics for hypotheses about measurement invariance for a one-factor model of somatic complaints analysed across ethnic samples.

Model	Additional free parameter(s)	χ^2_M	df_M	χ^2_D	df_D	RMSEA	CFI
1. Configural invariance	—	25.114**	10	—	—	.037 [.019, .055]	.991
2. Configural invariance	Bothered with Restless error covariance in African American group only	17.290*	9	6.824**	1	.029 [.004, .049]	.995
3. Full metric invariance	—	19.436	13	2.146	4	.021 [0, .039]	.996
4. Full scalar invariance	—	40.620**	17	21.184**	4	.035 [.021, .049]	.986
5. Partial scalar invariance	Intercept of Get Going indicator in both groups	24.076	16	16.544**	1	.021 [0, .038]	.995

Note: The RMSEA is reported with its 90% confidence interval.
*$p < .05$, **$p < .01$.

χ^2_D (13) = 19.436, p = .110, and all absolute correlation residuals are < .10 in both groups, so the hypothesis of equal factor loadings is supported. Also, the fit of Model 3 is not statistically worse than that of Model 2, the modified configural invariance model, χ^2_D (4) = 2.146, p = .709 (see Table 2).

In Model 4, the intercept of each indicator is constrained to equality across the groups, which tests the hypothesis of full scalar invariance. This model fails the chi-square test, χ^2_M (17) = 40.620, p = .001, and its relative fit is statistically worse than that of Model 3, for which the intercepts are freely estimated in both groups, χ^2_D (4) = 21.184, p < .001. For Model 4, the standardized mean residual for the Get Going indicator in the African American sample is statistically significant, z = 4.100, p < .001, so this model does not accurately predict the corresponding observed mean in this group.

In Model 5, the equality constraint on the intercept of the Get Going indicator is released (it is freely estimated in both groups). This model has reasonable overall fit to the data, χ^2_M (16) 24.076, p = .088, and its fit is comparatively better than that of Model 4, χ^2_D (1) = 16.544, p < .001. Also, the absolute correlation residuals are all < .10 in both groups. Based on these results, Model 5 is selected as the final invariance model. In sum, this model assumes full metric invariance but partial scalar invariance, specifically, all intercepts are equal across the groups except for the Get Going indicator. This difference in the intercept may reflect a systematic response style where the same level on the factor is associated with different observed means on the corresponding indicator. Controlling for this effect in the African American group makes possible a direct comparison of the factor means over two samples. An error covariance for a pair of indicators (Bothered, Restless) is estimated in the African American sample, but not in the White sample (i.e., it is assumed to be zero for this group).

These results support a weak form of strong factorial invariance, but also indicate that the factor may be measured somewhat differently by the five indicators across the groups. Whether these differences make this set of five items "unfair" cannot be determined here because, as mentioned, the evaluation of fairness depends on more than just statistical results. But if the goal were to derive a 5-item composite (total score) to summarize somatic complaints, then these results cast doubt on whether such a composite would have the same interpretation for White versus African American respondents. An option not explored here is to consider whether a composite based on a smaller number of items (< 5; i.e., one or more items are eliminated) would be more comparable over the groups, but see Gregorich (2006).

Reported in Table 3 are unstandardized estimates for the parameters of the covariance structure for Model 5 in both groups. Note in the table that the factor loading of each indicator is equal across the groups, which indicates full metric invariance. In contrast, the error and factor variances are freely estimated in both groups except for the error covariance between the Bothered and Restless indicators, which is estimated in the African American group only. Listed in Table 4 are unstandardized estimates for the mean structure in both groups. A total of four of five indicator intercepts are equal across the groups, but the estimate for the Get Going intercept in the White group is negative (−.063), but it is positive in the African American group (.226) (see Table 4). This result is consistent with a higher observed mean on the Get Going indicator in the African American groups compared with the White group (see Table 1). It could also indicate a systematic response style apart from the influence of the factor that leads to higher scores on this item in the African American sample. This difference is controlled when considering the mean contrast on the somatic complaints factor, which is

$$.445 - .421 = .024$$

Table 3. Unstandardized estimates for the covariance structure in the final one-factor model of somatic complaints analysed across ethnic samples.

	Sample	
Parameter	White	African American
Equality-constrained estimates		
Factor loadings		
Bothered	.770 (.032)	.770 (.032)
Restless	.708 (.031)	.708 (.031)
Get Going	1.305 (.038)	1.305 (.038)
Appetite	1.072 (.039)	1.072 (.039)
Effort	1.146 (.036)	1.146 (.036)
Unconstrained estimates		
Factor variances		
Somatic	.203 (.009)	.445 (.037)
Error variances and covariance		
Bothered	.377 (.014)	.382 (.039)
Restless	.323 (.012)	.504 (.049)
Get Going	.420 (.020)	.907 (.095)
Appetite	.588 (.022)	.639 (.066)
Effort	.364 (.016)	.379 (.047)
Bothered with Restless	—	.076 (.032)

Note: Standard errors are reported in parentheses, and $p < .05$ for all estimates. The estimated error correlation is .173.

(see Table 4), so the African American group has a higher factor mean than the White group by .024. The estimated factor variances in the two groups are .021 and .070, so we can estimate the magnitude of the factor mean contrast with a standardized mean difference as

$$\frac{.024}{\sqrt{(.021 + .070)/2}} = .11$$

That is, the factor mean contrast is only about 11% of the unweighted common standard deviation in magnitude, which indicates a relatively small effect size.

Table 4. Unstandardized estimates for the mean structure in the final one-factor model of somatic complaints analysed across ethnic samples.

	Sample	
Parameter	White	African American
Equality-constrained estimates		
Intercepts		
Bothered	.004 (.018)	.004 (.018)
Restless	−.051 (.017)	−.051 (.017)
Appetite	.156 (.022)	.156 (.022)
Effort	−.046 (.019)	−.046 (.019)
Unconstrained estimates		
Intercepts		
Get Going	−.063 (.021)	.226 (.070)
Factor means		
Somatic	.421 (.012)	.445 (.037)

Note: Standard errors are reported in parentheses, and $p < .05$ for all estimates except the Bothered intercept.

Extensions

Readers can find another empirical example of using MGCFA to evaluate measurement invariance in Millsap and Olivera-Aguilar (2012). Briefly mentioned next are works that deal with extensions to the basic hypothesis testing framework just considered. Chen, Sousa, and West (2005) described testing for invariance of second-order factor measurement models with a higher order factor without indicators specified to affect first order factors with indicators. Cheung and Lau (2012) outlined a method for invariance testing that relies on bootstrapped confidence intervals instead of the chi-square difference test. In computer simulation studies, Meade, Johnson, and Braddy (2008) concluded that group sizes of at least 400 may be needed for adequate statistical power in multiple-group CFA when testing for measurement invariance.

An MGCFA is a kind of multilevel analysis where scores are nested under the groups. Score dependencies within each group are explicitly modelled through the specification of the measurement model, but group membership per se otherwise has a relatively small role in standard MGCFA. Forer and Zumbo (2011) described an approach to test validation that involves a more rigorous application of true multilevel analyses for situations when there are theoretical grounds to examine both within-group and between-group effects. The latter may involve at least one level of data aggregation from individual cases (within groups) to larger social units (between groups), such as students within schools or siblings within families. In multilevel CFA, it may be possible to analyse separate measurement models at different levels, within versus between, or estimate *context effects*, which involve the regression of scores from the case level on predictors at the group level. For example, the student-to-teacher ratio over different schools may predict achievement levels of students within schools, and neighbourhood characteristics such as average income may affect the adjustment of siblings within families. The approach described by Forer and Zumbo (2011) potentially expands the scope of the kinds of hypotheses about measurement that can be tested. Kline (2011) gave an overview of multilevel SEM including multilevel CFA.

Acknowledgements

The author wishes to thank the three anonymous reviewers for their helpful suggestions.

Notes

1. Configural invariance should be distinguished from *dimensional invariance*, which requires only that indicators depend on the same number of factors across groups, but it does not also assume the same indicator-factor correspondence. Dimensional invariance only is incompatible with the concept of measurement invariance.
2. Standardized parameter estimates are not directly comparable over groups, especially when the groups have different ranges of individual differences on the observed or latent variables.
3. http://www.ats.ucla.edu/stat/mplus/paperexamples/gregorich/default.htm
4. http://psychology.concordia.ca/fac/kline/invariance.html

References

Aguinis, H. (2004). *Regression analysis for categorical moderators.* New York, NY: Guilford Press.

Blanton, H., & Jaccard, J. (2006). Arbitrary metrics in psychology. *American Psychologist, 61*, 27–41. doi:10.1037/0003-066X.61.1.27

Borsboom, D., Romeijn, J. W., & Wicherts, J. M. (2008). Measurement invariance versus selection invariance: Is fair selection possible? *Psychological Methods*, *13*, 75–98. doi:10.1037/1082-989X.13.2.75

Bovaird, J. A., & Koziol, N. A. (2012). Measurement models for categorical indicators. In R. H. Hoyle (Ed.), *Handbook of structural equation modeling* (pp. 495–511). New York, NY: Guilford Press.

Brown, T. A. (2006). *Confirmatory factor analysis for applied research*. New York, NY: Guilford Press.

Chen, F. F., Sousa, K. H., & West, S. G. (2005). Teacher's corner: Testing measurement invariance of second-order factor models. *Structural Equation Modeling*, *12*, 471–492. doi:10.1207/s15328007sem1203_7

Cheung, G. W., & Lau, R. S. (2012). A direct comparison approach for testing measurement invariance. *Organizational Research Methods*, *15*, 167–198. doi:10.1177/1094428111421987

Cheung, G. W., & Rensvold, R. B. (2002). Evaluating goodness-of-fit indexes for testing measurement invariance. *Structural Equation Modeling*, *9*, 233–255. doi:10.1207/S15328007SEM0902_5

DeShon, R. P. (2004). Measures are not invariant across groups without error variance homogeneity. *Psychology Science*, *46*, 137–149. Retrieved from http://www.pabst-publishers.de/psychology-science/

Ellis, P. D. (2010). *The essential guide to effect sizes: Statistical power, meta-analysis, and the interpretation of research results*. New York, NY: Cambridge University Press.

Forer, B., & Zumbo, B. D. (2011). Validation of multilevel constructs: Validation methods and empirical findings for the EDI. *Social Indicators Research*, *103*, 231–265. doi:10.1007/s11205-011-9844-3

Gregorich, S. E. (2006). Do self-report instruments allow meaningful comparisons across diverse population groups? Testing measurement invariance using the confirmatory factor analysis framework. *Medical Care*, *44* (Suppl. 3), S78–S94. doi:10.1097/01.mlr.0000245454.12228.8f

Grissom, R. J., & Kim, J. J. (2011). *Effect sizes for research: Univariate and multivariate applications* (2nd ed.). New York, NY: Routledge.

Gunnell, K. E., Wilson, P. M., Zumbo, B. D., Mack, D. E., & Crocker, P. R. E. (2012). Assessing psychological need satisfaction in exercise contexts: Issues of score invariance, item modification, and context. *Measurement in Physical Education and Exercise Science*, *16*, 219–236. doi:10.1080/1091367X.2012.693340

Harrington, G. M. (1984). An experimental model of bias in mental testing. In C. R. Reynolds & R. T. Brown (Eds.), *Perspectives on bias in mental testing* (pp. 101–138). New York, NY: Plenum.

Hayduk, L., Cummings, G., Boadu, K., Pazderka-Robinson, H., & Boulianne, S. (2007). Testing! testing! one, two, three – Testing the theory in structural equation models! *Personality and Individual Differences*, *42*, 841–850. doi:10.1016/j.paid.2006.10.001

Hoyle, R. H. (2012). Model specification in structural equation modeling. In R. H. Hoyle (Ed.), *Handbook of structural equation modeling* (pp. 126–144). New York, NY: Guilford Press.

Jensen, A. R. (1980). *Bias in mental testing*. New York, NY: Free Press.

Kazdin, A. (2006). Arbitrary metrics: Implications for identifying evidence-based treatments *American Psychologist*, *61*, 42–49. doi:10.1037/0003-066X.61.1.42

Kim, E. S., & Yoon, M. (2011). Testing measurement invariance: A comparison of multiple-group categorical CFA and IRT. *Structural Equation Modeling*, *18*, 212–228. doi:10.1080/10705511.2011.557337

Kline, R. B. (2010). *Principles and practice of structural equation modeling* (3rd ed.). New York, NY: Guilford Press.

Kline, R. B. (2011). Convergence of structural equation modeling and multilevel modeling. In M. Williams & W. P. Vogt (Eds.), *Handbook of methodological innovation* (pp. 562–589). Thousand Oaks, CA: Sage.

Kline, R, B. (2012). Assumptions of structural equation modeling. In R. Hoyle (Ed.), *Handbook of structural equation modeling* (pp. 111–125). New York, NY: Guilford Press.

Kline, R. B. (2013a). *Beyond significance testing: Statistics reform in the behavioral sciences*. Washington, DC: American Psychological Association.

Kline, R. B. (2013b). Exploratory and confirmatory factor analysis. In Y. Petscher & C. Schatschneider (Eds.), *Applied quantitative analysis in the social sciences* (pp. 171–207). New York, NY: Routledge.

Koh, K., & Zumbo, B. D. (2008). Multi-group confirmatory factor analysis for testing measurement invariance in mixed item format data. *Journal of Modern Applied Statistical Methods, 7*, 471–477. Retrieved from http://www.jmasm.com/

Lambdin, C. (2012). Significance tests as sorcery: Science is empirical – significance tests are not. *Theory & Psychology, 22*, 67–90. doi:10.1177/0959354311429854

Larry P. v. Riles, 343 F. Supp. 1306 (N.D. Cal. 1972) (order granting preliminary injunction), aff'd, 502 F.2d 963 (9th Cir. 1974), 495 F. Supp. 926 (N. D. Cal. 1979) (decision on merits), aff'd, No. 80-427 (9th Cir. Jan. 23, 1984), No. C-71-2270 RFP (Sept. 25, 1986) (order modifying judgment), 793 F.2d 969 (9th Cir. 1994).

Little, T. D., Slegers, D. W., & Card, N. A. (2006). A non-arbitrary method of identifying and scaling latent variables in SEM and MACS models. *Structural Equation Modeling, 13*, 59–72. doi:10.1207/s15328007sem1301_3

Lynam, D. R., Moffitt, T., & Stouthamer-Loeber, M. (1993). Explaining the relation between IQ and delinquency: Class, race, test motivation, or self-control? *Journal of Abnormal Psychology, 102*, 187–196. doi:10.1037//0021-843X.102.2.187

Matsueda, R. L. (2012). Key advances in the history of structural equation modeling. In R. H. Hoyle (Ed.), *Handbook of structural equation modeling* (pp. 17–42). New York, NY: Guilford Press.

Meade, A. W., Johnson, E. C., & Braddy, P. W. (2008). Power and sensitivity of alternative fit indices in tests of measurement invariance. *Journal of Applied Psychology, 93*, 568–592. doi:10.1037/0021-9010.93.3.568

Meade, A. W., & Lautenschlager, G. J. (2004). A comparison of item response theory and confirmatory factor analytic methodologies for establishing measurement equivalence/invariance. *Organizational Research Methods, 7*, 361–388. doi:10.1177/1094428104268027

Messick, S. (1998). Test validity: A matter of consequence. *Social Indicators Research, 45*, 35–44. doi:10.1023/A:1006964925094

Millsap, R. E., & Olivera-Aguilar, M. (2012). Investigating measurement invariance using confirmatory factor analysis. In R. H. Hoyle (Ed.), *Handbook of structural equation modeling* (pp. 380–392). New York, NY: Guilford Press.

Millsap, R. E., & Yun-Tein, J. (2004). Assessing factorial invariance in ordered-categorical measures. *Multivariate Behavioral Research, 39*, 479–515. doi:10.1207/S15327906MBR3903_4

Moons, K. G. M., Van Es, G. A., Deckers, J. W., Habbema, J. D. F., & Grobbee, D. E. (1997). Limitations of sensitivity, specificity, likelihood ratio, and Bayes' theorem in assessing diagnostic probabilities: A clinical example. *Epidemiology, 8*, 12–17. doi:10.1097/00001648-199701000-00002

Morison, P., White, S. H., & Feuer, M. J. (Eds.). (1996). *The use of IQ tests in special education decision making and planning: Summary of two workshops.* Washington, DC: National Academy Press.

Muthén, L. K., & Muthén, B. O. (1998–2010). *Mplus user's guide* (6th ed.). Los Angeles, CA: Authors.

Nimon, K., & Reio, T., Jr. (2011). Measurement invariance: A foundational principle for quantitative theory building. *Human Resource Development Review, 10*, 198–214. doi:10.1177/1534484311399731

Oliveri, M. E., Olson, B. D., Ercikan, K., & Zumbo, B. D. (2012). Methodologies for investigating item- and test-level measurement equivalence in international large-scale assessments. *International Journal of Testing, 12*, 203–223. doi:10.1080/15305058.2011.617475

Preacher, K. J., Curran, P. J., & Bauer, D. J. (2006). Computational tools for probing interactions in multiple linear regression, multilevel modeling, and latent curve analysis. *Journal of Educational and Behavioral Statistics, 31*, 437–448. doi:10.3102/10769986031004437

Radloff, L. S. (1977). The CES–D scale: A self-report depression scale for research in the general populations. *Applied Psychological Measurement, 1*, 385–401. Retrieved from http://apm.sagepub.com/

Reynolds, C. R. (1982). Methods for detecting construct and predictive bias. In R. A. Berk (Ed.), *Handbook of methods for detecting test bias* (pp. 199–227). Baltimore, MD: John Hopkins University Press.

Reynolds, C. R., & Kaiser, S. M. (1990). Bias in assessment of aptitude. In C. R. Reynolds & R. W. Kamphaus (Eds.), *Handbook of psychological and educational assessment of children* (pp. 611–653). New York, NY: Guilford Press.

Schmitt, N., & Kuljanin, G. (2008). Measurement invariance: Review of practice and limitations. *Human Resource Management Review, 18,* 210–222. doi:10.1016/j.hrmr.2008.03.003

Steenkamp, J.-B. E. M., & Baumgartner, H. (1998). Assessing measurement invariance in cross-national consumer research. *Journal of Consumer Research, 25,* 78–90. doi:10.1086/209528

Whitaker, B. G., & McKinney, J. L. (2007). Assessing the measurement invariance of latent job satisfaction ratings across survey administration modes for respondent subgroups: A MIMIC modeling approach. *Behavior Research Methods, 39,* 502–509. doi:10.3758/BF03193019

Wirth, R. J., & Edwards, M. C. (2007). Item factor analysis: Current approaches and future directions. *Psychological Methods, 12,* 58–79. doi:10.1037/1082-989X.12.1.58

Ziliak, S., & McCloskey, D. N. (2008). *The cult of statistical significance: How the standard error costs us jobs, justice, and lives.* Ann Arbor, MI: University of Michigan Press.

Zumbo, B. D. (2007). Three generations of DIF analyses: Considering where it has been, where it is now, and where it is going. *Language Assessment Quarterly, 4,* 223–233. Retrieved from http://www.tandfonline.com/loi/hlaq20

The formalization of fairness: issues in testing for measurement invariance using subtest scores

Dylan Molenaar and Denny Borsboom

University of Amsterdam, Amsterdam, The Netherlands

Measurement invariance is an important prerequisite for the adequate comparison of group differences in test scores. In psychology, measurement invariance is typically investigated by means of linear factor analyses of subtest scores. These subtest scores typically result from summing the item scores. In this paper, we discuss 4 possible problems related to this common practice. Specifically, we discuss (a) nonlinearity of the latent variable to subtest relation; (b) suboptimality of the total score as a proxy for the latent variable measured through the item scores; (c) non-normality of the subtest score; and (d) differences in the nature of the latent variable at the item level as compared to the latent variable at the subtest level. Additionally, we give guidelines to overcome these problems and illustrate the issues by analysing data that pertain to a performal IQ data set.

Introduction

In psychology and educational assessment, researchers often want to make inferences regarding properties like working memory, mood, extraversion, arithmetic ability, and perceptual organization. As researchers cannot observe these properties directly, they typically focus on observable indicators that are assumed to be determined by the properties of interest. For example, if we want to measure perceptual organization, we may consider the performance of a sample of subjects on the Block Design and Matrix Reasoning subtests of the Wechsler Adult Intelligence Scale III (WAIS-III; Wechsler, 1997), and take performance differences to reflect differences in perceptual organization (Edwards & Bagozzi, 2000).

Formal models designed to represent and test such measurement hypotheses are generically known as latent variable models (Bartholomew, 1987; Borsboom, 2005, 2008). The parameters of reflective measurement models represent measurement characteristics of the test or items, that is, specify how it relates the latent variables of interest to the indicators. Various measurement models are available; these differ in the structure of the latent and observed variables (e.g., categorical or continuous; see Batholomew, 1987; Mellenbergh, 1994a) and in the type of relation that connects them (e.g., monotonic, as in Ellis & Junker, 1997, or linear, as in Jöreskog, 1971). Popular measurement models include the linear factor model (Spearman, 1904, 1927; Thurstone, 1947), which links continuous item data to a continuous latent variable (Mellenbergh, 1994b), and the two-parameter logistic model (2PL; Birnbaum, 1968), which links dichotomous item data to a continuous latent variable.

As Lord (1980) suggested, meaningful interpretations of observed mean differences, in terms of the latent variables in the model, are facilitated if the same measurement properties hold in the samples under consideration. For a parametric model, this implies that the parameters in the measurement model are the same across groups. This idea was developed by B. O. Muthén (1989) and especially Mellenbergh (1989) and Meredith (1993) to construct the theoretical framework of measurement invariance. Measurement invariance holds if and only if all subjects with the same position on the latent variable have the same observed score distribution, regardless of their group membership. This idea is completely general and applies to all kinds of measurement models, including nonparametric item response theory (IRT) models and latent class models. If group differences in observed scores exist conditional on the latent variable, however, the scores display violations of measurement invariance, also known as differential item functioning (DIF) in the IRT literature. Although formally speaking these concepts designate the same property, in this paper we will generally speak of DIF when discussing individual items, and of measurement invariance with respect to subtests, since this terminology has become common in the literature (see Millsap, 2011). Violations of measurement invariance are designated as bias if they introduce unwanted distortions in the inferences made in the measurement process (this need not be the case in all settings; e.g., see Borsboom, 2006).

In the case of DIF or lack of measurement invariance, observed differences between groups do not necessarily reflect differences on the latent variable. In this case, it is likely that unintended latent variables have contributed to the measurement process, which may implicate validity problems (Messick, 1989). For instance, the "Information" subtest of the WAIS is consistently found to be biased in favour of males (e.g., Dolan et al., 2006; Jensen & Reynolds, 1983; Van der Sluis, Posthuma, et al., 2006). Such bias could possibly be due to the overrepresentation of questions that require solving physics problems. If so, the average male advantage on this subtest is not due to a higher verbal ability – the latent variable that the information subtest is purported to measure – but due to more knowledge about physics (since, on average, males tend to favour courses like physics more often than females do in secondary school). In addition to unintended latent variables that are measured by a test or item, bias could be introduced by differences in research settings that exist across groups. For instance, Wicherts, Dolan, and Hessen (2005) showed that bias can be introduced by altering test instructions in different groups. Specifically, in a sample of female students, an arithmetic test was preluded by stating that females do less well on arithmetic tests as compared to males, while in another sample of female students this statement was omitted. Wicherts et al. found that the different instruction lowered the average score of the former group, indicating that bias was introduced in the former group.

The above definition of test bias has not been uncontroversial in the literature. Where measurement invariance denotes equality of measurement models across samples, an alternative definition given by Cleary (1968) states that a test is biased when the regression of an external criterion (e.g., grade point average) on the test score (e.g., an IQ score) diverges across groups. This definition has been used – or is being used – in influential guides including the Standards for Educational and Psychological Testing (see Borsboom, Romeijn, & Wicherts, 2008). In addition, predictive invariance has been used as operationalization of test bias in a number of (empirical) studies (e.g., Aguinis & Smith, 2007; Evers, Te Nijenhuis, & Van der Flier, 2005; Gamliel & Cahan, 2007; Hunter & Schmidt, 2000; Neisser et al., 1996; Rushton & Jensen, 2005; Sackett, Borneman, & Connely, 2008; Sackett, Schmitt, Ellington, & Kabin, 2001). However, as argued in multiple sources (Borsboom et al., 2008; Millsap, 1997, 1998, 2008; Wicherts & Millsap, 2009), predictive invariance does not necessarily imply the absence of test bias. Specifically, when predictive invariance holds, severe bias can be present (e.g., Wicherts & Millsap, 2009). Borsboom et al. (2008) concluded that measurement invariance should be preferred over predictive invariance to test for item or test bias because (a) predictive invariance implies a violation of bias as defined by Mellenbergh (1989), which is unacceptable, whereas measurement invariance does not violate this definition; (b) tests on predictive invariance are ambiguous as they depend on the choices concerning the criterion variables; (c) predictive invariance can lead to opposite results when the causal direction between the criterion and the test scores are reversed (i.e., when the test is used as criterion and the criterion is used as test). In this paper, we therefore espouse the definition of bias in terms of lack of measurement invariance or – similarly – the presence of DIF.

Statistical procedures to test for the presence of measurement invariance are well developed (see Millsap, 2011, for an overview). Traditionally, tests on measurement bias originate in factor analysis (Meredith, 1964; Thomson & Lederman, 1939; Thurstone, 1947). The linear factor model is a measurement model that links a continuously distributed latent variable to a set of continuous observed variables. In psychology, the linear factor model is arguably the most widely used method to test for item bias in case of power tests like intelligence and ability tests. For power tests, data are generally dichotomous (scored 1: correct and 0: incorrect). Therefore, the linear factor model is not strictly suitable for these data. Researchers have, however, focused on the analysis of summed item scores, or item parcels, to make the data more suitable for factor analysis. Reasons for using factor analysis lie primarily in the large number of subtests and items that are featured in typical power tests, which make item-level tests more difficult unless samples are very large. Consider for instance the WAIS. The WAIS-III (Wechsler, 1997) contains 14 subtests, each of which consists of 40 to 60 items. An item-level measurement model like the 2PL model would require a second-order structure with 14 first-order latent variables and 4 second-order latent variables. Fitting such a model and comparing its parameters across groups is computationally infeasible. By taking sum scores for each subtest, and using the linear factor model for the analysis, the model simplifies to a linear model with only 4 first-order latent variables, which is numerically less demanding and can be fitted using widely available software. Thus, there may be a reasonable justification for using factor models in such cases, even though one knows that they cannot strictly be correct.

Although the procedure of taking summed item scores or item parcels is valuable from a practical point of view, several problems arise in applications of the linear factor model to summed item scores when testing for measurement invariance. In the present paper, we analyse these problems and suggest ways to address them. Specifically, we discuss problems associated with (a) nonlinearity of the latent variable to subtest relation, (b) suboptimality of the sum score as a proxy for the latent variable underlying the item scores, (c) non-normality of the subtest score, and (d) differences in the nature of the latent variable as it applies to the item level, as compared to the latent variable that applies to the subtest level. We provide guidelines to evaluate whether factor analysis can be applied safely and whether alternative methods should be considered, such as methods based on item response theory (IRT, e.g., the 2PL model).

An outline of this paper is as follows: We first introduce the linear factor model and discuss how a typical test on measurement invariance is executed. Next, we discuss problems with multi-group factor analyses of total scores. We then illustrate our main points on a dataset that pertains to performal intelligence. We end with some general recommendations with respect to tests for measurement invariance in power tests.

Linear factor analysis and measurement invariance

Linear factor analysis is a statistical method to investigate the hypothesized factor structure for a set of observed variables. In factor analysis, the observed data are linearly regressed on a set of latent variables through a set of factor loadings (i.e., the regression weights), intercepts, and residuals. In doing so, the covariance matrix of the data is modelled in terms of the factor loadings, the residual variances, and the (co)variances of the latent variables. In addition, the mean vector of the observed data can be modelled in terms of the factor loadings, the intercepts and – in multi-group applications – the means of the latent variables.[1] Note that in confirmatory factor analysis – as discussed in this paper – the structure of the factor loadings is typically assumed to be given. That is, it is assumed that we have prior information that can be used to determine which items load on (i.e., are regressed on) which of the common factors. To investigate whether the hypothesized factor model gives an adequate description of the data, various model fit indices can be consulted (see, for an overview, e.g., Schermelleh-Engel, Moosbrugger, & Müller, 2003).

Measurement invariance involves the sequential application of increasingly restrictive factor models to the observed data of multiple groups (Meredith, 1993; see, e.g., Horn & McArdle, 1992; Widaman & Reise, 1997). To enable application of these models, a multivariate normal distribution is assumed for the data (Meredith, 1993), implying a normal distribution for all subtests. The models that subsequently are fitted to the data are described next.

The first step, *configural invariance*, involves the question whether the same factor structure holds within each group under investigation. To this end, the hypothesized factor structure is fitted to the data of all groups and goodness of fit is established. Note that all parameters of the factor model are allowed to vary between groups. The only restriction in place is that the factor loading configuration is equal across groups. The next step, *metric invariance*, involves the question whether the factor loadings are invariant across groups. To this end, factor loadings are constrained to be equal across groups, and the deterioration of model fit is established. When measurement invariance holds, model fit should not deteriorate significantly and goodness-of-fit measures (like the root mean square error of approximation [RMSEA] and Akaike's information criterion [AIC], which take into account model parsimony) should indicate that the model does not fit worse than the preceding model.

Next, *equal residual variances* are specified between the groups (Lubke & Dolan, 2003). Again, when measurement invariance holds, this model should be favoured by the model fit indices. The final step is to test for *strict measurement invariance* (Meredith, 1993). In this model, the intercepts are equated across groups, and the factor means are freed in all groups but an arbitrary reference group, allowing for factor mean differences across groups (Sörbom, 1974). To establish measurement invariance, one needs to justify the conclusion that the strict factorial invariance model is the best fitting model among all models considered, in terms of the model fit criteria. The strict factorial invariance model is the only factor model among those considered above that guarantees measurement invariance (Meredith, 1993). All of the other models considered are consistent with violations of measurement variance and hence do not guarantee accurate inferences from observed differences between groups to latent differences.

In the ideal case, each model fits better than the preceding model in terms of the fit indices like the RMSEA, or the model fit does not deteriorate significantly, in terms of a likelihood ratio test. In such cases, the strict measurement invariance model may be preferred over the less parsimonious models (Dolan, 2000). In the case that a model fits worse than the preceding model, modification indices could be inspected, which could shed a light on the causes of misfit. If misfit is limited to a few parameters, these could be freed across groups, and valid comparisons may still be made on the basis of the subset of items or subtests that do satisfy measurement invariance. In case of too many parameters that violate invariance, measurement invariance should be rejected. Importantly, this does not disqualify the use of tests for all purposes; for instance, one could still legitimately compare the sign of the correlation between factors across groups as long as the relation between latent and observed variables is monotonic in both groups. However, inferences to latent mean differences from observed mean differences are typically jeopardized in the presence of bias, as in the use of tests for selection purposes that involve members of different groups.

Possible confounds when testing for bias on summed item scores

The most important measurement instruments in psychology are power tests, like intelligence and ability tests, and self-report questionnaires, like mood and personality questionnaires. Items of a power test typically result in dichotomous item responses (correct vs. incorrect). As a result, naturally appropriate measurement models for data gathered with power tests are IRT models like the Rasch model (Rasch, 1960) or the 2PL model (Birnbaum, 1968). In IRT models, however, the relation between the observed item scores and the latent variable is modelled by an S-shaped curve (generally a logistic function or a normal ogive function). This function is called the item characteristic curve (ICC) and, in the case of the Birnbaum (1968) model, is characterized by two parameters: item discrimination (the slope of the curve) and item difficulty (the location of the mid-point of the curve on the latent variable continuum). In case of the Rasch model, all item discriminations are assumed to be equal.

Thus, here we advocate the use of IRT models like the multi-group Rasch model and the multi-group 2PL model to test for measurement invariance. We note, however, that alternative methods are available that are appropriate for discrete item-level data but that do not depend on IRT. These methods include, for instance, the Mantel-Haenszel approach (MH; Mantel & Haenszel, 1959; see, for related approaches, Dorans & Kulick, 1986; Shealy & Stout, 1993) and the logistic regression approach (Swaminathan & Rogers, 1990). A more elaborate overview can be found elsewhere (Millsap, 2011; Osterlind & Everson, 2009; Penfield & Camilli, 2007). Most of the methods, like the MH and the logistic regression approach, test for an association between group membership and item response using the sum score to correct for differences on the underlying construct. As the sum score plays a key role in these procedures, most of these alternative methods are vulnerable to the same criticism as below. On the contrary, no parametric assumptions need to be imposed (e.g., latent variable distributions and local independence).

Thus, as discussed above, in practice, researchers rely heavily on the sum score in testing for measurement invariance. That is, all items of the same subtest are summed and analysed as continuous variables in the linear factor model. In such cases, the investigator purposefully misspecifies the measurement model, which may lead to various problems.

Nonlinearity of the latent variable to subtest relation

An important problem is pointed out by Tucker-Drob (2009) and illustrated in Figure 1. Figure 1 shows the relationship between the latent variable and the total score on 20, 40, and 60 items that follow a Rasch model. Three scenarios are considered: (a) the difficulties

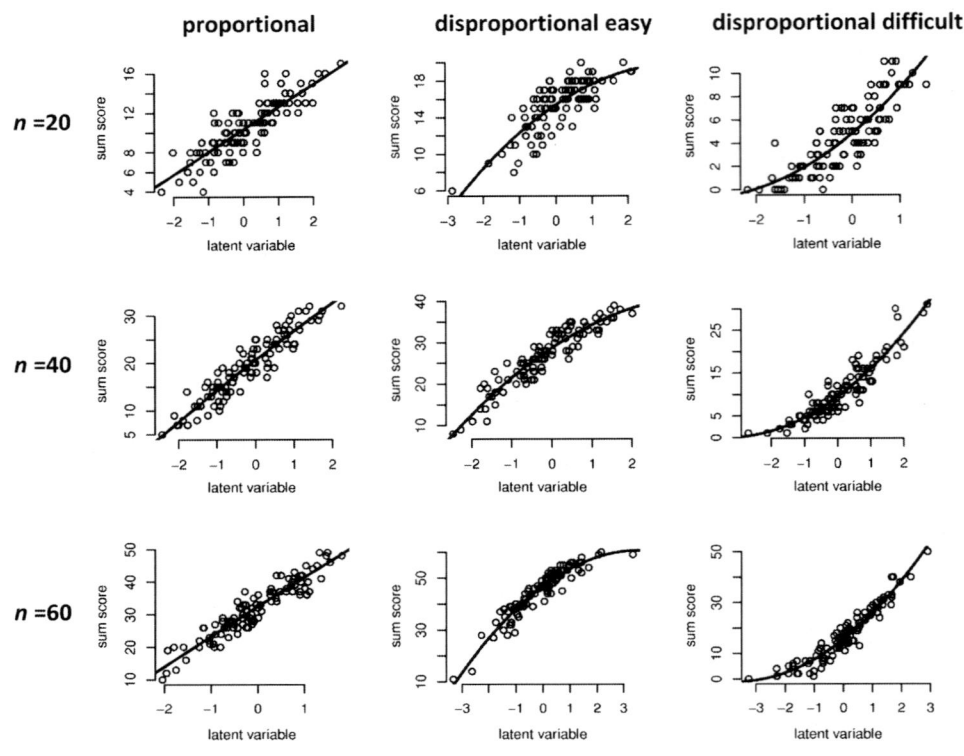

Figure 1. Relation between the summed item scores and the latent variable when the items follow a Rasch model where the item difficulties are (a) proportionally varied, (b) have a disproportional number of difficult items, and (c) have a disproportional number of easy items. Cases are depicted for 20, 40, and 60 items.

of the items are proportionally varied (equal amount of difficult and easy items); (b) there are a disproportional number of difficult items; and (c) there are a disproportional number of easy items. As can be seen, in the first scenario the function approximates a linear function reasonably well (although strict linearity is not attainable due to the fact that the total score is bounded from below and from above). For the second and third scenarios, however, the relation between the sum score and the latent variable becomes strongly nonlinear due to a floor and a ceiling effect, respectively. Such nonlinearity is problematic for the application of factor analysis to testing measurement invariance. For instance, Bauer (2005) showed analytically that, when an invariant nonlinear relation between the observed and latent variables underlies the data, but the linear factor model is applied, tests on MI will be distorted. As a result, the factor loadings and intercepts will diverge across groups; see Bauer (2005) for a detailed explanation of the expected parameter values in the groups under nonlinearity.

An important implication of Figure 1 and the results by Bauer (2005) is that, in the analysis of total scores, spurious nonlinearity can arise due to over- or underrepresentation of difficult and easy items, and that this nonlinearity can result in wrongfully rejecting measurement invariance. In very large samples, measurement invariance would in fact be expected to be generally violated: Because the relation between total score and latent variable cannot be strictly linear as a matter of principle, rejecting measurement invariance is guaranteed as the sample size approaches infinity. Severe violations of linearity also occur when dichotomous items have different discrimination parameters, as can be seen

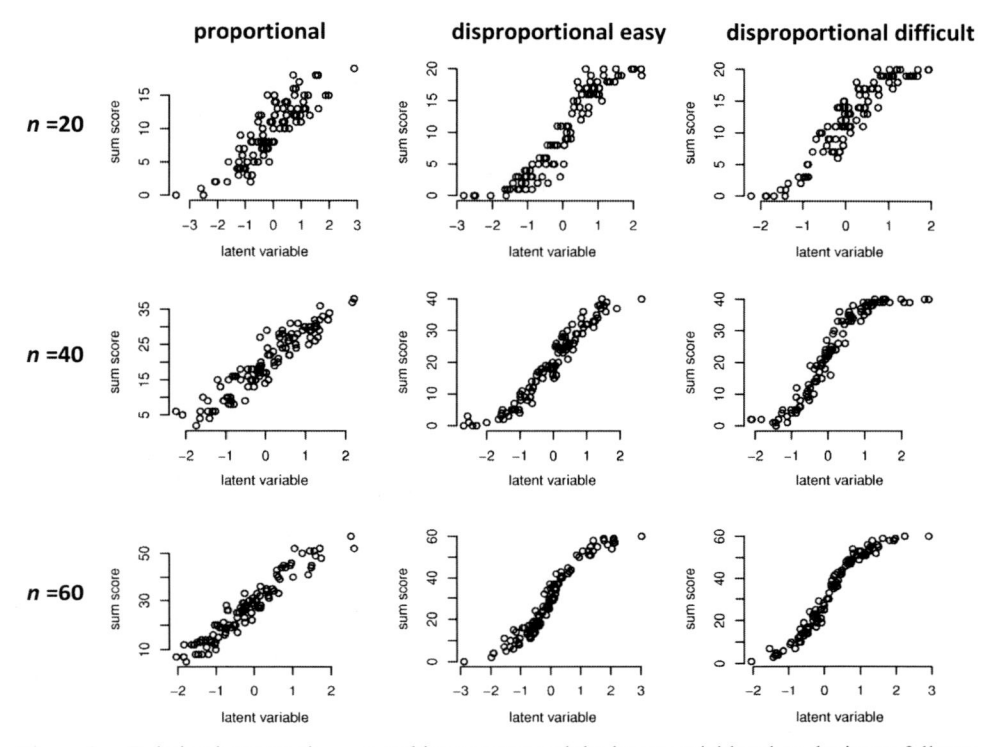

Figure 2.   Relation between the summed item scores and the latent variable when the items follow a two-parameter logistic model where the item discriminations (a) do not differ between items, (b) differ mildly, and (c) differ substantially across items. Cases are depicted for 20, 40, and 60 items.

in Figure 2. In that case, the relation between the latent variable and the summed item scores has an S shape. Thus, nonlinearity can arise when a sample is characterized by restriction of range, for example, in case of the application of an intelligence test to a sample of highly educated subjects. In Figure 2, subjects will be mainly positioned on the upper end of the latent variable, which will typically result in stronger nonlinearity.

The total score as a proxy for the latent variable

In executing measurement invariance tests at the total score level, one basically assumes that the relevant total score is a good proxy for a first-order latent variable that is measured directly by the items of a subtest. Thus, when one enters a total score into a factor analysis routine, one typically assumes that the items themselves are unidimensional. To the extent that this is not the case, violations of measurement invariance at the subtest level are very hard to interpret, because they may arise either as a result of item bias or because of erroneous assumptions regarding the dimensionality of the item scores.

Ideally, one would in fact have a Rasch model that holds at the item level, because in this case the unweighted total score is a sufficient statistic for the latent variable. This means that, conditional on the total score, the item scores are independent of the latent variable, so that the total score contains all relevant information with regard to the latent variable distribution (Andersen, 1973). However, when the Rasch model is violated, summing item scores will discard some information about the discriminatory ability of the items. A weighted sum score, where the item scores are weighted by their discriminatory power, may in this case provide a better proxy, as this weighted score would be a sufficient statistic for the latent variable if the weights were known (see e.g., Verhelst & Glas, 1995). However, discriminatory power of the items, which regulates their weights in computing the weighted score, is a parameter that needs to be estimated. In addition, a weighted total score is still suboptimal, as estimated discrimination is only an approximation to the true discriminatory power of an item.

A practical solution is not to estimate weights at all, but instead rely on the robustness of the total score, which is guaranteed to be monotonically related to the latent variable provided all the individual items are (i.e., has monotone likelihood ratio; see Grayson, 1988). However, although these results guarantee certain regularity properties of comparisons of individuals that belong to the same population (specifically, the expected latent variable score is strictly higher for people with higher total scores), they do not guarantee that the ICCs are equal across groups and hence do not guarantee measurement invariance – especially not when a misspecified factor model is fitted. A related issue in using the total score is that a lack of measurement invariance on the item level, that is, DIF, is not necessarily expressed on subtest level. It is possible that DIF cancels out at the level of the total score (Borsboom, 2005), or that the power to detect DIF on the subtest level is small. Thus, if DIF is present at item level, it need not be present at the subtest level.

The exact relation between measurement invariance at the item level and at the subtest level is therefore not as simple as one may think. Even if a unidimensional IRT model holds across groups, this does not guarantee that the total score will have an invariant relation to the latent variable, particularly if the groups differ in the location or variance of the latent distribution. Further research into this issue would be useful; however, it would seem safe to say that a minimum requirement for testing measurement invariance using subtest scores is evidence that the items of the relevant subtests are themselves unidimensional. If this is not the case, then all bets are off with respect to measurement invariance tests through applications of the linear factor model.

Non-normality of the subtest scores

In essence, summed dichotomous item scores are count data. Count data are seldom characterized by a normal distribution, because the data are bounded from above and from below. More appropriate distributions for count data include the Poisson distribution or the lognormal distribution. In single-group applications, it is known that non-normality in the data causes biased parameter estimates and goodness-of-fit measures of the factor models (Curran, West, & Finch, 1996).

In case of testing for measurement invariance, this could be problematic, especially when departures from normality differ between the groups under investigation. For instance, an invariant measurement model may underlie the data of two groups, but due to a mean difference on the latent variable, the total score distribution could be less normal in the high-scoring group as compared to the low-scoring group. This is illustrated in Figure 3, where total scores are depicted for a reference group (Group 1) and an advantaged group (Group 2) which features a higher location of the latent variable distribution. Note again, that in this case, measurement invariance holds across the groups.

As can be seen, the shape of the distributions differs across the groups, which is due to the fact that the sum score is bounded between zero and the number of items. Therefore, the advantage of Group 2 over Group 1 does not simply result in a shift of the distribution across the x-axis, but instead results in a distribution of a different shape. This may

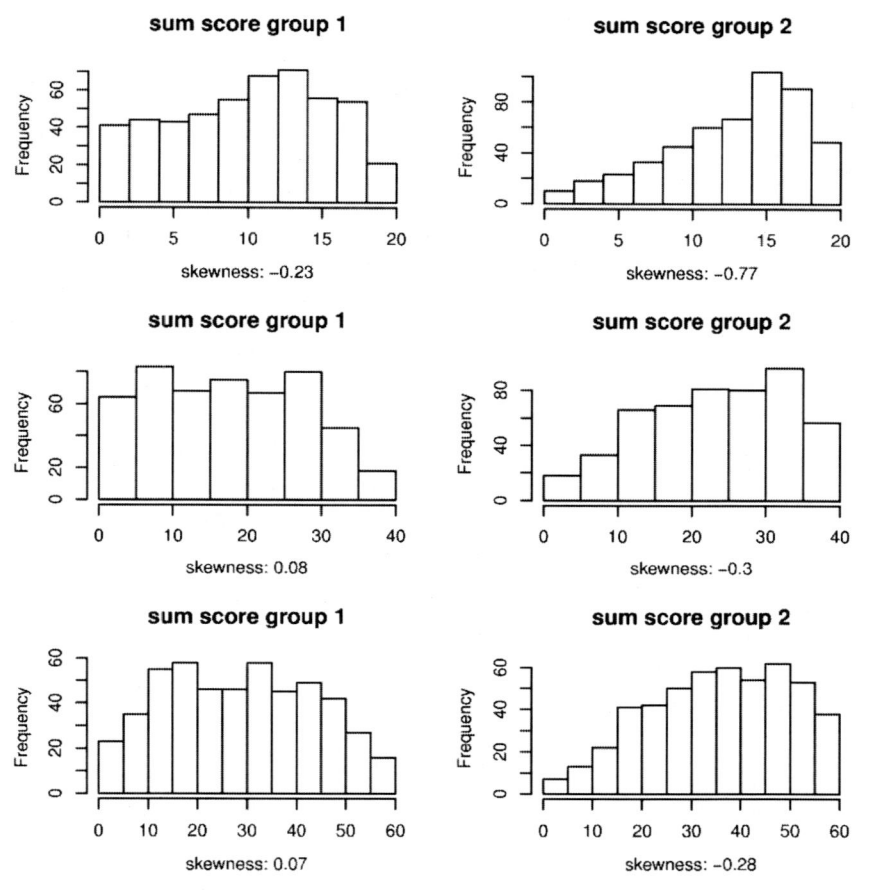

Figure 3.   Summed item score distribution in two groups for 20, 40, and 60 items, where Group 2 has mean advantage on the latent variable as compared to Group 1.

distort the fit of the linear factor model (as pointed out by Curran et al., 1996) to a different extent in both groups, resulting in biased results.

Different nature of the latent variables

When testing for measurement invariance in the linear factor model, multiple subtest scores are needed, as a single subtest cannot be tested for bias. As a consequence, multiple subtests are used to measure the same (more general) second-order construct. For instance, if we have an IQ test battery, and we are interested in testing for measurement invariance for the Information subtest of the WAIS, we also need to consider other subtests of the same domain, for example, Vocabulary and Comprehension. As a result, we test the subtest Information for bias with respect to a general latent variable like verbal intelligence. If we had conducted the analysis on item level, that is, if we had submitted the item scores of the Information subtest to a DIF analysis, we would have tested this subtest for bias with respect to the latent variable "general knowledge".

Many researchers would say that these tests answer somewhat different questions, as "general knowledge" is part of, but certainly not equal to, "verbal intelligence". This is also illustrated in Figure 4. The circles represent subscales that consist of items. Overlap between circles denotes that the respective subtest scores share variance. Now, consider the subscale that is represented by the upper left circle. If we test this subtest for bias at the item level, we investigate whether we can fairly compare subjects on the basis of the striped area, that is, the part that represents the variance of only one of the subtests. If we test for bias at the subtest level, however, we need to take into account the other three subtests, and we are actually investigating whether we can compare subjects on the basis of the black area, that is, the variance that is common to all subtests.

Thus, unless the items are unidimensional across all subtests (i.e., a unidimensional model would fit the responses to all items analysed jointly), measurement invariance with respect to the item level is not the same as measurement invariance at the subtest level: The latent variable that is conditioned on in the definition of measurement invariance (Meredith, 1993) is not identical in both cases. This is consistent with the fact that measurement invariance is a property of test scores rather than of tests; however, in many cases researchers use the invariance properties of subtest scores to say something about the fairness of the test in general. Since any test is essentially a collection of items, it is not entirely clear to what extent such generalizations should be considered to be supported.

Illustration

To illustrate the above points, we analysed both item-level data and subtest-level data of four performal subtests of the Dutch version of the *Intelligenz Struktur Test* (IST; Amthauer,

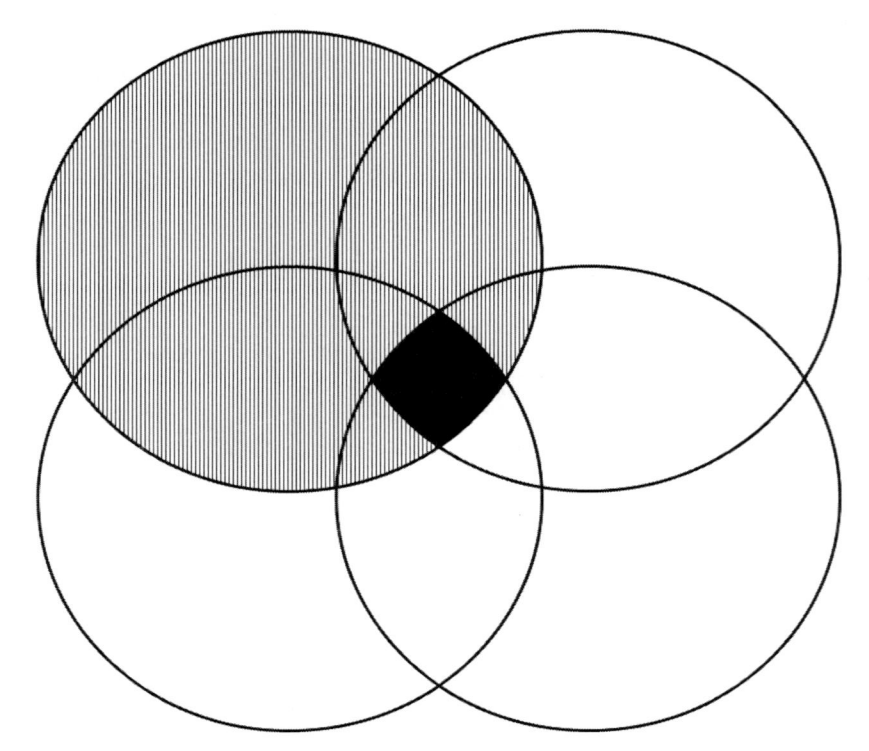

Figure 4.   Schematic representation of the nature of the latent variables in an item analysis and in a subtest analysis. Circles represent variance in subtests; overlap represents a correlation between subtests.

Table 1. Correlations for the four subtests for males and females (males below diagonal).

	FC	DR	AR	MR
FC	1.00	0.33	0.06	0.39
DR	0.47	1.00	0.08	0.36
AR	0.18	0.13	1.00	0.10
MR	0.40	0.39	0.14	1.00

Brocke, Liepmann, & Beauducel, 2001). These subtests concern: Figure Completion (FC), Dice Rotation (DR), Arithmetic Reasoning (AR), and Matrix Reasoning (MR), consisting of 20 items each (scored correct: 1, incorrect: 0), and were completed by 1,473 psychology freshman for course credit (428 males; 1,045 females). For the subtest AR, we omitted the first two items, as none of the subjects answered these items incorrectly. See Table 1 for the correlations among the subtest scores and Table 2 for the means and standard deviations.

On these data, we first conducted a nonlinear factor analyses to assess whether we could assume a linear measurement model for the sum scores. Next, we tested measurement invariance with respect to gender in the linear factor model, using the summed item scores for each subtests. We also tested for predictive invariance. Next, we tested the items of each subtest on measurement invariance in a two-parameter logistic item response model. To asses model fit, we relied on the RMSEA, comparative fit index (CFI), and AIC. In addition, we used a likelihood ratio test (LRT) to test restrictions across models on significance. For all tests, we will use a nominal level of significance of 0.01.

Analyses at the subtest level: testing measurement invariance

To first investigate nonlinearity, we tested whether the factor-to-subtest relationship was nonlinear. To this end, we fitted a nonlinear single-factor model to the subtest data. Results are represented in Table 3. As can be judged from the standard errors of the parameter estimates, in the male group, subtest FC is characterized by nonlinear factor loadings ($p = .002$). However, in the female group, all factor loadings are linear.

Next, we started the actual measurement analyses. Results are represented in Table 4. First, we fitted a single-factor model to the data in both groups. This baseline model, denoted configural invariance (Model 1), in which the parameters are free to vary across groups, fitted well, $\chi^2(4) = 2.09$, $p = 0.72$, RMSEA = 0.00. Next, we introduced equality constraints for the factor loadings, denoted metric invariance (Model 2). This did not affect the model fit significantly, as judged by the likelihood ratio test (LRT; $p = 0.09$). In addition, the RMSEA and CFI showed good model fit. AIC showed a minor deterioration, but the difference was so small that we considered it neglectable. We conclude that metric invariance is tenable.

Table 2. Means and standard deviations of the four subtest scores for males and females.

		FC	DR	AR	MR
Males	Mean	11.91	11.47	9.70	11.12
	SD	3.63	4.64	6.72	3.23
Females	Mean	11.43	10.08	7.34	11.72
	SD	3.42	4.22	5.91	2.97

Table 3.   Results of nonlinear factor analysis of subtest-level data.

Parameter(s)	subtest	Males	Females
linear loadings	FC	1.000	1.000
	DR	1.136 (0.181)	1.171 (0.105)
	AR	0.566 (0.163)	0.390 (0.138)
	MR	0.701 (0.115)	1.002 (0.142)
nonlinear loadings	FC	−0.052 (0.018)	−0.040 (0.022)
	DR	−0.009 (0.030)	0.038 (0.021)
	AR	−0.060 (0.056)	−0.049 (0.068)
	MR	−0.049 (0.023)	−0.047 (0.024)
intercepts	FC	12.265 (0.244)	11.586 (0.146)
	DR	11.537 (0.353)	9.931 (0.170)
	AR	10.111 (0.524)	7.527 (0.314)
	MR	11.460 (0.225)	11.906 (0.124)
residual variance	FC	6.069 (1.154)	7.725 (0.635)
	DR	12.553 (1.507)	12.416 (0.708)
	AR	42.642 (2.006)	34.260 (0.844)
	MR	6.874 (0.669)	4.788 (0.616)
Factor variance		6.907 (1.327)	3.920 (0.661)

Note: Standard errors are in brackets.

We proceeded by restricting the residual variance to be equal across groups (Model 3a). The likelihood ratio test indicated that the restrictions were tenable ($p = 0.02$), however, the RMSEA showed a drop in model fit as it nearly doubled. We therefore consulted the modification indices. These indicated that for subtest AR, the restriction was possibly too stringent. We therefore freed this parameter (Model 3b). This resulted in an improvement in model fit: The RMSEA decreased to a level comparable with that of Model 2, and the likelihood ratio showed no significant difference as compared to Model 2 ($p = 0.37$). In addition, AIC indicated that Model 3b was the best fitting as compared to the previous models. Inspection of the results indicated that, in the male sample, subtest AR was associated with a residual variance of 43.18, and in the female sample this variance equalled 34.21. We therefore concluded that equal residuals were tenable for all subtests but AR, which had a significantly larger residual in the male sample.

In the next step, we tested for strict factorial invariance (Model 4a). This model showed a significant deterioration in model fit, as indicated by the likelihood ratio ($p < .001$), the CFI, AIC, and RMSEA. We consulted the modification indices to diagnose the source of the misfit. Subtest MR was associated with the largest modification index. However,

Table 4.   Testing for measurement invariance: model fit statistics for the subtest-level analysis.

		χ^2	df	LRT models	$\chi^2(df)$	RMSEA	CFI	AIC
1	Configural Invariance	2.09	4	–	–	0.000	1.00	32779.44
2	Metric Invariance	8.56	7	2 vs 1	6.47 (3)	0.017	1.00	32779.91
3a	Equal residual variances	20.02	11	3a vs 2	11.46 (4)	0.033	0.99	32783.77
3b	– variance AR free	11.70	10	3b vs 2	3.14 (3)	0.015	1.00	32777.05
4a	Strict MI	111.18	13	4a vs 3b	99.48 (3)	0.101	0.835	32870.53
4b	– intercept MR freed	47.48	12	4b vs 3b	35.78 (2)	0.063	0.94	32808.83
4c	– intercept AR freed	20.42	11	4c vs 3b	8.72 (1)	0.034	0.98	32783.77

freeing the relevant intercept (Model 4b) did not improve model fit sufficiently, that is, likelihood ratio was still significant as compared to Model 3b ($p < 0.001$), and the AIC, RMSEA, and CFI were too high as compared to the previous models. The intercept of MR was estimated to be 11.12 in the male sample and 12.53 in the female sample. After consulting the modification indices, we freed the intercept of subtest AR (Model 4c). Again, model fit did not improve sufficiently, that is, the likelihood ratio was still significant as compared to Model 3b ($p = 0.003$), and AIC, RMSEA, and CFI were still worse as compared to Models 1, 2, and 3b. The intercept of AR was estimated to be 9.70 in the male sample and 7.71 in the female sample. Despite the fact that model fit was still insufficient, we could not free more intercepts (as with four subtests the minimal number of intercepts required for strict factorial invariance equals two. Freeing an additional intercept causes the mean model to be saturated, that is, in this case the number of parameters equals the number of observed means).

Therefore, the general conclusion of these analyses is that strict factorial invariance is not tenable. This means that we cannot assume measurement invariance for these subtests. At least subtest MR and AR are associated with intercept differences, with a higher intercept for the males for subtest AR, and a larger intercept for females on the MR subtest. In addition, subtest AR is associated with a residual variance that differs across males and females, with the larger variance in the male sample. Finally, it is likely that the intercepts of FC and/or DR also differed between the samples, but we were not able to test for this due to the presence of already two intercept differences.

Analyses at the subtest level: testing predictive invariance

To illustrate that predictive invariance does not necessarily imply the absence of test bias, which is not always fully appreciated in the literature on fairness, we tested the four subtests for predictive invariance. To do so, we considered the scores of the subjects on a memory subtest of the IST. This subtest (ME) consisted of 33 items measuring the ability to memorize pictures, numbers, and words. We took this subtest and used it as a criterion in the test on predictive invariance. For each subtest, an ordinary least squares regression model was fitted with the memory test, ME, as dependent variable, and the corresponding subtest as independent variable. Also included in each regression model was the effect of gender and the interaction effect between gender and the subtest score.

For predictive invariance to hold, the same regression model should hold in both groups, that is, the effect of gender should be insignificant (implying equal intercepts), and the interaction effect should be insignificant (implying equal factor loadings). All subtest variables were standardized in the total sample to prevent spurious interactions. Results are represented in Table 5. As can be seen, predictive invariance held for FC and MR, as both the interaction effect and the gender effect were non-significant. For DR

Table 5. Tests on Predictive Invariance for each subtest.

	Intercept	Main effect	Gender	Interaction
FC	−0.10 (0.05)	**0.33 (0.04)**	0.14 (0.06)	−0.07 (0.05)
DR	**−0.14 (0.05)**	**0.30 (0.04)**	**0.18 (0.06)**	−0.12 (0.05)
AR	−0.12 (0.05)	**0.18 (0.04)**	**0.16 (0.06)**	−0.03 (0.05)
MR	−0.02 (0.05)	**0.38 (0.04)**	0.03 (0.05)	−0.06 (0.05)

Note: Effects that significant at $\alpha = 0.01$ are in bold face.

and AR, predictive invariance did not hold, as intercepts differed significantly between males and females, with the higher intercept in the female group for both subtests.

Analysis at the item level

For the analysis at the item level, we used the R-package "difR" (Magis, Béland, Tuerlinckx, & De Boeck, 2010). Specifically, within this package, we used the Raju method (Raju, 1988, 1990), which involves a test on the signed area between the item characteristic functions in two groups. If this area departs significantly from 0, measurement invariance does not hold for that item, that is, the item is said to show DIF.

Results are represented in Table 6. As evident from the table, subtest FC contains 6 items with a p value smaller than 0.01, and subtest DR contains 1 significant item. For AR, none of the p values exceeds the nominal level of significance, and for subtest MR 10 items are significant according to the Raju method. As we did multiple testing, conclusions should be drawn with care as the number of false positives increases when a large number of statistical tests are conducted. However, a clear pattern is visible in Table 6, that is, the items from subtest DR and AR are largely unbiased, while some items of FC are associated with DIF. In addition, subtest MR shows a considerable extent of DIF.

Comparison of the item-level and subtest-level analyses

In Table 7, we provide an overview concerning the subtest analyses on measurement invariance, the item-level analysis on DIF, and the analysis on predictive invariance.

Table 6. Testing for measurement invariance: model fit statistics for the item-level analysis.

item no.	FC		DR		AR		MR	
	χ_1^2	p	χ_1^2	p	χ_1^2	p	χ_1^2	p
1	9.12	**0.003**	0.31	0.577	–	–	103.84	**<0.001**
2	2.43	0.119	1.08	0.300	–	–	0.08	0.773
3	9.99	**0.002**	1.00	0.320	0.10	0.753	1.61	0.206
4	2.56	0.110	1.82	0.178	3.20	0.074	14.36	**<0.001**
5	7.51	**0.006**	0.17	0.683	5.02	0.025	0.81	0.367
6	6.25	0.012	1.23	0.266	5.06	0.024	9.67	**0.002**
7	5.76	0.017	3.03	0.082	1.04	0.308	1.04	0.309
8	3.13	0.077	1.99	0.159	0.16	0.691	0.88	0.349
9	73.27	**<0.001**	1.10	0.296	0.83	0.363	3.39	0.065
10	6.76	**0.009**	0.09	0.767	3.80	0.052	0.26	0.607
11	1.32	0.252	6.40	0.011	0.11	0.741	9.00	**0.003**
12	4.20	0.040	0.13	0.716	0.77	0.382	35.52	**<0.000**
13	6.81	**0.009**	0.13	0.718	1.85	0.173	57.30	**<0.000**
14	0.25	0.619	1.39	0.240	2.96	0.085	22.66	**<0.000**
15	0.17	0.680	9.73	**0.002**	2.31	0.129	75.52	**<0.000**
16	0.08	0.779	2.96	0.085	3.61	0.057	42.25	**<0.000**
17	0.72	0.396	0.62	0.431	3.20	0.073	21.62	**<0.000**
18	0.30	0.582	2.40	0.120	0.01	0.915	51.70	**<0.000**
19	1.32	0.250	2.53	0.113	0.16	0.686	30.47	**<0.000**
20	0.25	0.618	0.32	0.572	1.93	0.165	0.10	0.757

Note: χ_1^2 is the Raju's method test statistic, p is the corresponding p value. All p values smaller than 0.01 are in bold face.

Table 7. Comparison of the results concerning bias using the different methods.

Subtest	Measurement Invariance	Predictive Invariance	DIF
FC	bias	no bias	bias
DR	no bias	bias	no bias
AR	bias	bias	no bias
MR	bias	no bias	bias

We first note that the results concerning predictive invariance yield a pattern that is exactly opposite to that shown by the measurement invariance analyses. That is, when a subtest is flagged as biased by the item analysis, the predictive invariance analysis labels this item as fair, and vice versa. The predictive invariance analysis and the measurement invariance analysis only agree on the AR subtest. Both methods indicated this subtest as biased. These results illustrate the fact that one cannot assume predictive invariance and measurement invariance to be exchangeable or even mutually supportive (Borsboom et al., 2008).

Next, we compare the results concerning DIF at the item level and measurement invariance at the subtest level. For the MR subtest, the results agree. That is, both analyses indicate that this subtest is biased. Figure 5 represents the item characteristic curves for the male and female samples for the biased items as flagged in Table 6. For almost all items, the females have a slight advantage, as items are mostly easier for this sample (Item 4 is the sole exception). In the subtest analysis, we further found an intercept difference on subtest MR, where the higher intercept was associated with the female sample. This is consistent with the observation that all items are easier in the female sample.

In the DIF and measurement invariance analysis results of subtest AR, an inconsistency occurs. This subtest was flagged by the measurement invariance analyses as being biased (due to a larger residual variance and intercept in the male sample). However, the item analyses revealed no bias in this subtest. Figure 6 suggests an explanation for this inconsistency. In the figure, the subtest scores are plotted for the male and female samples. As can be seen, the distribution of the AR test in the male sample is severely non-normal with a clear ceiling effect, possibly causing a higher residual variance and intercept in this sample.

For the FC and DR subtests, results are difficult to compare. It is unclear from the subtest analysis which of the two is associated with an intercept difference. However, given that the subtest analysis correctly picked up the bias in subtest MR, it is likely that the intercept difference is associated with FC, as the item analysis showed some bias in this subtest.

Thus, comparing the subtest and item analysis revealed some consistency in case of subtest MR, and some large inconsistency in case of the subtest AR. Inconsistencies in the results concerning AR are likely due to violations of normality, clearly illustrating why one should be cautious in analysing total scores when testing for measurement invariance. Finally, results of the predictive invariance analyses were largely inconsistent with results of the other methods. This clearly bolsters earlier critiques concerning the use of predictive invariance to investigate item or test bias.

Discussion

In this paper, we discussed the effects of testing for measurement invariance on summed item scores. We identified four possible problems that may jeopardize inferences concerning measurement invariance: nonlinearity, information loss in the sum score, non-normality,

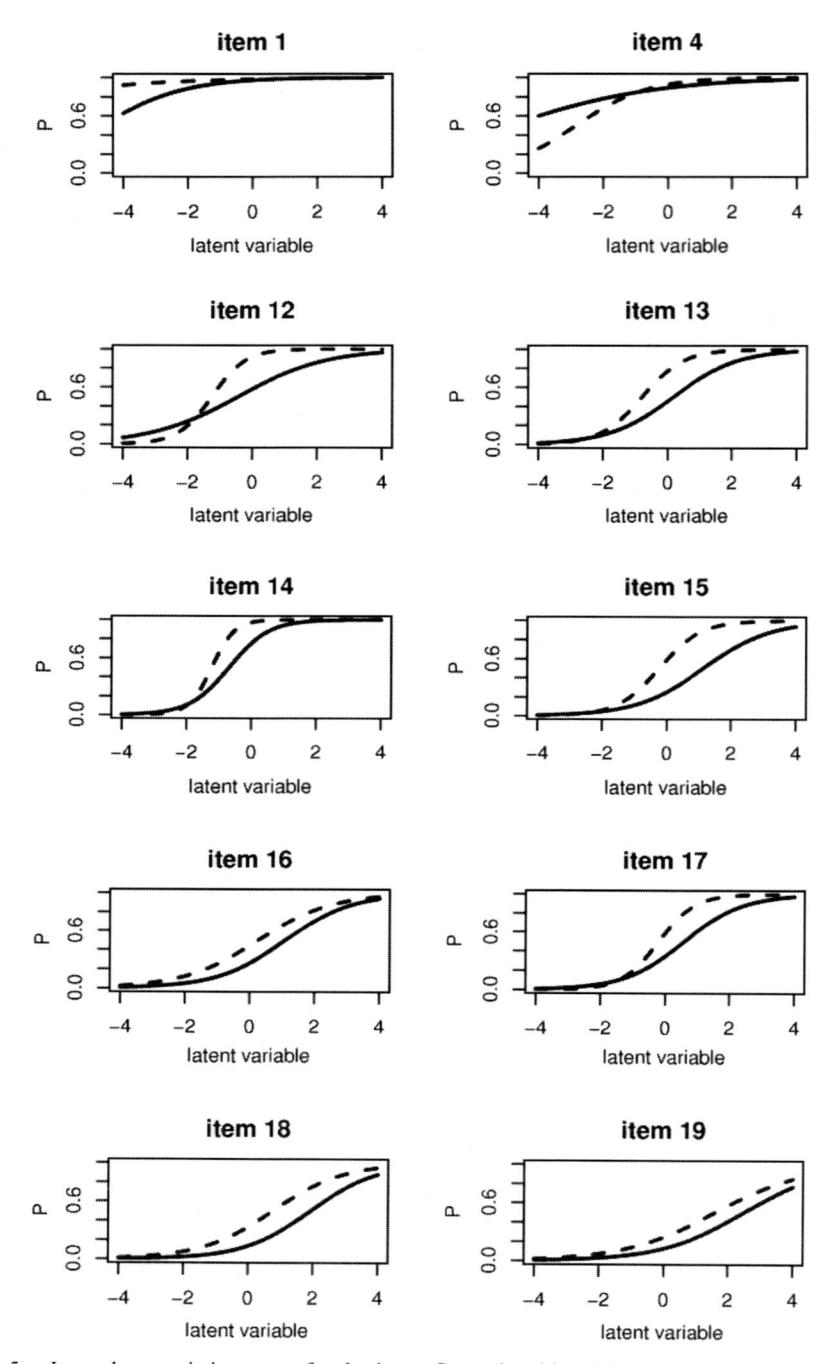

Figure 5. Item characteristic curves for the items flagged as biased in subtest MR for males (solid line) and females (striped line).

and the different nature of the latent variable at item and subtest levels. In a real data set, we showed that inconsistencies in the results for measurement invariance tests were clearly present, and at least some of these inconsistencies could be traced to the problems we

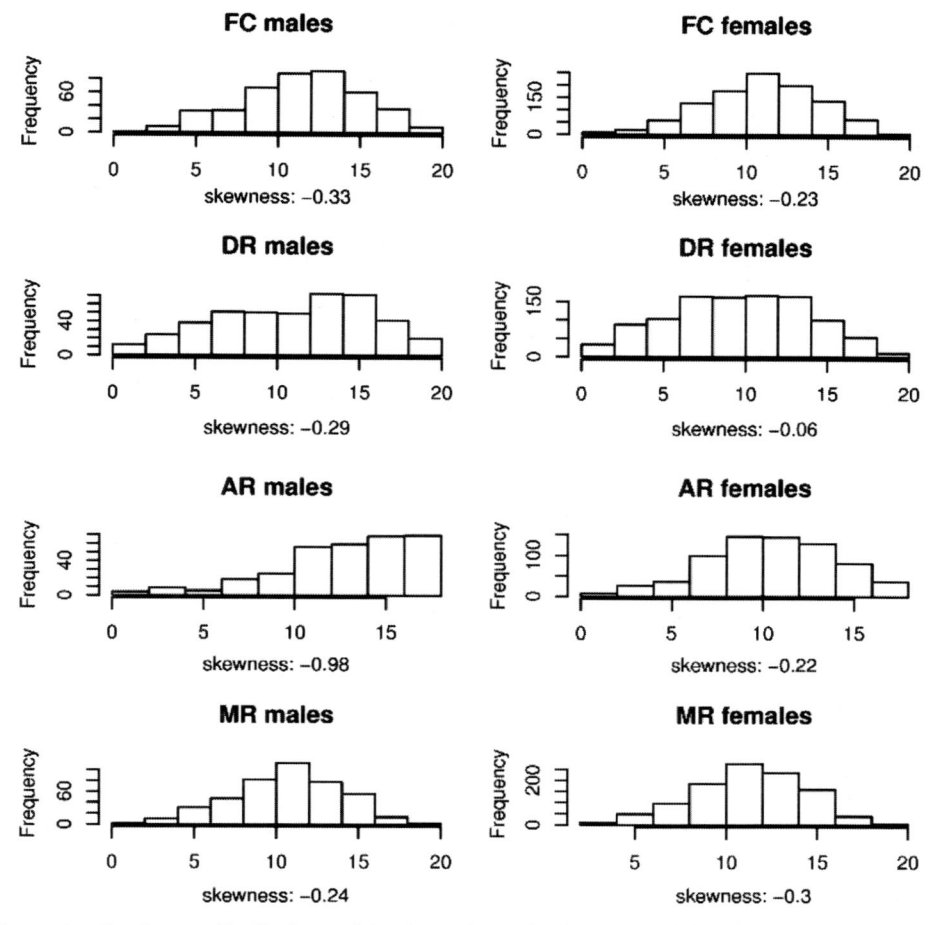

Figure 6.   Total score distributions of the four subtests in the male and female sample.

discussed. This shows that caution is warranted when analysing measurement invariance using linear factor models that are applied to total scores.

While we focused on testing measurement invariance on sum scores, results do generally also hold for Likert scales data. That is, analogous to the sum score (Figures 1 and 2), the problem of nonlinearity can also arise in Likert scales when the answer options of the scale are disproportionately used by the subjects. This problem is also referred to as "poor scaling" of the measurement (Molenaar & Dolan, 2012; Van der Sluis, Dolan, Neale, Boomsma, & Posthuma, 2006). A related problem with Likert scales is "censoring" (Tobin, 1958) in which the majority of a sample obtains the highest or lowest possible score. Censoring will result in non-normality by definition, which in turn may distort tests on measurement invariance as discussed in this paper with respect to the sum score. See also Lubke and Muthén (2004), who demonstrated this in simulated Likert scale data. Finally, as with the sum score, treating Likert scales as continuous variables is also associated with the problem of information loss. When Likert scales are analysed with an appropriate IRT model, for example, the graded response model (Samejima, 1969), so-called category thresholds are taken into account. These parameters model the distances between the answer categories on the latent continuum (which are not necessarily the same in case of ordinal data). By treating the Likert scale data as continuous, however, distances between adjacent categories are assumed to be equal. Again, this can influence tests on measurement invariance (see Lubke & Muthén, 2004).

Importantly, we do not discourage the use of factor analysis in tests on measurement invariance. As we argued in the introduction, in some circumstances such analyses are necessitated by the circumstances. Also, the hypotheses tested in item-level and subtest-level studies of measurement invariance may not precisely align. This means that there may be situations in which one is primarily interested in the invariance properties of subtests, and does not care much for the invariance properties of items. On the other hand, we have rarely come across a serious substantive of methodological motivation that would apply in this kind of situation. It rather seems that many researchers take measurement invariance of items and subtests to be alternative formulations of the same hypothesis (i.e., that the *test* is fair – a hypothesis which, ironically, is tested in neither of the approaches).

The problem of differences in the nature of the latent variable in the item analyses and in the subtest analyses presents an interesting conceptual puzzle. Even a multidimensional IRT model will not necessarily lead to results comparable to the linear factor model, as the factor model strictly focuses on higher order latent variables which differ from the lower order latent variables analysed in IRT. With respect to this problem, it might be concluded that the linear factor model and the IRT model indeed address different hypotheses concerning measurement invariance. Reasoning further along these lines, one could argue that the linear factor model (as applied to summed item scores) indirectly tests a structural hypothesis; namely, that the relation between the lower order latent variable in the IRT analysis and the higher order latent variable in the factor model is the same across groups. So viewed, the hypothesis tested in the linear factor model approach is not a measurement hypothesis at all. On the other hand, there is no a priori reason to limit the definition of an indicator to item responses; total scores are, after all, observable just as well. Reasoning in this direction, therefore, one would suggest that that the linear factor model does in fact test the invariance of a measurement relation, be it a different one from the IRT modelling approach. This is the position we favour.

The problem of how to sum item scores to obtain the best subtest score for the subsequent factor modelling endeavour is open to debate. If we accept the previous conclusion that IRT and factor analysis address different questions, we may in fact take many routes to construct total scores. For instance, we may take factor scores from a Rasch model or a 2PL model and submit these to factor analysis. To profitably do so, however, we would typically want to assume that DIF is absent at the item level to enable the adequate estimation of factor scores in both groups. Then, however, the question arises whether these estimated factor scores are necessarily measurement invariant if they are based on invariant IRT models. This is likely to differ from model to model, and presents an interesting avenue for further research.

As a practical guideline, we have some suggestions following from the present undertaking. First, when analysing summed item scores, tests on nonlinearity should be routinely considered. These tests are currently straightforward in the Mplus program (L. K. Muthén & Muthén, 2007). Alternatively, as suggested by Bauer (2005), plots between all pairs of item scores can be considered. These should all be approximately linear for the linear factor model to be tenable. As we illustrated in our data analyses, when no apparent nonlinearity is found, one can be more confident in using the linear factor model to test for measurement invariance. When significant nonlinearity is found, it could be safer to use either item-level analyses or reside on the nonlinear factor model. A second suggestion is that classical test theory item characteristics could be considered to roughly gauge whether the item difficulties are distributed proportionally across the latent variable scale; if this is not the case, linearity is unlikely. To judge whether the distribution of the item difficulties is proportional, uniform QQ-plots of the proportion correct could be considered or a Kolmorogov-Smirnov test for uniform distributions could be conducted (both can be done in SPSS). In addition, the item-total correlations could be considered to get an idea about the differences in discrimination across items. If these correlations are roughly equal (e.g., as judged by their confidence intervals), this would indicate that item discrimination does not differ importantly across item, and the sum score can be more confidently used in a linear factor analysis (given normality and proportionally distributed item difficulties). However, when item-total correlations differ across items, it is better to reside on item-level analysis. A final recommendation is that the total score is ideally based on a large number of items, which will typically make the assumption of a normal distribution more plausible due to the central limit theorem.

Acknowledgements

The research by Dylan Molenaar and Denny Borsboom was made possible by a Top Talent grant and a VIDI grant from the Netherlands Organization for Scientific Research (NWO). We thank Harry Vorst for the data used in the application.

Note

1. Note that the common factor means are only identified in multi-group models given a sufficient number of invariant intercepts (Sörbom, 1974).

References

Aguinis, H., & Smith, M. E. (2007). Understanding the impact of test validity and bias on selection errors and adverse impact in human resource selection. *Personnel Psychology, 60*, 165–199.

Amthauer, R., Brocke, B., Liepmann, D., & Beauducel, A. (2001). *I-S-T 2000R. Intelligenz-Struktur-Test 2000R*. Göttingen, Germany: Hogrefe.

Andersen, E. B. (1973). Asymptotic properties of conditional maximum-likelihood estimators. *Journal of the Royal Statistical Society, Series B, 32*, 283–301.

Bartholomew, D. J. (1987). *Latent variable models and factor analysis*. London, UK: Griffin.

Bauer, D. J. (2005). The role of nonlinear factor-to-indicator relationships in tests of measurement equivalence. *Psychological Methods, 10*, 305–316.

Birnbaum, A. (1968). Some latent trait models and their use in inferring an examinee's ability. In E. M. Lord & M. R. Novick (Eds.), *Statistical theories of mental test scores* (pp. 397–479). Reading, MA: Addison Wesley.

Borsboom, D. (2005). *Measuring the mind: Conceptual issues in contemporary psychometrics*. Cambridge, UK: Cambridge University Press.

Borsboom, D. (2006). When does measurement invariance matter? *Medical Care, 44*, S176–S181.

Borsboom, D. (2008). Latent variable theory. *Measurement, 6*, 25–53.

Borsboom, D., Romeijn, J. W., & Wicherts, J. M. (2008). Measurement invariance versus selection invariance: Is fair selection possible? *Psychological Methods, 13*, 75–98.

Cleary, T. A. (1968). Test bias: Prediction of grades of Negro and White students in integrated colleges. *Journal of Educational Measurement, 5*, 115–124.

Curran, P. J., West, S. G., & Finch, J. F. (1996). The robustness of test statistics to nonnormality and specification error in confirmatory factor analysis. *Psychological Methods, 1*, 16–29.

Dolan, C. V. (2000). Investigating Spearman's hypothesis by means of multi-group confirmatory factor analysis. *Multivariate Behavioral Research, 35*, 21–50.

Dolan, C. V., Colom, R., Abad, F. J., Wicherts, J. M., Hessen, D. J., & Van der Sluis, S. (2006). Multi-group covariance and mean structure modeling of the relationship between WAIS-III common factors and gender and educational attainment in Spain. *Intelligence, 34*, 193–210.

Dorans, N. J., & Kulick, E. (1986). Demonstrating the utility of the standardization approach to assessing unexpected differential item performance on the Scholastic Aptitude Test. *Journal of Educational Measurement*, *23*, 355–368.

Edwards, J. R., & Bagozzi, R. P. (2000). On the nature and direction of relationships between constructs and measures. *Psychological Methods*, *5*, 155–174.

Ellis, J. L., & Junker, B. W. (1997). Tail-measurability in monotone latent variable models. *Psychometrika*, *62*, 495–523.

Evers, A., Te Nijenhuis, J., & Van der Flier, H. (2005). Ethnic bias and fairness in personnel selection: Evidence and consequences. In A. Evers, N. Anderson, & O. F. Voskuijl (Eds.), *The Blackwell handbook of personnel selection* (pp. 306–328). Oxford, UK: Blackwell.

Gamliel, E., & Cahan, S. (2007). Mind the gap: Between-group differences and fair test use. *International Journal of Selection and Assessment*, *15*, 273–282.

Grayson, D. (1988). Two-group classification in latent trait theory: Scores with monotone likelihood ratio. *Psychometrika*, *53*, 383–392.

Horn, J. L., & McArdle, J. J. (1992). A practical and theoretical guide to measurement invariance in aging research. *Experimental Aging Research*, *18*, 117–144.

Hunter, J. E., & Schmidt, F. L. (2000). Racial and gender bias in ability and achievement tests. *Psychology, Public Policy, and Law*, *6*, 151–158.

Jensen, A. R., & Reynolds, C. R. (1983). Sex differences on the WISC-R. *Personality and Individual Differences*, *4*, 223–226.

Jöreskog, K. G. (1971). Statistical analysis of sets of congeneric tests. *Psychometrika*, *36*, 109–133.

Lubke, G. H., & Dolan, C. V. (2003). Can unequal residual variances across subpopulations mask differences in residual means in the common factor model? *Structural Equation Modeling*, *10*, 175–192.

Lubke, G. H., Muthén, B. O. (2004). Applying multigroup confirmatory factor models for continuous outcomes to Likert scale data complicates meaningful group comparisons. *Structural Equation Modeling*, *11*, 514–534.

Lord, F. M. (1980). *Applications of item response theory to practical testing problems*. Hillsdale, NJ: Lawrence Erlbaum Associates.

Magis, D., Beland, S., Tuerlinckx, F. & De Boeck, P. (2010). A general framework and an R package for the detection of dichotomous differential item functioning. *Behavior Research Methods*, *42*, 847–862.

Mantel, N., & Haenszel, W. (1959). Statistical aspects of the analysis of data from retrospective studies of disease. *Journal of the National Cancer Institute*, *22*, 719–748.

Mellenbergh, G. J. (1989). Item bias and item response theory. *International Journal of Educational Research*, *13*, 127–143.

Mellenbergh, G. J. (1994a). Generalized linear item response theory. *Psychological Bulletin*, *115*, 300–307.

Mellenbergh, G. J. (1994b). A unidimensional latent trait model for continuous item responses. *Multivariate Behavioral Research*, *29*, 223–236.

Meredith, W. (1964). Notes on factorial invariance. *Psychometrika*, *29*, 177–185.

Meredith, W. (1993). Measurement invariance, factor analysis, and factorial invariance. *Psychometrika*, *58*, 525–543.

Messick, S. (1989). Validity. In R. L. Linn (Ed.), *Educational measurement* (pp. 13–103). Washington, DC: American Council on Education and National Council on Measurement in Education.

Millsap, R. E. (1997). Invariance in measurement and prediction: Their relationship in the single-factor case. *Psychological Methods*, *2*, 248–260.

Millsap, R. E. (1998). Group differences in regression intercepts: Implications for factorial invariance. *Multivariate Behavioral Research*, *33*, 403–424.

Millsap, R. E. (2008). Invariance in measurement and prediction revisited. *Psychometrika*, *72*, 461–473.

Millsap, R. E. (2011). *Statistical approaches to measurement invariance*. New York, NY: Routledge.

Molenaar, D., & Dolan, C. V. (2012). Substantively motivated extensions of the traditional latent trait model. *Netherlands Journal of Psychology*, *67*, 48–57.

Muthén, B. O. (1989). Latent variable modeling in heterogeneous populations. *Psychometrika*, *54*, 557–585.

Muthén, L. K., & Muthén, B. O. (2007). *Mplus User's Guide* (5th ed.). Los Angeles, CA: Authors.

Neisser, U., Boodoo, G., Bourchard, T. J., Boykin, A. W., Brody, N., Ceci, S. J., ... Urbina, S. (1996). Intelligence: Knowns and unknowns. *American Psychologist*, *51*, 77–101.

Osterlind, S. J., & Everson, H. T. (2009). *Differential item functioning* (2nd ed.). Thousand Oaks, CA: Sage.

Penfield, R. D., & Camilli, G. (2007). Differential item functioning and item bias. In C. R. Rao & S. Sinharay (Eds.), *Handbook of statistics: Vol. 26. Psychometrics* (pp. 125–167). Amsterdam, The Netherlands: Elsevier.

Raju, N. S. (1988). The area between two item characteristic curves. *Psychometrika*, *53*, 495–502.

Raju, N. S. (1990). Determining the significance of estimated signed and unsigned areas between two item response functions. *Applied Psychological Measurement*, *14*, 197–207.

Rasch, G. (1960). *Probabilistic models for some intelligence and attainment tests*. Copenhagen, Denmark: Danmarks Paedogogiske Institut.

Rushton, J. P., & Jensen, A. R. (2005). Thirty years of research on race differences in cognitive ability. *Psychology, Public Policy, and Law*, *11*, 235–294.

Sackett, P. R., Borneman, M. J., & Connelly, B. S. (2008). High-stakes testing in higher education and employment: Appraising the evidence for validity and fairness. *American Psychologist*, *63*, 215–227.

Sackett, P. R., Schmitt, N., Ellington, J. E., & Kabin, M. B. (2001). High-stakes testing in employment, credentialing, and higher education: Prospects in a post-affirmative action world. *American Psychologist*, *56*, 302–318.

Samejima, F. (1969). *Estimation of latent ability using a response pattern of graded scores* (Psychometric Monograph, No. 17). Richmond, VA: Psychometric Society. Retrieved from http://www.psychometrika.org/journal/online/MN17.pdf

Schermelleh-Engel, K., Moosbrugger, H., & Müller, H. (2003). Evaluating the fit of structural equation models: Tests of significance and descriptive goodness-of fit measures. *Methods of Psychological Research*, *8*, 23–74.

Shealy, R., & Stout, W. (1993). A model-based standardization approach that separates true bias/DIF from group ability differences and detects test bias/DIF as well as item bias/DIF. *Psychometrika*, *58*, 159–194.

Sörbom, D. (1974). A general method for studying differences in factor means and factor structure between groups. *British Journal of Mathematical and Statistical Psychology*, *27*, 229–239.

Spearman, C. (1904). "General intelligence" objectively determined and measured. *American Journal of Psychology*, *15*, 201–293.

Spearman, C. E. (1927). *The abilities of man: Their nature and measurement*. New York, NY: Macmillan.

Swaminathan, H., & Rogers, H. J. (1990). Detecting differential item functioning using logistic regression procedures. *Journal of Educational Measurement*, *27*, 361–370.

Thomson, G. H., & Lederman, W. (1939). The influence of multivariate selection on the factorial analysis of ability. *British journal of psychology*, *29*, 288–305.

Thurstone, L. L. (1947). *Multiple factor analysis*. Chicago, IL: university of Chicago Press.

Tobin, J. (1958). Estimation of relationships for limited dependent variables. *Econometrica*, *26*, 24–36.

Tucker-Drob, E. M. (2009). Differentiation of cognitive abilities across the life span. *Developmental Psychology*, *45*, 1097–1118.

Van der Sluis, S., Dolan, C. V., Neale, M. C., Boomsma, D. I., & Posthuma, D. (2006). Detecting genotype-environment interaction in monozygotic twin data: Comparing the Jinks & Fulker test and a new test based on marginal maximum likelihood estimation. *Twin research and Human Genetics*, *9*, 377–392.

Van der Sluis, S., Posthuma, D., Dolan, C. V., De Geus, E. J. C., Colom, R., & Boomsma, D. I. (2006). Gender differences on the Dutch WAIS-III. *Intelligence*, *34*, 273–289.

Verhelst, N. D., & Glas, C. A. W. (1995). The one-parameter logistic model. In G. H. Fischer & I. W. Molenaar (Eds), *Rasch models: Foundations, recent developments, and applications.* (pp. 215–237). New York, NY: Springer.

Wechsler, D. (1997). *Wechsler Adult Intelligence Scale- III (WAISIII)*. San Antonio, TX: Psychological Corporation.

Wicherts, J. M., Dolan, C. V., & Hessen, D. J. (2005). Stereotype threat and group differences in test performance: A question of measurement invariance. *Journal of Personality and Social Psychology*, *89*, 696–716.

Wicherts, J. M., & Millsap, R. E. (2009). The absence of underprediction does not imply the absence of measurement bias. *American Psychologist, 64,* 281–283.

Widaman, K. F., & Reise, S. P. (1997). Exploring the measurement invariance of psychological instruments: Applications in the substance use domain. In K. J. Bryant & M. Windle (Eds.), *The science of prevention: Methodological advances from alcohol and substance abuse research* (pp. 281–324). Washington, DC: American Psychological Association.

Generalizability theory and the fair and valid assessment of linguistic minorities

Guillermo Solano-Flores[a] and Min Li[b]

[a]University of Colorado, Boulder, CO, USA; [b]University of Washington, Seattle, WA, USA

We discuss generalizability (G) theory and the fair and valid assessment of linguistic minorities, especially emergent bilinguals. G theory allows examination of the relationship between score variation and language variation (e.g., variation of proficiency across languages, language modes, and social contexts). Studies examining score variation across items administered in emergent bilinguals' first and second languages show that the interaction of student and the facets (sources of measurement error) item and language is an important source of score variation. Each item poses a unique set of linguistic challenges in each language, and each emergent bilingual individual has a unique set of strengths and weaknesses in each language. Based on these findings, G theory can inform the process of test construction in large-scale testing programmes and the development of testing models that ensure more valid and fair interpretations of test scores for linguistic minorities.

Introduction

Generalizability (G) theory is a psychometric theory of measurement error that allows partitioning score variance according to multiple sources. It addresses the extent to which the scores obtained by examinees in a test can be generalized to make precise, valid inferences related to the construct that the test is intended to measure. It evaluates how reliable and valid score interpretations of measurement conditions are for the construct of interest (Brennan, 2000, 2001; Kane, 1982).

Formally presented by Cronbach and his colleagues (Cronbach, Gleser, Nanda, & Rajaratnam, 1972) as an extension of classical test theory and further developed by other scholars (Brennan, 2001; Shavelson & Webb, 1981, 1991; Webb, Shavelson, & Haertel, 2007), G theory conceptualizes measurement error in terms of sampling of measurement conditions. A score from a given measurement is a sample from a universe of admissible observations – the collection of scores in all possible measurement conditions relevant to measuring the construct and to making generalizations about the object of measurement (Kane, 1982). Often, in the context of educational testing, that object of measurement is the student (see Cardinet, Tourneur, & Allal, 1976).

G theory addresses the fact that student scores vary not only due to individual differences in the knowledge or skills measured, but also due to multiple sources of measurement error. In a perfect world, test scores would vary only due to the students' measured skill or knowledge. In the real world, test scores reflect both the construct measured and many construct-irrelevant factors that affect student performance. G theory makes it possible to determine the extent to which precise generalizations and decisions about students can be made from test scores by allowing examination of the extent to which scores vary due to student and to various sources of measurement error.

Surprisingly, while G theory is 40 years old, approaches intended to address fairness in the testing of linguistic minorities have been developed based exclusively on classical test theory and item response theory. Of course, G theory has been used many times in the assessment of language skills (such as conversational skills in testing situations that involve social interaction), to identify the optimal number of tasks, raters, testing occasions, and so forth, needed to obtain reliable measures of language proficiency (e.g., Bachman, Lynch, & Mason, 1995; Brennan, Gao, & Colton, 1995; Lee, 2006; Lynch & McNamara, 1998; Van Weeren & Theunissen, 1987). That is an obvious application of the theory in assessment endeavours involving constructed-response tasks and the use of human judgement to assess performance. What is new is the treatment of language – the language of testing – as a source of score variation and the establishment of a clear link between score variance and language variation as key to addressing reliability and validity.

In this paper, we discuss the use of G theory in the assessment of linguistic minorities based on research that, for a bit over a decade, we have conducted to examine reliability and validity in the testing of linguistic minorities. It is not our intent to render a formal, exhaustive discussion of the theory; other sources exist for that purpose (Brennan, 2001; Haertel, 2006; Shavelson & Webb, 1991, 2009; Webb et al., 2007). Rather, we discuss how, because of its attention to sampling, the theory provides a robust methodological foundation for addressing fairness – a concept that is elusive and difficult to operationalize (see Solano-Flores, 2011a).

For the purpose of this paper, the term *linguistic minorities* is used to refer to populations of students whose first language is different from the language predominantly used in the society in which they live, the schools they attend, or the tests they are given, and which are developing their second language as they continue developing their first language. Typically, linguistic minorities have less power in a society, or their first language is less prestigious than the predominant language (see Wardhaugh, 2002). Also typically, their need for developing a second language is circumstantial (see Valdés & Figueroa, 1994); it is a consequence of historical, trans-generational factors such as forced migration (e.g., due to war or financial stress) or the imposition of a new language in a society (e.g., colonization).

According to this perspective, an individual who is learning a foreign language by choice in formal courses or who voluntarily migrates to a country in which this language is used is not part of a language minority (Solano-Flores & Trumbull, 2008). While there are important commonalities between developing a second language and learning a foreign language, important differences must be recognized that are relevant to valid testing (Brown, 2007). Some of these differences entail cognitive aspects of information processing that favour bilingual over monolingual individuals (see Bialystok, Craik, Green, & Gollan, 2009); others are related to society and power (see Cummins, 2000).

We refer to individuals belonging to linguistic minorities as *bilingual*. While the common usage of this term implies full command of two languages, individuals who are fully proficient in their two languages are very rare. In sociolinguistics, *bilingual* describes an individual who has developed or is developing two languages regardless of the level of command in each language (Wei, 2000).

Most of the research reported in this paper has been conducted with linguistic minority populations of students in the United States referred to as *English language learners*

(ELLs). We use, as a synonym to *ELL*, the term *emergent bilingual*, proposed by García and Kleifgen (2010), to emphasize the fact that, "through school and through acquiring English, these children become *bilingual*, able to continue to function in their home language as well as in English – their new language and that of school" (García & Kleifgen, 2010, p. 2). While, unfortunately, the use of this term is not as widespread as *ELL*, it is consistent with the notion that consideration of their two languages is critical to attaining valid testing for linguistic minorities.

In the first section of this paper, we discuss the basic concepts of G theory. Then, we provide a brief history of the applications of the theory in the assessment of linguistic minorities in terms of the interaction of student, item, and language. In the third section, we discuss empirical research on the use of the theory as a tool for examining the link between score variation and language variation due to both language proficiency and dialect. In the fourth section, we discuss how, because of its capability to address uncertainty, G theory can contribute to the improvement of assessment systems. Finally, we discuss the implications of this research and ways in which G theory can be used to promote more fair and valid testing for linguistic minorities. In the final comments section, we discuss how G theory is different from and similar to item response theory in its approach to addressing fairness in the testing of linguistic students.

Basic concepts in G theory

Measurement error

The notion of random and systematic error is critical to understanding the contribution of G theory in the field of measurement. In classical theory, measurement error is defined as the difference between true score and the student's observed score; it is thought of as being random in nature. In contrast, G theory distinguishes between random and systematic error; it considers both types of error when estimating the measurement error. Random error is inconsistent, difficult to predict, and beyond control (e.g., student guessing or the noise outside of the room where students are tested). Systematic error consistently affects the students' scores due to the characteristics of the test (e.g., an item is more difficult than other items or a rater is more lenient than other raters in assigning scores to students' responses).

Both classical theory and G theory estimate reliability based on the percentage of score variation. However, while in classical theory the reliability coefficient is the proportion of observed score variance relative to true score variance, in G theory the reliability coefficient is defined as the proportion of score variance attributable to student relative to the total score variance due to both student and various sources of measurement error. In addition, while classical test theory only allows estimation of the reliability coefficient for one type of error at a time (e.g., inter-rater reliability or internal consistency), G theory can determine the amount of score variability associated with multiple sources of error simultaneously.

Analysis of variance is commonly used in G theory to calculate the estimated mean squared deviations, which then allows estimation of measurement error due to the main and interaction effect of multiple sources or error.[1] The sum of error associated with student (e.g., the student-by-item interaction or the student-by-rater interaction) contributes to the relative measurement error. The sum of error due to all sources of measurement error is referred to as absolute measurement error.

These two types of measurement error are corresponded with two types of test decisions, relative and absolute. *Relative decisions* are associated with norm-referenced interpretations of scores; they are concerned with the consistency of scores in ranking students according to differences in their knowledge and skills (i.e., examining whether different raters rank students consistently). The *generalizability coefficient* (ρ^2) for relative decisions is computed by considering random measurement error and is equivalent to the reliability coefficient in classical theory.

Absolute decisions are associated with criterion-referenced interpretations of scores; they are concerned with indexing the exact level of students' knowledge and skills – the level of knowledge of a given domain. The *dependability coefficient* (Φ) is computed by considering both random and systematic measurement error and informs about the validity of test scores – the extent to which valid inferences about the students' knowledge and skills can be made based on their scores.

Facets and designs

In G theory, the term *facet* is used to refer to each of the characteristics (factors) used to generate the universe of observations. Item, test form, rater, mode of administration, sequence of administration, format, occasion, and language (the language in which a test is administered) are examples of the many possible facets involved in an assessment. Each facet has various categories called *conditions*. For example, in a test of 10 open-ended items scored by three raters, two facets are involved, item with 10 conditions and rater with 3 conditions.

The 10 items and the three raters are assumed to be samples of all the possible items and raters drawn from the universe of observations defined by the facet item (i) and the facet rater (r). A two-facet design of student (s), item, and rater, denoted $s \times i \times r$, can be used to estimate the error due to sampling of the measurement conditions from the universe of observations and partition the score variation into the following sources:

s

i

r

si

sr

ir

sir,e

The last term, sir,e refers to error due to the interaction of student, item, and rater confounded with unexplained random error.

Three issues concerning facets need to be considered in G theory designs. The first two have to do with the actions needed to take to properly compute reliability estimates; the third one involves sampling. First, facets can be *fixed* or *random* depending, respectively, on whether the universe from which the particular measurement is sampled includes finite or infinite conditions of the universe of observations to which generalizations are to be made. Suppose that an assessment specialist is interested in examining the reliability of a reading assessment that involves judgements made by raters. The district uses four reading teachers as raters. Rater should be treated as a fixed facet if the district does not plan to expand the pool of raters beyond the set of four individuals it has hired to rate the students' performance. However, if the district anticipates to recruit more teachers as raters in the future, then rater would have to be treated as a random facet.

Second, facets can be either crossed or nested with the object of measurement (student in most cases) or other facets in any designs. *Crossed* refers to the case in which all the sampled conditions of any facet are present for all students and for all conditions of any other facet. In contrast, *nested* refers to the fact that only some of the sampled conditions of a given facet are present. In the example above, rater is a crossed facet if the four raters score the responses of all students. But if, for practical reasons, students' responses were scored by different sets of raters, then rater would be nested within student (which is denoted as $r{:}s$) because not all of the conditions of the facet *rater* (i.e., not all the individuals that act as raters) are represented for all the conditions in the object of measurement. This particular design with a crossed facet (item) and a nested facet (rater) considers the following five sources of score variation:

s

i

$r{:}s$

si

$ir{:}s,e$

A third issue stems from the fact that, for certain facets, only one particular level or condition is represented in a G study design. Such facets are called *hidden*. In the example of the 10 items scored by three raters, the items were administered in English (and, more precisely, a particular dialect of English), in a paper-and-pencil format, and on a particular occasion. Language, format, and occasion are hidden facets because, although they are not specified in the design, only one condition of each is represented in it. It is impossible to estimate the amount of score variation hidden facets may account for (Cronbach, Linn, Brennan, & Haertel, 1997; Shavelson, Ruiz-Primo, & Wiley, 1999). Thus, to increase the dependability of generalizations when there are hidden facets that are especially relevant to the construct measured or the population assessed, it is necessary to increase the size of the samples of observations for facets included in the design (see Ruiz-Primo, Baxter, & Shavelson, 1993).

Generalizability and decision studies

G theory distinguishes between *generalizability (G) studies* and *decision (D) studies*. The purpose of a G study is to obtain the ρ^2 coefficient or both the ρ^2 and Φ coefficients for a measurement that has taken place. In contrast, the purpose of a D study is to obtain, based on the magnitude of the estimated variance components observed in the G study, those coefficients for measurements that have not occurred.

D studies can be thought of as simulations based on empirical data obtained from the G studies. These simulations aim to determine the ρ^2 and Φ coefficients that can be obtained if the sample sizes of some facets are changed or if different assumptions are made about the conditions of some facets (i.e., as nested or crossed, or as random or fixed). In the example of a test with 10 items scored by three raters, a series of D studies can be conducted to examine the ρ^2 and Φ coefficients even with studies different from the original G study. That is the case when the test consists of only 5 items scored by the same three raters (i.e., s x i x r random design, $n_i' = 5$ and $n_r' = 3$) or when the test consists of 5 items and different sets of two raters score each student's responses (i.e., $(r{:}s)$ x i random design, $n_i' = 5$ and $n_r' = 2$). Thus, D studies enable test developers to determine the optimal combination of samples of observations that are needed to obtain dependable scores.

Language variation and score variation

Language dominance and the interaction of student, item, and language

The use of G theory in the assessment of linguistic minorities came about as an unplanned outcome of a project concerned with fairness in the testing of ELLs. The project's goal was to assemble a sampler of responses given by Grade 4 and Grade 5 ELL students to science and mathematics items when they were tested in their native, first language (L1) and when they were tested in English, their second language (L2). The sampler was to be used as a material to train teachers who participated as raters of constructed-response items in large-scale testing programmes (Solano-Flores, Lara, Sexton, & Navarrete, 2001). The sampler was intended to address the fact that, in the USA, ELLs are included in these testing programmes after a few years of schooling, in spite of the fact that they have not developed the kind of English proficiency they need to benefit from schooling and to demonstrate knowledge in tests administered in English (see Hakuta, 2000). Since the majority of teachers in the US are monolingual English speakers, with little to no formal preparation in the education of linguistic minorities (Darling-Hammond & Sykes, 2003), many teachers who participate as raters may need support to become sensitive to the fact that ELLs may possess the knowledge being assessed but cannot demonstrate it in L2. Although the features of the responses given by ELLs in English often look as incomprehensible, they often reflect cultural and first language influences. A careful examination of their responses beyond superficial features (e.g., spelling patterns) and based on knowledge of these influences may contribute to making better interpretations of ELLs' responses and fair scoring decisions.

We selected released science and mathematics test items used in the National Assessment of Educational Progress (NAEP; a national, large-scale assessment programme in the US) and had teams of bilingual teachers translate them into the L1 of three groups of students: native speakers of Spanish, Haitian-Creole, and Mandarin Chinese. We gave the same set of items to students from these groups in L1 and in L2. Then, we had the teachers score the students' responses in the two languages. Appropriate actions were taken to ensure that students were given the two language versions of the same items in two different occasions and in random order and to ensure that raters could not tell when two responses to a given item were from the same student. We had the teachers translate the students' responses in L1 into English, so that we could compare the responses' features in addition to their scores.

Common sense would lead to think that the ELLs' responses to the items would be consistently better (and their scores higher) in L1 than in L2. However, we did not observe such a pattern. We concluded that ELLs' performance on tests administered in two languages was instable. The scores from tests given to ELLs in either L1 or in L2 might give an inaccurate picture of the achievement of ELLs. Important information about the students' knowledge of the construct measured appeared to be missed by testing ELLs in each language.

We performed certain analyses to examine this instability across languages. The conventional approach focusing on the statistical significance of any differences between scores on the items administered in L1 and scores on the items administered in L2 did not seem to be appropriate as, due to the instability mentioned above, any differences across languages would cancel out. Thus, we used reasonings from G theory to examine score variation. The theory allowed us to identify the score variance components for three types of sources of score variation: (a) student (s) – the object of measurement; (b) three facets: rater (r), item (i), and language (l); and (c) the interactions: s x r; s x i; s x l; r x i; r x l; i x l; s x r x i; s x r x l; s x i x l; r x i x l; s x r x i x l,e.

We observed that the largest percentage of the total score variance across the three linguistic groups was that due to the interaction, s x i x l. This indicated that some students performed better on some items administered in their L1, whereas other students performed better on items administered in their L2. In addition to knowledge of the content, the responses of ELLs to the items appeared to be shaped by the interaction of their varying weaknesses and strengths in L1, their varying weaknesses and strengths in L2, the linguistic challenges and affordances of items given in L1, and the linguistic challenges and affordances of items given in L2.

These findings are consistent with the notion that the bilingual individual is not two monolinguals in one (Valdés & Figueroa, 1994) and with the notion that language in bilinguals can be thought of as a system that integrates both L1 and L2 (Cummins, 2000). At the lexical level, for example, the vocabulary of emergent bilinguals is distributed across L1 and L2. "Some of the vocabulary possessed by bilingual children is encoded in L1 but not in L2, and vice versa" (Oller, Pearson, & Cobo-Lewis, 2007, p. 192); some of it is encoded in both L1 and L2.

Testing students with the same set of items in two languages is key to investigating how language variation affects the validity of measures of academic achievement for ELLs (Solano-Flores & Li, 2006, 2008, 2009a, 2009b). Notice, however, that this approach differs from research and practice in ELL testing, which has used two-sided, L1 and L2 versions of the same tests. In our approach, giving the same set of items in two languages (although not simultaneously) is not a test format. Rather, it is part of a strategy intended to devise testing models for linguistic minorities.

Additional evidence on the ways in which score variance is influenced by the heterogeneity of linguistic minorities comes from research using between-group designs (i.e., designs including both ELL and non-ELL students) with s x i models. For example, there is evidence that the amount of measurement error contributed by different facets in the assessment of reading skills may be different for ELLs and non-ELLs (Li & Brennan, 2007). Notice, however, that, while this between-group design allows comparison of the patterns of score variability across linguistic groups, it does not allow examination of score variability across languages.

An important aspect of our G theory-based approach is the treatment of language as a random facet. Conventional wisdom would lead to think that language is a fixed facet simply because, in the testing of emergent bilinguals, students can be tested only in two languages – L1 and L2. However, while there are only two languages of interest, only a few of their multiple features (e.g., vocabulary, grammar, discourse, etc.) are represented in each particular item given in each language. Items can be thought of as samples of the language in which they are written. If language were a fixed facet, an item could be written only in one way. In reality, saying that an item is administered in a given language is to say that it is written in one of many (undetermined or infinite) possible ways.

Testing across languages and dialects

Knowledge from the fields of sociolinguistics and bilingual development provides a conceptual basis for interpreting the results of the G studies described above. Mainly, the considerable inconsistency of ELL students' performance across items administered in different languages can be accounted for by the fact that linguistic minorities are tremendously heterogeneous. Multiple patterns of dominance in L1 and L2 result, among other things, from multiple personal life experiences (e.g., migration, first-language influences, type of exposure to L2, interaction with ELL peers) and schooling histories (e.g., in bilingual or English-only programmes, length of schooling).

These multiple life experiences and schooling histories can be examined in terms of language dominance and dialect. First, against popular beliefs, ELLs are not necessarily more proficient in L1 than in L2 for all language modes – listening, speaking, reading, and writing (Baker, 2001). Classifications of students based on a reduced number of levels of English proficiency without reference to language modes fail to properly describe the linguistic skills of emergent bilinguals. This is especially the case for reading and writing – skills more likely to be learned at school than at home.

Second, languages are not systems of communications used exactly in the same way by all their users. Instead, languages vary either moderately or considerably across individuals, communities, cultures, ages, genders, education levels, socioeconomic strata, geographical regions, and times in history (Wolfram, Adger, & Christian, 1999). All speakers of a given language speak dialects of that language. Even the most prestigious form of a language, for example, standard English, is a dialect. Contrary to the common use of the term, a dialect is not an imperfect variety of a language. A wealth of evidence shows that even the least prestigious dialects of a language are as complex systems of conventions as the most prestigious ones (see Baker, 2001; Crystal, 1997).

Decisions on testing linguistic minorities in L1 or in L2 rarely take into account the tremendous linguistic heterogeneity due to dialect. Moreover, test development practices view dialect as a threat to the validity that can be addressed by ensuring that tests are written in a standard version of a language. In reality, a standard version of a test privileges the users of that dialect, thus becoming a potential source of bias against the users who are unfamiliar with that dialect (Solano-Flores, 2006).

To examine more carefully score variation due to language and also to determine if dialect is an important source of measurement in the testing of linguistic minorities, we conducted a series of studies using the same methods described in the section above and new samples of Grade 4 and Grade 5 ELLs who were native speakers of Haitian-Creole (Solano-Flores & Li, 2006) and native speakers of Spanish (Solano-Flores & Li, 2009b). We created a mathematics test with NAEP released items. For each linguistic group, we used the same design. Students from two cities participated in this study. A sample of students from City A was tested across languages, English, and a standard version of L1. A second sample of students (also from City A) was tested with the same standard version of L1 and a local version of L1 (L1-City A). A third sample of students, from City B, was tested with the standard version of L1 and its own local version of L1 (L1-City B).

The standard dialect version of L1 was created by a translation company. In contrast, the local dialect versions of L1 were created by teachers who taught in the same schools attended by the participating students. With facilitation from project staff, these teachers were asked to create a translation that reflected the ways in which L1 was used in their schools and communities. These teachers did not teach the students whose responses they scored. A series of random s x r x i x l model and random s x r x i x dialect (d) model G studies (see Figure 1) revealed that the amount of measurement error due to the interaction of student, item, and dialect (s x i x d) for students tested across dialects could be as large as the amount of measurement error due to the interaction of s x i x l for students tested across languages.

Testing models

We also performed a series of G and D studies using random s x r x i models (see Figure 2) assuming testing students in one language (i.e., either English or the first language) and testing in one dialect (either the standard or the local dialect) of the first language.

Table 1 shows the results for Hispanic students of Mexican origin/cultural heritage, native speakers of Spanish from a state on the West Coast of the US. For each language or dialect, the results include each source of score variation, its corresponding estimated

Variance components:

$$\sigma^2_{sril} = \sigma^2_s + \sigma^2_r + \sigma^2_i + \sigma^2_l + \sigma^2_{sr} + \sigma^2_{si} + \sigma^2_{sl} + \sigma^2_{ri} + \sigma^2_{rl} + \sigma^2_{il} + \sigma^2_{sri} + \sigma^2_{srl} + \sigma^2_{sil} + \sigma^2_{ril} + \sigma^2_{sril,e}$$

Relative decisions:

$$\rho^2 = \frac{\sigma^2_s}{\sigma^2_s + \sigma^2_\delta} = \frac{\sigma^2_s}{\sigma^2_s + \sigma^2_{sr} + \sigma^2_{si} + \sigma^2_{sl} + \sigma^2_{sri} + \sigma^2_{srl} + \sigma^2_{sil} + \sigma^2_{sril,e}}$$

Absolute decisions:

$$\Phi = \frac{\sigma^2_s}{\sigma^2_s + \sigma^2_\Delta} = \frac{\sigma^2_s}{\sigma^2_s + \sigma^2_r + \sigma^2_i + \sigma^2_l + \sigma^2_{sr} + \sigma^2_{si} + \sigma^2_{sl} + \sigma^2_{ri} + \sigma^2_{rl} + \sigma^2_{il} + \sigma^2_{sri} + \sigma^2_{srl} + \sigma^2_{sil} + \sigma^2_{ril} + \sigma^2_{sril,e}}$$

Figure 1. *s* x *r* x *i* x *l* (**s**tudent x **r**ater x **i**tem x **l**anguage) random model design. Substitute *l* by *d* for the *s* x *r* x *i* x *d* (**s**tudent x **r**ater x **i**tem x **d**ialect) random model design.

variance component, and the rounded percentage of the total score variance produced. The table also shows the relative and absolute errors and the relative and absolute decisions coefficients and the minimum test length – minimum number of items – needed to obtain an absolute decisions coefficient of at least .80. This minimum test length was determined through D studies based on the estimated variance components obtained from the G studies.

Consistently, the major source of score variation was due to the *s* x *i* interaction, which accounted for about the same percentage of the total score variation (57% to 70%) for both students tested across languages and across dialects of their first language. For Student Sample 1, about the same number of items (19 and 18) would be needed to obtain dependable scores if the test were to be administered in English or in Spanish. For Student Sample 2, many more items (26) would be needed to obtain dependable scores if the test were to be administered in the local version of Spanish than in the standard version of Spanish (16 items).

Table 2 shows the ρ^2 and Φ coefficients obtained for ELLs, native speakers of Haitian-Creole, from two cities on the West Coast of the US (Solano-Flores & Li, 2006). For Student Sample 1 (tested across languages), 10 items and about 20 items would be needed to obtain dependable scores (at least $\Phi = .80$) if they were tested respectively in standard English only and in standard Haitian-Creole only. The results for Student Samples 2 and 3 (tested each

Variance components:

$$\sigma^2_{sri} = \sigma^2_s + \sigma^2_r + \sigma^2_i + \sigma^2_{sr} + \sigma^2_{si} + \sigma^2_{ri} + \sigma^2_{sri,e}$$

Relative decisions:

$$\rho^2 = \frac{\sigma^2_s}{\sigma^2_s + \sigma^2_\delta} = \frac{\sigma^2_s}{\sigma^2_s + \sigma^2_{sr} + \sigma^2_{si} + \sigma^2_{sri,e}}$$

Absolute decisions:

$$\Phi = \frac{\sigma^2_s}{\sigma^2_s + \sigma^2_\Delta} = \frac{\sigma^2_s}{\sigma^2_s + \sigma^2_r + \sigma^2_i + \sigma^2_{sr} + \sigma^2_{si} + \sigma^2_{ri} + \sigma^2_{sri,e}}$$

Figure 2. *s* x *r* x *i* (**s**tudent x **r**ater x **i**tem) random model design.

Table 1. Estimated variance components and percentage of score variation for students tested in one language (Student Sample 1) and for students tested in one dialect of the native language (Student Sample 2). Random s x r x i model: English language learners, native Spanish Speakers.

| Source of Score Variation | n | Student Sample 1: Tested in one Language | | | | | | | Student Sample 2: Tested in one Dialect of the First Language | | | | | | |
| | | English (Standard) | | | Spanish (Standard) | | | Standard Spanish | | | Mexican (Local) Spanish | | |
		EVC	%[a]	MinimumTest Length[b]	EVC	%[a]	MinimumTest Length[b]	EVC	%[a]	MinimumTest Length[b]	EVC	%[a]	MinimumTest Length[b]
s	30	0.02705	18		0.02403	19		0.02655	20		0.01949	13	
r	4	0.00014	0		0[c]	0		0[c]	0		0	0	
i	10	0.01148	8		0.00395	3		0.00579	4		0.01784	12	
sr		0.00028	0		0.00048	0		0[c]	0		0.00003	0	
si		0.10032	67		0.08768	70		0.09504	70		0.10100	68	
ri		0	0		0.00012	0		0.00009	0		0.00014	0	
sri,e		0.01151	8		0.00971	8		0.00762	6		0.00927	6	
Total variance		0.1508	100		0.1260	100		0.1351	100		0.1478	100	
Relative error		0.1121			0.0979			0.1027			0.1103		
Absolute error		0.1237			0.1019			0.1085			0.1283		
ρ^2		0.194			0.197			0.205			0.150		
Φ		0.179		19	0.191		18	0.197		16	0.132		26

Notes: Source: Solano-Flores & Li (2009b). [a]Percentages may not add up to 100 due to rounding. [b]The minimum test length is the estimated number of items needed to obtain an absolute decisions coefficient ϕ = .80, assuming one rater. [c]Small negative value set to zero.

Table 2. Relative and absolute decision coefficients by test length for a sample of students tested across languages (Sample 1) and two samples of students tested across dialects (Sample 2 and Sample 3). Random s x i x r model: English language learners, native Haitian-Creole Speakers.

| Test Length | Student Sample 1: Tested in one Language | | | | Student Sample 2: Tested in one Dialect of the First Language | | | | Student Sample 3: Tested in one Dialect of the First Language | | | |
| | English (Standard) | | Haitian-Creole (Standard) | | Standard Haitian-Creole | | Local (City A) Haitian-Creole | | Standard Haitian-Creole | | Local (City B) Haitian-Creole | |
	ρ^2	Φ	ρ^2	Φ	ρ^2	Φ	ρ^2	Φ	ρ^2	Φ	ρ^2	Φ
10	.83	.82	.77	.74	.72.	.70	.80	.79	.73	.69	.73	.70
20	.91	.90	.87	.85	.84	.83	.89	.89	.84	.82	.84	.81
30	.94	.93	.91	.90	.88	.88	.92	.92	.89	.87	,89	.87

Source: Solano-Flores & Li (2006).

across Standard Haitian-Creole and the local dialect of Haitian-Creole) are not consistent. For Student Sample 2, about 10 items would be needed to obtain dependable scores if the test were administered in the local dialect of Haitian-Creole, whereas a bit fewer than 20 items would be needed if the test were administered in the standard dialect of Haitian-Creole. In contrast, for Student Sample 3, comparable dependability coefficients would be obtained by testing them in either the standard or the local dialect of Haitian-Creole.

These findings speak to the limitations of testing policies, which are based on blanket approaches in which all emergent bilinguals are treated in the same way. Even within the same broad linguistic group, different groups of ELLs benefit differently from being tested in L1 or in L2 or in different dialects of L1. To produce valid measures of academic achievement for linguistic minorities, testing policies and practices need to be sensitive to language variation, including dialect and local usage of language.

Our studies examining the relationship between test score variation and dialect variation have been limited to dialects of the ELL students' first language. An important aspect yet to be investigated is the relationship between test score variation and English dialect variation – score variation across items administered in standard English and the students' local dialect of English. We have evidence that localizing items originally created in standard English (i.e., adapting their linguistic features to the characteristics of the English used in the schools) is an effective form of testing accommodation for ELLs (Solano-Flores et al., 2007). However, the magnitude of the s x i x d interaction (or the differences in magnitude of the s x i interaction for items administered in different English dialects) is yet to be investigated. Information from this research could be relevant not only to the testing of ELL students but also to the testing of native English speakers who are users of non-standard forms of English.

G theory and the improvement of assessment systems

Uncertainty and the testing of English language learners

Uncertainty is a recurring issue in all aspects of the testing of linguistic minorities (Solano-Flores, 2008). This uncertainty results not only from the heterogeneity of linguistic groups but also from the limited ability of assessment systems to address this diversity. Three aspects in the process of testing can be identified in which the testing of linguistic minorities is flawed due to this limited ability – the ways in which ELL populations are specified, the inadequacy of testing practices, and the ways in which research findings concerning ELL testing are used (Solano-Flores, 2009).

Regarding population misspecification, the No Child Left Behind Act of 2001 defines an ELL based on language background and level of English proficiency according to a limited set of language proficiency measures (Abedi, 2007). These criteria, which may be insufficient to address the complexity of language proficiency, produce a spurious dichotomy of students as either proficient or not proficient in English and may lead to multiple false positive and false negative ELL classifications (Abedi, 2008; Solano-Flores & Gustafson, in press).

Regarding inadequate testing practices, actions intended to minimize the effect of limited language proficiency as a threat to test validity constitute sources of measurement error themselves (Solano-Flores, 2009). Testing accommodations are a case in point. The term *testing accommodation* is used to refer to any of the multiple modifications in the ways in which tests are administered with the purpose of minimizing limited language proficiency as a threat to the validity of the test scores for ELLs by supporting these students to gain access to the content of the items without giving away their content or giving ELL students an unfair advantage over non-ELL students (Abedi, Hofstetter, & Lord, 2004; Young & King, 2008).

Due to the fact that emerging bilinguals have multiple patterns of language dominance (Bialystok, 2001), not all testing accommodations serve ELLs in the same way (see Kopriva, Koran, & Hedgspeth, 2007; Rivera, Collum, Willner, & Sia, 2006). For example, a testing accommodation consisting of reading aloud the directions of a test in students' L1 may be effective only for some students. In addition, some educators in charge of providing the accommodation may not be well qualified for that task. It would be unrealistic to expect that assessment systems have the mechanisms needed to ensure appropriate fidelity of implementation or even the collection on information on fidelity of implementation with the level of detail needed to screen or select individuals who provide testing accommodations.

The notion that actions intended to address language issues are sources of measurement error is critical in the design of testing policy in assessment systems. Thus, by conducting investigations examining both score differences and differences in the magnitudes of the generalizability and dependability coefficients obtained when accommodations are and are not provided, it is possible to evaluate the effectiveness of testing practices intended to address language.

Regarding overgeneralization, policy and practice informed by research in ELL testing may fail to consider the multiple contextual factors that are relevant to language and language usage. This overgeneralization results from the tendency to look for simple, cost-effective testing approaches. However, as discussed above, what works for some individuals or communities to reduce the impact of limited proficiency in the language of testing does not work for other individuals or communities, even if they belong to the same broad linguistic group.

Addressing uncertainty in assessment systems

From our perspective, the key to more fair and valid assessment for linguistic minorities lies in recognizing the uncertainty that results from the heterogeneity of linguistic groups, the instability of language phenomena, and the limited effectiveness of assessment systems to deal with or even account for the multitude of factors associated with that diversity and that instability (Solano-Flores & Gustafson, in press). Because it is about estimating score variation contributed by various sources, G theory allows linking the technical properties of academic achievement measures to the effectiveness of assessment systems.

An investigation on the linguistic background of individuals who participate as raters in large-scale assessment programmes illustrates this (Kachchaf & Solano-Flores, 2012). We were interested in examining the extent to which the linguistic background of raters may influence the quality of the scoring of native Spanish-speaking ELL students' responses to short-answer, open-ended mathematics items administered in English. More specifically, we intended to examine if the quality of the scoring was better among bilingual (English-Spanish) raters who were native speakers of Spanish than among bilingual (English-Spanish) raters who were native speakers of English.

We conducted a series of $s \times l \times i \times (r{:}b)$ random model G studies (see Figure 3) in which rater (r) was treated as nested in rater's language background (b) – a bilingual teacher acting as a rater could be either native English speaker or native Spanish speaker, not both. We observed a negligible score variation due to the main and interaction effect of $r{:}b$ (i.e., the $r{:}b$ nested effect). We concluded that the language background of bilingual raters in the scoring of ELL students' responses to items administered in English is not critical to obtaining reliable measures of academic achievement, provided that the responses scored are responses to open-ended items. However, we also cautioned against overgeneralization: The type of items used to assess students (e.g., long-answer, constructed-response items and multiple-choice items) and other hidden facets (e.g., the type of scorer training and the type of scoring rubrics used to score the responses) limit the generalizations of these findings. Also, future research should consider an important condition of rater's language background not included in this study: monolingual, native English speakers. A large amount of measurement error due to $r{:}b$ might be observed when the sample of raters includes both bilingual individuals and monolingual, English-speaking individuals.

G studies can inform assessment systems about the effectiveness of testing accommodations. In the US, NAEP and the majority of state assessment systems authorize the use of testing accommodations to test ELLs. Altogether, more than 70 forms of testing

Variance components:

$$\sigma^2_{slir{:}b} = \sigma^2_s + \sigma^2_l + \sigma^2_i + \sigma^2_b + \sigma^2_{r{:}b} + \sigma^2_{sl} + \sigma^2_{si} + \sigma^2_{sb} + \sigma^2_{sr{:}b} + \sigma^2_{li} + \sigma^2_{lb} + \sigma^2_{lr{:}b} + \sigma^2_{ib} + \sigma^2_{ir{:}b} + \sigma^2_{sli} + \sigma^2_{slb}$$
$$+ \sigma^2_{slr{:}b} + \sigma^2_{sib} + \sigma^2_{sir{:}b} + \sigma^2_{lib} + \sigma^2_{lir{:}b} + \sigma^2_{slib} + \sigma^2_{slir{:}b,e}$$

Relative decisions:

$$\rho^2 = \frac{\sigma^2_s}{\sigma^2_s + \sigma^2_\delta} = \frac{\sigma^2_s}{\sigma^2_s + \sigma^2_{sl} + \sigma^2_{si} + \sigma^2_{sb} + \sigma^2_{sr{:}b} + \sigma^2_{sli} + \sigma^2_{slb} + \sigma^2_{slr{:}b} + \sigma^2_{sib} + \sigma^2_{sir{:}b} + \sigma^2_{slib} + \sigma^2_{slir{:}b,e}}$$

Absolute decisions:

$$\Phi = \frac{\sigma^2_s}{\sigma^2_s + \sigma^2_\Delta} = \sigma^2_s / (\sigma^2_s + \sigma^2_l + \sigma^2_i + \sigma^2_b + \sigma^2_{r{:}b} + \sigma^2_{sl} + \sigma^2_{si} + \sigma^2_{sb} + \sigma^2_{sr{:}b} + \sigma^2_{li} + \sigma^2_{lb} + \sigma^2_{lr{:}b} + \sigma^2_{ib} + \sigma^2_{ir{:}b}$$
$$+ \sigma^2_{sli} + \sigma^2_{slb} + \sigma^2_{slr{:}b} + \sigma^2_{sib} + \sigma^2_{sir{:}b} + \sigma^2_{lib} + \sigma^2_{lir{:}b} + \sigma^2_{slib} + \sigma^2_{slir{:}b,e})$$

Figure 3. $s \times l \times i \times (r{:}b)$ (student x language of testing x item x rater: linguistic background of rater) random model design.

accommodations are used in the US, ranging from allowing students to provide their answers verbally to seating them in areas in which they are less likely to be distracted (Rivera et al. 2006). Some of these accommodations are not defensible, and evidence on effectiveness exists only for a limited number (e.g., item linguistic simplification, computer-administered glossaries) (Abedi, Lord, Hofstetter, & Baker, 2001; Pennock-Roman & Rivera, 2011; Sireci, Li, & Scarpati, 2003).

The effectiveness of testing accommodations for ELLs can be examined not only in terms of score differences in within-group designs in which students are tested with and without the accommodations. Also, effectiveness can be examined in terms of score variability due to the facet, format (f) (i.e., presence or absence of the accommodation) in within-group designs in which students are given the same sets of items with and without the accommodations.

We have used G studies to examine the effectiveness of vignette illustrations as a form of testing accommodation for ELLs (Solano-Flores, 2011b; Solano-Flores, Nguyen-Le, & Wang, 2012). We designed illustrations intended to visually support ELLs to gain access to the content of items by representing some of the elements of the contextual information provided in the stem of multiple-choice science items; then we added the illustrations to the text of the items without modifying the text. We gave the same set of items to ELL and non-ELL students, with and without illustrations according to the within-group design mentioned above. The percentage of score variation due to $s \times i \times f$ is an indication of the extent to which the effectiveness of this form of accommodation is shaped by the interaction of the characteristics of the items, the characteristics of the illustrations, and the characteristics of the students – both their knowledge of the content assessed and their ability to interpret the illustrations.

G studies can also inform assessment systems about the pertinence of testing linguistic minorities in their native languages. An investigation on the feasibility and limitations of testing Mexican Indian populations in their native languages (Backhoff, Solano-Flores, & Contreras-Niño, 2012) illustrates this application. With project staff facilitation, Mayan-speaking bilingual (Spanish-Mayan) educators translated and culturally adapted into the peninsular Mayan language and culture mathematical reasoning items originally developed and administered in Spanish by the National Institute for Educational Evaluation in Mexico for Spanish-speaking students. Also with project staff facilitation, these educators wrote items in Mayan with the same content and format specifications as their item counterparts in Spanish. The tests were then administered to Mayan students in three language versions to samples of native Mayan-speaking students, Spanish, Mayan-translated and culturally adapted, and Mayan-original. A student x item x version x rater random design was used to examine score variability due to these sources of score variation and their interaction.

Consistent with findings for other ELLs, we observed that the largest source of measurement error was the interaction of student, item, and version. As with other linguistic minority groups, Mayan students are tremendously heterogeneous in their strengths and weaknesses in their first and second languages, and items in each language pose them with different sets of linguistic challenges. Decisions concerning the language in which linguistic minority students should be tested needs to be based on considering the numbers of items needed to obtain adequate generalizability and dependability coefficients in each language.

Final comments

In this paper, we have discussed the contributions of G theory to fairness in the testing of linguistic minorities. Because of its capability to address language as a facet that contributes to score variability, the theory makes it possible to develop testing models that are consistent with the notion of an integrated language system in bilinguals. Also, the theory makes it possible to develop testing models that address the well-known fact that bilinguals vary tremendously as to their proficiency in each language mode (listening, speaking, reading, and writing) in their first language and in their second language.

Unlike item response theory (IRT)-based approaches to detecting item linguistic and cultural bias, G theory-based approaches to addressing language do not require the use of a reference group (e.g., mainstream, non-ELL students). Validity is addressed in terms of the proper sample of observations needed to make appropriate generalizations of test scores about the students' knowledge or skills. Also, unlike IRT-based approaches, G theory-based approaches do not assume population homogeneity (Solano-Flores, 2006). Indeed, G theory-based approaches enable test developers to address the uncertainty that results from linguistic heterogeneity, imprecise information about the characteristics of ELLs, and the poor implementation of testing policies (Solano-Flores, 2008). Finally, while IRT-based approaches are, in practice, costly and difficult to implement with large numbers of items and under tight timelines, G theory-based approaches are easy to implement because they focus on the size of samples of observations. The two theories address language in different ways; they are mutually complementary.

A word about the value of different designs in the assessment of linguistic minorities is in order. While the use of s x i x l designs allows examination of the link between language variation and score variation, their use is restricted to the context of research. In practice, it would be unrealistic to expect assessment systems to conduct G studies examining the language of testing as a facet, mainly because most of the ELLs are tested in English. However, assessment systems could perform G studies with s x i designs for tests administered in English. We believe that routine examination of the dependability of academic achievement measures for ELL students with different levels of English proficiency using a simple s x i design would contribute significantly to more valid and fair assessment for linguistic minorities.

The most important lesson learned from our research on G theory and the assessment of linguistic minorities has to do with the notion that, in many G theory-based studies, the variance component interpreted as s x i interaction results from the instability of student performance (see Cronbach et al., 1997). Findings from our research indicate that, in the case of linguistic minorities, a great deal of this instability results from the multiple patterns of language dominance among emergent bilinguals and the multiple sets of linguistic challenges posed by test items. Recognizing language as a hidden facet when emergent bilingual students are tested in one language is critical to the fair and valid testing of linguistic minorities. More dependable measures for these students can be obtained by simply increasing the number of items in a test.

If we are serious about ensuring fairness in the assessment of ELLs, two actions need to be taken routinely as part of the process of assessment development. First, ELL students should be included during the pilot stages of assessment development, along with their non-ELL counterparts, so that data on performance are available for both groups. Against common beliefs, ELLs can participate in pilot stages of test development by both responding to tests *administered in English* or responding to cognitive interviews *conducted in English* on the ways in which they interpret the items and respond to them (Prosser & Solano-Flores, 2010). This capability, seldom recognized by educators and test developers, results from the fact that, while they may not have developed the academic language needed to fully benefit from instruction in their second language, ELLs acquire in a relatively short time the basic conversational skills embedded in context that they need to interact with peers and adults (Hakuta, 2000).

Second, the generalizability and dependability coefficients for non-ELL students and ELL students with different levels of proficiency should be examined separately. Then, the minimum number of items comprising a test to be administered to the entire population (both ELL and non-ELL students) should be determined based on the generalizability and dependability coefficients obtained for the subpopulation of ELLs for which a greater amount of measurement error is observed. This is a simple, cost-effective method that can produce more reliable and valid measures of academic achievement for ELLs.

As can be seen, G theory allows operationalization of fairness through the proper representation of linguistic minorities and the proper sampling of observations. It is up to the assessment systems to incorporate G theory-based approaches as part of their practices intended to examine the technical quality of interpretations of test scores.

Note

1. Other statistical methods have been used in estimating the variance components (and their standard errors), such as the re-sampling approach (e.g., Brennan, Harris, & Hanson, 1987; Wiley, 2001) and the Bayesian approach (e.g., Brennan, 2001).

References

Abedi, J. (2007). English language proficiency assessment and accountability under the NCLB Title III: An overview. In J. Abedi (Ed.), *English language proficiency in the nation: Current status and future practice* (pp. 3–10). Davis, CA: University of California, Davis.

Abedi, J. (2008). Classification system for English language learners: Issues and recommendations. *Educational Measurement: Issues and Practice, 27*(3), 17–31.

Abedi, J., Hofstetter, C. H., & Lord, C. (2004). Assessment accommodations for English language learners: Implications for policy-based empirical research. *Review of Educational Research, 74*, 1–28.

Abedi, J., Lord, C., Hofstetter, C., & Baker, E. (2001). Impact of accommodation strategies on English language learners' test performance. *Educational Measurement: Issues and Practice, 19*(3), 16–26.

Bachman, L. F., Lynch, B. K., & Mason, M. (1995). Investigating variability in tasks and rater judgments in a performance test of foreign language speaking. *Language Testing, 12*, 239–257.

Backhoff, E., Solano-Flores, G., & Contreras-Niño, L. A. (2012, October). *Aplicación piloto de 30 reactivos del Excale-00/PM en poblaciones mayas: Quinto reporte de investigación. Proyecto: "Pertinencia de la Traducción y Adaptación de las Pruebas Excale de Preescolar a la Lengua Maya"* [Analysis of a 30-item test administered to pre-school Mayan students: Fifth research report. Project: "Feasibility of translating and adapting EXCALE pre-school tests into the Mayan language"]. Submitted to the National Institute for Educational Evaluation, Universidad Autónoma de Baja California, Ensenada, Baja California, Mexico.

Baker, C. (2001). *Foundations of bilingual education and bilingualism* (4th ed.) Clevedon, UK: Multilingual Matters.

Bialystok, E. (2001). *Bilingualism in development: Language, literacy, and cognition.* Cambridge, UK: Cambridge University Press.

Bialystok, E., Craik, F. I. M., Green, D. W., & Gollan, T. H. (2009). Bilingual minds. *Psychological Science in the Public Interest, 10*, 80–129.

Brennan, R. L. (2000). (Mis) conception about generalizability theory. *Educational Measurement: Issues and Practice, 19*(1), 5–10.

Brennan, R. L. (2001). *Generalizability theory.* New York, NY: Springer Verlag.

Brennan, R. L., Gao, X., & Colton, D. A. (1995). Generalizability analyses of Work Keys listening and writing tests. *Educational and Psychological Measurement, 55*, 157–176.

Brennan, R. L., Harris, D. J., & Hanson, B. A. (1987). *The bootstrap and other procedures for examining the variability of estimated variance components in testing contexts* (ACT Research Report 87-7). Iowa City, IA: ACT.

Brown, H. D. (2007). *Principles of language learning and teaching* (5th ed.). Boston, MA: Addison Wesley & Longman.

Cardinet, J., Tourneur, Y., & Allal, L. (1976). The symmetry of generalizability theory: Applications to educational measurement. *Journal of Educational Measurement, 13*, 119–135.

Cronbach, L. J., Gleser, G. C., Nanda, H., & Rajaratnam, N. (1972). *The dependability of behavioral measurements*. New York, NY: Wiley.

Cronbach, L. J., Linn, R. L. Brennan, R. L., & Haertel, E. H. (1997). Generalizability analysis for performance assessments of student achievement or school effectiveness. *Educational and Psychological Measurement, 57*, 373–399.

Crystal, D. (1997). *The Cambridge encyclopedia of language* (2nd ed.). Cambridge, UK: Cambridge University Press.

Cummins, J. (2000). *Language, power and pedagogy*. Clevedon, UK: Multilingual Matters.

Darling-Hammond, L., & Sykes, G. (2003). Wanted: A national teacher supply policy for education: The right way to meet the "Highly Qualified Teacher" challenge. *Education Policy Analysis Archives, 11*(33). Retrieved from http://epaa.asu.edu/epaa/v11n33/

García, O., & Kleifgen, J. A. (2010). *Educating emergent bilinguals: Policies, programs, and practices of English language learners*. New York, NY: Teachers College Press.

Haertel, E. H. (2006). Reliability. In R. L. Brennan (Ed.), *Educational measurement* (4th ed., pp. 65–110). Wesport, CT: American Council on Education.

Hakuta, K. (2000). *How long does it take English learners to attain proficiency?* (University of California Linguistic Minority Research Institute. Policy Reports). Santa Barbara, CA: Linguistic Minority Research Institute. Retrieved from http://repositories.cdlib.org/lmri/pr/hakuta

Kachchaf, R., & Solano-Flores, G. (2012). Rater language background as a source of measurement error in the testing of English language learners. *Applied Measurement in Education, 25*, 167–172.

Kane, M. T. (1982). A sampling model of validity. *Applied Psychological Measurement, 6*, 125–160.

Kopriva, R., Koran, J., & Hedgspeth, C. (2007). Addressing the importance of systematically addressing student needs and test accommodations. In C. Cahalan Laitusis & L. L. Cook (Eds.), *Large-scale assessment and accommodations: What works?* (pp. 145–165). Arlington, VA: Council for Exceptional Children.

Lee, Y. (2006). Dependability of scores for a new ESL speaking assessment consisting of integrated and independent tasks. *Language Testing, 23*, 131–166.

Li, D., & Brennan, R. L. (2007). *A multi-group generalizability analysis of a large-scale reading comprehension test* (Center for Advanced Studies in Measurement and Assessment Research. Report No. 25, August). College of Education Iowa City, IA, University of Iowa. Retrieved from http://www.education.uiowa.edu/centers/docs/casma-research/25casmareport.pdf?sfvrsn=0

Lynch, B. K., & McNamara, T. F. (1998). Using G-theory and many-facet Rasch measurement in the development of performance assessments of the ESL speaking skills of immigrants. *Language Testing, 15*, 158–180.

Oller, D. K., Pearson, B. Z., & Cobo-Lewis, A. B. (2007). Profile effects in early bilingual language and literacy. *Applied Psycholinguistics, 28*, 191–230.

Pennock-Roman, M., & Rivera, C. (2011). Mean effects of test accommodations for ELLs and non-ELLs: A meta-analysis of experimental studies. *Educational Measurement: Issues and Practice, 30*(3), 10–28.

Prosser, R. R., & Solano-Flores, G. (2010, April). *Including English language learners in the process of test development: A study on instrument linguistic adaptation for cognitive validity*. Paper presented at the Annual Conference of the National Council of Measurement in Education, Denver, CO.

Rivera, C., Collum, E., Willner, L. N., & Sia, J. K., Jr. (2006). Study 1: An analysis of state assessment policies regarding the accommodation of English language learners. In C. Rivera & E. Collum (Eds.), *State assessment policy and practice for English language learners: A national perspective* (pp. 1–136). Mahwah, NJ: Erlbaum.

Ruiz-Primo, M. A., Baxter, G. P., & Shavelson, R. J. (1993). On the stability of performance assessments. *Journal of Educational Measurement, 30*, 41–53.

Shavelson, R. J., Ruiz-Primo, M. A., & Wiley, E. W. (1999). Notes on sources of sampling variability in science performance assessments. *Journal of Educational Measurement, 36,* 61–71.

Shavelson, R. J., & Webb, N. M. (1981). Generalizability theory: 1973–1980. *British Journal of Mathematical and Statistical Psychology, 34,* 133–166.

Shavelson, R. J., & Webb, N. M. (1991). *Generalizability theory: A primer.* Newbury Park, CA: Sage.

Shavelson, R. J., & Webb, N. M. (2009). Generalizability theory and its contribution to the discussion of the generalizability of research findings. In K. Ercikan & W. M. Roth (Eds.), *Generalizing from educational research* (pp.13–32). New York, NY: Routledge.

Sireci, S. G., Li, S., & Scarpati, S. (2003). *The effects of test accommodation on test performance: A review of the literature* (Center for Educational Assessment Research Report No. 485). Amherst, MA: University of Massachusetts at Amherst.

Solano-Flores, G. (2006). Language, dialect, and register: Sociolinguistics and the estimation of measurement error in the testing of English-language learners. *Teachers College Record, 108,* 2354–2379.

Solano-Flores, G. (2008). Who is given tests in what language by whom, when, and where? The need for probabilistic views of language in the testing of English language learners. *Educational Researcher, 37,* 189–199.

Solano-Flores, G. (2009). The testing of English language learners as a stochastic process: Population misspecification, measurement error, and overgeneralization. In K. Ercikan & W. M. Roth (Eds.), *Generalizing from educational research* (pp. 33–48). New York, NY: Routledge.

Solano-Flores, G. (2011a). *Assessing the cultural validity of assessment practices: An introduction.* In M. R. Basterra, E. Trumbull, & G. Solano-Flores (Eds.), *Cultural validity in assessment: Addressing linguistic and cultural diversity* (pp. 3–21). New York, NY: Routledge.

Solano-Flores, G. (2011b, April). *Development of illustrations as image supports for English language learners in large-scale testing: A report on the procedure for designing vignette illustrations.* Paper presented at the CADRE ELL-STEM Roundtable session "Advancing English Language Learners in Science and Math: Realizing the Promise" at the Annual Meeting of the American Educational Research Association, New Orleans, LA.

Solano-Flores, G., & Gustafson, M. (in press). Assessment of English language learners: A critical, probabilistic, systemic view. In M. Simon, K. Ercikan, & M. Rousseau (Eds.), *Improving large scale assessment in education: Theory, issues, and practice* (pp. 87–109). New York, NY: Taylor & Francis Routledge.

Solano-Flores, G., Lara, J., Sexton, U., & Navarrete, C. (2001). *Testing English language learners: A sampler of student responses to science and mathematics test items.* Washington, DC: Council of Chief State School Officers.

Solano-Flores, G., & Li, M. (2006). The use of generalizability (G) theory in the testing of linguistic minorities. *Educational Measurement: Issues and Practice 25*(1), 13–22.

Solano-Flores, G., & Li, M. (2008). Examining the dependability of academic achievement measures for English-Language Learners. *Assessment for Effective Intervention, 33,* 135–144.

Solano-Flores, G., & Li, M. (2009a). Generalizability of cognitive interview-based measures across cultural groups. *Educational Measurement: Issues and Practice, 28*(2), 9–18.

Solano-Flores, G., & Li, M. (2009b). Language variation and score variation in the testing of English language learners, native Spanish speakers. *Educational Assessment, 14,* 1–15.

Solano-Flores, G., Li, M., Speroni, C., Rodriguez, J., Basterra, M., & Dovholuk, G. (2007, April). *Comparing the properties of teacher-adapted and linguistically-simplified test items for English language learners.* Paper presented at the Annual Meeting of the American Educational Research Association, Chicago, IL.

Solano-Flores, G., Nguyen-Le, K., & Wang, C. (2012, July). *Linking generalizability and effectiveness in the evaluation of testing accommodations for English language learners.* Paper presented at the symposium "Limits of Generalizing in Psychological Research" organized by Kadriye Ercikan, International Congress of Psychology in Cape Town, South Africa.

Solano-Flores, G., & Trumbull, E. (2008). In what language should English language learners be tested? In R. J. Kopriva (Ed.), *Improving testing for English language learners* (pp. 169–200). New York, NY: Routledge.

Valdés, G., & Figueroa, R. A. (1994). *Bilingualism and testing: A special case of bias.* Norwood, NJ: Ablex.

Van Weeren, J., & Theunissen, T. J. J. M. (1987).Testing pronunciation: An application of generalizability theory. *Language Learning, 37,* 109–122.

Wardhaugh, R. (2002). *An introduction to sociolinguistics.* (4th ed.). Malden, MA: Blackwell.

Webb, N. M., Shavelson, R. J., & Haertel, E. H. (2007). Reliability coefficients and generalizability theory. In C. R. Rao & S. Sinharay (Ed.), *Handbook of statistics, Volume 26: Psychometrics* (pp. 81–124). Amsterdam, The Netherlands: Elsevier.

Wei, L. (2000). Dimensions of bilingualism. In L. Wei (Ed.), *The bilingualism reader* (pp. 3–25). New York, NY: Routledge.

Wiley, E. W. (2001). *Bootstrap strategies for variance component estimation: Theoretical and empirical results* (Unpublished doctoral dissertation). Stanford University, Stanford, CA.

Wolfram, W., Adger, C. T., & Christian, D. (1999). *Dialects in schools and communities.* Mahwah, NJ: Lawrence Erlbaum Associates.

Young, J. W., & King, T. C. (2008). *Testing accommodations for English language learners: A review of state and district policies.* New York, NY: The College Board.

Index

Note: Page numbers in *italics* represent tables
Page numbers in **bold** represent figures
Page numbers followed by 'n' refer to notes